LYLE PRICE GUIDE
DOLLS
& TOYS

The publishers wish to express their sincere thanks to the following for their involvement and assistance in the production of this volume:

Editor	TONY CURTIS
Text By	EELIN McIVOR
Editorial	ANNETTE CURTIS
	DONNA RUTHERFORD
	JACQUELINE LEDDY
Art Production	CATRIONA DAY
	NICKY FAIRBURN
	DONNA CRUICKSHANK
Graphics	FRANK BURRELL
	JAMES BROWN
	EILEEN BURRELL

Illustrations
Page 1 - 'Ski Rolf' by E.P. Lehmann. (Lawrence Fine Art) £1,265
Page 3 - A Kammer & Reinhardt bisque doll. (Greenslades) £200
      A Composition 'Red Riding Hood' doll. (Greenslades) £190

A CIP catalogue record for this book is available from the British Library.

ISBN 86248-141-4

Copyright © Lyle Publications MCMXCII
Glenmayne, Galashiels, Scotland.

Typeset by Word Power, Auchencrow, Berwickshire
Printed and bound in Great Britain by
Butler & Tanner Ltd, Frome and London

LP

LYLE PRICE GUIDE
DOLLS
& TOYS

TONY CURTIS

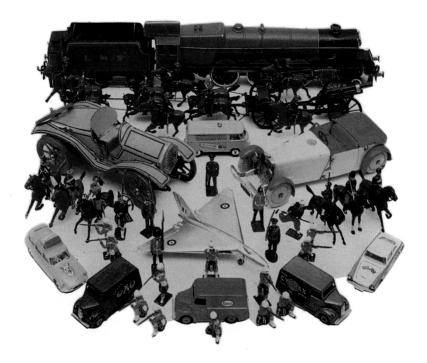

CONTENTS

JUST £14.95

With comprehensive illustrations, descriptions and up to date prices for over 3,000 items, this Lyle Price Guide provides a unique and indispensable work of reference for anyone interested in the art and artefacts of these fascinating and stimulating periods.

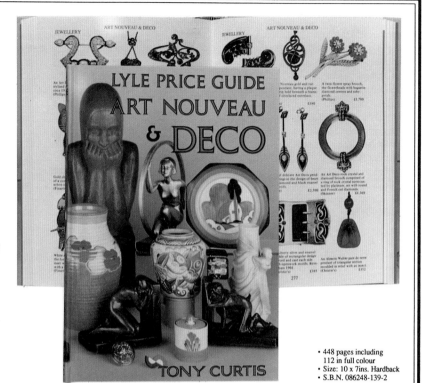

• 448 pages including 112 in full colour
• Size: 10 x 7ins. Hardback
• S.B.N. 086248-139-2

• 448 pages including 112 in full colour
• Size: 10 x 7ins. Hardback
• S.B.N. 086248-140-6

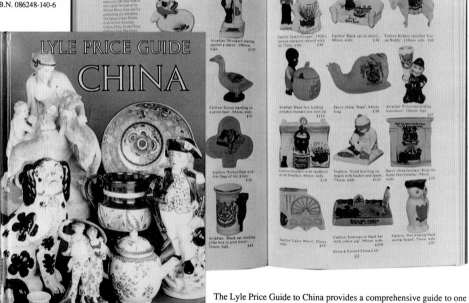

The Lyle Price Guide to China provides a comprehensive guide to one of the most popular and fascinating subjects with over 3,000 examples of everything from Arita to Zsolnay, carefully selected to give a broad representation of each factory's output.

Acknowledgements

AB Stockholms Auktionsverk, Box 16256, 103 25 Stockholm, Sweden
Abbots Auction Rooms, The Auction Rooms, Campsea Ash, Woodbridge, Suffolk
Abridge Auction Rooms, Market Place, Abridge, Essex RM4 1UA
Allen & Harris, St Johns Place, Whiteladies Road, Clifton, Bristol BS8 2ST
Jean Claude Anaf, Lyon Brotteaux, 13 bis place Jules Ferry, 69456 Lyon, France
Anderson & Garland, Marlborough House, Marlborough Crescent, Newcastle upon Tyne NE1 4EE
Antique Collectors Club & Co. Ltd, 5 Church Street, Woodbridge, Suffolk IP 12 1DS
Auction Team Köln, Postfach 50 11 68, D-5000 Köln 50 Germany
Auktionshause Arnold, Bleichstr. 42, 6000 Frankfurt a/M, Germany
Barber's Auctions, Woking, Surrey
Bearnes, Rainbow, Avenue Road, Torquay TQ2 5TG
Biddle & Webb, Ladywood Middleway, Birmingham B16 0PP
Bigwood, The Old School, Tiddington, Stratford upon Avon
Black Horse Agencies, Locke & England, 18 Guy Street, Leamington Spa
Boardman Fine Art Auctioneers, Station Road Corner, Haverhill, Suffolk CB9 0EY
Bonhams, Montpelier Street, Knightsbridge, London SW7 1HH
Bonhams Chelsea, 65–69 Lots Road, London SW10 0RN
Bonhams West Country, Dowell Street, Honiton, Devon
British Antique Exporters, School Close, Queen Elizabeth Avenue, Burgess Hill, Sussex
William H Brown, The Warner Auction Rooms, 16–18, Halford Street, Leicester LE1 1JB
Butterfield & Butterfield, 220 San Bruno Avenue, San Francisco CA 94103, USA
Butterfield & Butterfield, 7601 Sunset Boulevard, Los Angeles CA 90046, USA
Central Motor Auctions, Barfield House, Britannia Road, Morley, Leeds, LS27 0HN
H.C. Chapman & Son, The Auction Mart, North Street, Scarborough.
Christie's (International) SA, 8 place de la Taconnerie, 1204 Genève, Switzerland
Christie's Monaco, S.A.M, Park Palace 98000 Monte Carlo, Monaco
Christie's Scotland, 164–166 Bath Street Glasgow G2 4TG
Christie's South Kensington Ltd., 85 Old Brompton Road, London SW7 3LD
Christie's, 8 King Street, London SW1Y 6QT
Christie's East, 219 East 67th Street, New York, NY 10021, USA
Christie's, 502 Park Avenue, New York, NY 10022, USA
Christie's, Cornelis Schuytstraat 57, 1071 JG Amsterdam, Netherlands
Christie's SA Roma, 114 Piazza Navona, 00186 Rome, Italy
Christie's Swire, 1202 Alexandra House, 16–20 Chater Road, Hong Kong
Christie's Australia Pty Ltd., 1 Darling Street, South Yarra, Melbourne, Victoria 3141, Australia
A J Cobern, The Grosvenor Sales Rooms, 93b Eastbank Street, Southport PR8 1DG
Cooper Hirst Auctions, The Granary Saleroom, Victoria Road, Chelmsford, Essex CM2 6LH
Nic Costa/Brian Bates, 10 Madely Street, Tunstall
The Crested China Co., Station House, Driffield, E. Yorks YO25 7PY
Clifford Dann, 20/21 High Street, Lewes, Sussex
Julian Dawson, Lewes Auction Rooms, 56 High Street, Lewes BN7 1XE
Dee & Atkinson, The Exchange Saleroom, Driffield, Nth Humberside YO25 7LJ
Diamond Mills & Co., 117 Hamilton Road, Felixstowe, Suffolk
Dowell Lloyd & Co. Ltd, 118 Putney Bridge Road, London SW15 2NQ
Downer Ross, Charter House, 42 Avebury Boulevard, Central Milton Keynes MK9 2HS
Hy. Duke & Son, 40 South Street, Dorchester, Dorset
Du Mouchelles Art Galleries Co., 409 E. Jefferson Avenue, Detroit, Michigan 48226, USA
Duncan Vincent, 105 London Street, Reading RG1 4LF
Sala de Artes y Subastas Durán, Serrano 12, 28001 Madrid, Spain
Eldred's, Box 796, E. Dennis, MA 02641, USA
Ewbanks, Welbeck House, High Street, Guildford, Surrey, GU1 3JF
Fellows & Son, Augusta House, 19 Augusta Street, Hockley, Birmingham
Finarte, 20121 Milano, Piazzetta Bossi 4, Italy
John D Fleming & Co., 8 Fore Street, Dulverton, Somerset
G A Property Services, Canterbury Auction Galleries, Canterbury, Kent
Galerie Koller, Rämistr. 8, CH 8024 Zürich, Switzerland
Galerie Moderne, 3 rue du Parnasse, 1040 Bruxelles, Belgium
Geering & Colyer (Black Horse Agencies) Highgate, Hawkhurst, Kent
Glerum Auctioneers, Westeinde 12, 2512 HD's Gravenhage, Netherlands
The Goss and Crested China Co., 62 Murray Road, Horndean, Hants PO8 9JL
Graves Son & Pilcher, 71 Church Road, Hove, East Sussex, BN3 2GL
W R J Greenslade & Co., 13 Hammet Street, Taunton, Somerset, TA1 1RN
Peter Günnemann, Ehrenberg Str. 57, 2000 Hamburg 50, Germany
Halifax Property Services, 53 High Street, Tenterden, Kent
Halifax Property Services, 15 Cattle Market, Sandwich, Kent CT13 9AW
Hampton's Fine Art, 93 High Street, Godalming, Surrey
Hanseatisches Auktionshaus für Historica, Neuer Wall 57, 2000 Hamburg 36, Germany
Andrew Hartley Fine Arts, Victoria Hall, Little Lane, Ilkley

Hauswedell & Nolte, D-2000 Hamburg 13, Pöseldorfer Weg 1, Germany
Giles Haywood, The Auction House, St John's Road, Stourbridge, West Midlands, DY8 1EW
Heatheringtons Nationwide Anglia, The Amersham Auction Rooms, 125 Station Road, Amersham, Bucks
Muir Hewitt, Halifax Antiques Centre, Queens Road/Gibbet Street, Halifax HX1 4LR
Hobbs & Chambers, 'At the Sign of the Bell', Market Place, Cirencester, Glos
Hobbs Parker, Romney House, Ashford, Ashford, Kent
Hotel de Ventes Horta, 390 Chaussée de Waterloo (Ma Campagne), 1060 Bruxelles, Belgium
Jacobs & Hunt, Lavant Street, Petersfield, Hants. GU33 3EF
James of Norwich, 33 Timberhill, Norwich NR1 3LA
P Herholdt Jensens Auktioner, Rundforbivej 188, 2850 Nerum, Denmark
G A Key, Aylsham Saleroom, Palmers Lane, Aylsham, Norfolk, NR11 6EH
Kunsthaus am Museum, Drususgasse 1–5, 5000 Köln 1, Germany
Kunsthaus Lempertz, Neumarkt 3, 5000 Köln 1, Germany
Lambert & Foster (County Group), The Auction Sales Room, 102 High Street, Tenterden, Kent
W.H. Lane & Son, 64 Morrab Road, Penzance, Cornwall, TR18 2QT
Langlois Ltd., Westway Rooms, Don Street, St Helier, Channel Islands
Lawrence Butler Fine Art Salerooms, Marine Walk, Hythe, Kent, CT21 5AJ
Lawrence Fine Art, South Street, Crewkerne, Somerset TA18 8AB
Lawrence's Fine Art Auctioneers, Norfolk House, 80 High Street, Bletchingley, Surrey
David Lay, The Penzance Auction House, Alverton, Penzance, Cornwall TA18 4KE
Brian Loomes, Calf Haugh Farm, Pateley Bridge, North Yorks
Lots Road Chelsea Auction Galleries, 71 Lots Road, Chelsea, London SW10 0RN
R K Lucas & Son, Tithe Exchange, 9 Victoria Place, Haverfordwest, SA61 2JX
Duncan McAlpine, Stateside Comics plc, 125 East Barnet Road, London EN4 8RF
John Maxwell, 75 Hawthorn Street, Wilmslow, Cheshire
May & Son, 18 Bridge Street, Andover, Hants
Morphets, 4–6 Albert Street, Harrogate, North Yorks HG1 1JL
D M Nesbit & Co, 7 Clarendon Road, Southsea, Hants PO5 2ED
Onslow's, Metrostore, Townmead Road, London SW6 2RZ
Outhwaite & Litherland, Kingsley Galleries, Fontenoy Street, Liverpool, Merseyside L3 2BE
J R Parkinson Son & Hamer Auctions, The Auction Rooms, Rochdale, Bury, Lancs
Phillips Manchester, Trinity House, 114 Northenden Road, Sale, Manchester M33 3HD
Phillips Son & Neale SA, 10 rue des Chaudronniers, 1204 Genève, Switzerland
Phillips West Two, 10 Salem Road, London W2 4BL
Phillips, 11 Bayle Parade, Folkestone, Kent CT20 1SQ
Phillips, 49 London Road, Sevenoaks, Kent TN13 1UU
Phillips, 65 George Street, Edinburgh EH2 2JL
Phillips, Blenstock House, 7 Blenheim Street, New Bond Street, London W1Y 0AS
Phillips Marylebone, Hayes Place, Lisson Grove, London NW1 6UA
Phillips, New House, 150 Christleton Road, Chester CH3 5TD
Pinney's, 5627 Ferrier, Montreal, Quebec, Canada H4P 2M4
Pooley & Rogers, Regent Auction Rooms, Abbey Street, Penzance
Rennie's, 1 Agincourt Street, Monmouth
Riddetts, Richmond Hill, Bournemouth
Ritchie's, 429 Richmond Street East, Toronto, Canada M5A 1R1
Derek Roberts Antiques, 24–25 Shipbourne Road, Tonbridge, Kent TN10 3DN
Rogers de Rin, 79 Royal Hospital Road, London SW3 4HN
Russell, Baldwin & Bright, The Fine Art Saleroom, Ryelands Road, Leominster HR6 8JG
Sandoes Nationwide Anglia, Tabernacle Road, Wotton under Edge, Glos GL12 7EB
Schrager Auction Galleries, 2915 North Sherman Boulevard, Milwaukee, WI 53210, USA.
Selkirk's, 4166 Olive Street, St Louis, Missouri 63108, USA
Skinner Inc., Bolton Gallery, Route 117, Bolton MA, USA
Southgate Auction Rooms, Munro House, Cline Road, New Southgate, London N11.
Henry Spencer, 40 The Square, Retford, Notts. DN22 6DJ
G E Sworder & Son, Northgate End Salerooms, 15 Northgate End, Bishop Stortford, Herts
Taviner's of Bristol, Prewett Street, Redcliffe, Bristol BS1 6PB
Tennants, 27 Market Place, Leyburn, Yorkshire
Thomson Roddick & Laurie, 24 Lowther Street, Carlisle
Thomson Roddick & Laurie, 60 Whitesands, Dumfries
Venator & Hanstein, Cäcilienstr. 48, 5000 Köln 1, Germany
T Vennett Smith, 11 Nottingham Road, Gotham, Nottingham NG11 0HE
Duncan Vincent, 105 London Road, Reading RG1 4LF
Wallis & Wallis, West Street Auction Galleries, West Street, Lewes, E. Sussex BN7 2NJ
Ward & Morris, Stuart House, 18 Gloucester Road, Ross on Wye HR9 5BN
Warren & Wignall Ltd, The Mill, Earnshaw Bridge, Leyland Lane, Leyland PR5 3PH
Dominique Watine-Arnault, 11 rue François 1er, 75008 Paris, France
Wells Cundall Nationwide Anglia, Staffordshire House, 27 Flowergate, Whitby YO21 3AX
Woltons, 6 Whiting Street, Bury St Edmunds, Suffolk IP33 1PB
Woolley & Wallis, The Castle Auction Mart, Salisbury, Wilts.SP1 3SU
Austin Wyatt Nationwide Anglia, Emsworth Road, Lymington, Hants SO41 9BL
Yesterday Child, 118 Islington High Street, London N11 8EG

DOLLS & TOYS

One of the great delights of dolls and toys must be their nostalgia value. Another must be that they are so much more accessible to the average person than many other types of antiques. For you don't have to be a specialist or collector, or indeed, know very much about them. Even the complete layman will feel a frisson of excitement when turning the pages of such a book as this, for there is every chance that, there before him, he will find his own favourite childhood toy, which even now may still be up there in the attic.

Despite this accessibility, however, dolls and toys can really no longer be seen as being firmly at the cheaper end of the collectables scale. True, most of the major auction houses hold their doll and toy sales at their more 'popular' branches – Christie's at South Ken., for example, and Phillips at West Two, rather than at King Street or Blenstock House, but some of the prices now being fetched would not disgrace these more august surroundings. Take, for example, that Steiff dual plush 1920s teddy bear that sold for £55,000 at Sotheby's, or £47,000 for a Märklin tinplate carousel toys at Christie's, or even the staggering $231,000 paid for a George Brown 'Charles' tinplate hosereel, making it the world's most expensive toy. But even humble toy cars now regularly fetch sums into four figures.

Of course, the variations are vast. Many of the real high fliers – the Charles II doll at £71,500 or the Gustav Vichy pumpkin eater automaton which sold at Christie's for £22,000, were never intended to be played with by children. Rather they were made for rich society ladies or to delight royal courts. Sadly, but understandably, the value of many other items are also dependent on their condition. Few of the exquisite Jumeau dolls which fetch the highest sums today were ever subjected to the rough and tumble of the nursery, and to make real money even your Dinky cars have to be in mint condition and accompanied by their original box. On the other hand, if a piece such as a rocking horse is worn, faded and obviously much loved and played with, there is no point in trying to restore it to its first pristine condition, for messing about with the original paintwork, for example, slashes the value immediately. The same is true of just about any type of toy.

With regard to dolls, bisque heads were particularly susceptible to damage, and replacements were common. These will obviously detract from the value. A smoother area of bisque is often also indicative of restoration, while even the slightest crack can halve the value of a doll.

With regard to tinplate and mechanical toys, repainting and resoldering of joints also detract from value. It is always worth checking that tabs, where they exist, have not been opened. Patent marks often help with dating such toys; look for the last date, and the toy will normally have been made within ten years of that.

There is nostalgia too in the fact that so many of these now-sought-after toys were made by companies now no longer in existence. Most were European and some of the greatest, Meccano, Dinky, Lines Bros. for example, were British, and went to the wall when overwhelmed by the onslaught of cheap Far Eastern imports. It is probably fair to say that, with the possible exception of Japanese robots, none of their successors can hope to achieve the cachet which these earlier models enjoy in collectors' circles. Even when the names have reemerged following convoluted buy-outs and take-overs, the resulting products are mostly now made in Hong Kong and Macau or the like, and somehow just do not seem the same.

A rare Marklin rabbit automaton with carriage, circa 1910, 11in. tall.
(Christie's) £5,143

9

A rare early Donald Duck puppet made
from plaster, the earliest known example
in puppet form, made by Munzberg,
Germany in 1937, 17cm. high.
(Auction Team Koeln)   £1,850

A tinplate toy in the form of a Mickey
Mouse organ grinder with Minnie
dancing on top, circa 1930, 8in. high.
(G.E. Sworder)   £1,320

Fruit Seller, a leather-headed clockwork musical automaton modelled as a Negro holding a tray, 24in. high, by Vichy. (Christie's) £8,800

Little Girl Magician, a bisque-headed clockwork musical automaton, 16½in. high by Renou, circa 1900. (Christie's) £6,600

A bisque-headed bebe, with open/closed mouth, fixed blue eyes, blonde mohair wig, 19in. high, impressed Bru Jne 6. (Christie's) £15,400

A bisque-headed clockwork musical automaton, 14in. high, head impressed FIG by Vichy, circa 1890. (Christie's) £3,520

A Bing tinplate four seat open Phaeton, German, circa 1904, with trademark in front of rear seats, hand painted in red and brown, lined in gold, 'buttoned' mustard yellow seats, yellow spoked wheels with black rubber tyres, with large detachable paraffin headlamp, two spotlamps, small rear lamp, adjustable front wheels, clockwork motor driving rear wheels, with key, 13in. long.
(Sotheby's)   £6,160

A Bing hand painted tinplate taxi, German, circa 1909, finished in scarlet and maroon, with grey roof, lined gold and yellow, with hinged rear doors, headlamps and spotlamp, handbrake, clockwork motor driving rear wheels, working taxi meter, lithographed trademark plaque to rear, yellow spoked wheels and replacement white rubber tyres, 27cm. overall.   (Sotheby's)   £5,280

A large Carette lithographed tinplate limousine, German, circa 1911, finished in green, lined black and white, black roof with luggage rack and black running boards, brake and reverse levers, headlamps and sidelamps, spoked metal wheels with white rubber tyres, bevelled glass to windows, hinged opening rear doors, nickel-plated radiator surround, steering wheel, clockwork motor driving rear wheels, composition driver figure and two female passengers, 15¾in. long.   (Sotheby's)   £5,500

A Carette tinplate hand painted two seater 'high class motor car', German, circa 1909, hand painted in pale green, lined red, with maroon 'buttoned' seat, adjustable front wheels, handbrake, four original nickelled lamps, white rubber tyred spoked wheels, bevelled glass windscreen, and with original uniformed composition driver, 10in. long overall.   (Sotheby's)   £4,620

Lutz for Marklin Clockwork, 'Toulouse', circa 1880, 61cm. long.
(Christie's)   £12,100

Marklin Clockwork, 'Connecticut', first series, circa 1900, 72cm. long.
(Christie's)   £11,550

Marklin electric, 'Kaiser Wilhelm Der Grosse', circa 1909, 117cm. long. This model was the largest Marklin liner and would run with two 4 volt batteries for seven hours. (Christie's S. Ken)   £33,000

An extremely fine contemporary early 19th century French prisoner-of-war bone and horn model of a forty-six gun Royal Naval frigate, 10in. x 13½in. Complete with bound masts, yards with stun's'l booms, detailed standing and running rigging with standards at the mastheads and White Ensign at the mizzen and deck details including carved and painted figurehead, carved hair-rails, brass anchors with bone stocks, cat-heads, belaying rails, capstan, gratings, companionway, double ship's wheel, upper deck guns in slides and three ship's boats with thwarts, one in stern davits. (Christie's)   £16,500

Dinky pre-war 28d delivery van Oxo Beef At Its Best, 1st type.
(Christie's)   £1,540

A Chad Valley lithographed tinplate double deck greenline bus, lithographed green, with
yellow roof, as a number 721 Aldgate and Brentwood service, with hollow tin wheels,
detachable roof, passengers at windows, 10in. long.
(Sotheby's)   £1,045

A Toschi Grand Prix Ferrari racing car toy, Italian, circa 1959, hand painted in red, with
Ferrari emblems, black rubber tyres, adjustable windscreen, clockwork motor driving
rear wheels, originally made as a promotional gift bearing a miniature bottle of the Toschi
company's liquor in the driver's seat, in original cardboard box, 22in. long overall.
(Sotheby's)   £2,310

A Marusan Ford Sedan, Japanese, 1950's, chromed surface, plastic windscreen, black
rubber tyres, adjustable front wheels, friction drive to rear wheels, 13in. long.
(Sotheby's)   £1,870

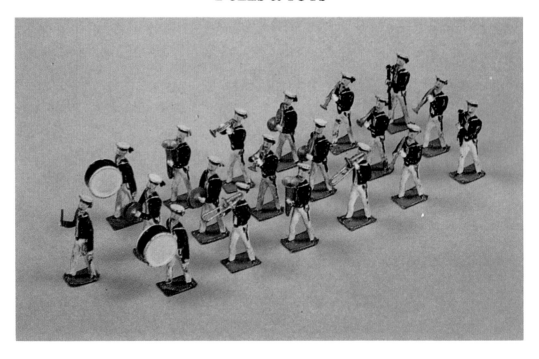

Heyde for Marklin, hand-painted cast lead German Naval band of 19 pieces, circa 1912.
(Christie's S. Ken)   £4,400

Rare Britains Set 1339, Royal Horse Artillery at the gallop, in the original box.
(Phillips)   £7,000

A Royal Horse Artillery Gun Team in painted wood and composition by Sonnenberg, circa 1870.   (Phillips)   £3,600

Rare Britains Set 131, of 281 figures, including infantrymen, bandsmen, sailors and Camel Corps soldiers, in original box with two lift-out trays.
(Phillips)   £10,000

A scarce Lutz tinplate horse drawn Phaeton, German, circa 1880, hand-painted in blue and black, lined in yellow and pale blue, red lined yellow undercarriage and spoked wheels, interior in cream lined red with flower spray to passenger footwell, cotton canopy, carriage lamps, horsebar, with a bisque headed and a painted composition figure, and complete with two hide covered horses with leather tack, wooden snouts and glass eyes, 13in. (Sotheby's)   £4,620

The famous George Brown tinplate 'Charles' hose reel, circa 1875, finished in royal blue and white with beautiful hand-painted decorative scroll work, twin brass bells and large cast wheels, probably the rarest early American tin toy known to exist, 23in. long. (Christie's)   £127,050

A magnificent early French tinplate horsedrawn open double decker tram, circa 1890, hand-painted in dark green and black with yellow and red piping, destination side boards reading 'Ville de Marseille'—'Longchamp Joliette', by the Compagnie Generale de Omnibus, with double open ended stairways, top and interior seating, railings, cast yellow wheels, five open windows on each side, and fretwork decorations, pulled by a pair of brown metal horses in livery, trotting with small wheels for easy movement, 42in. long overall.   (Christie's)   £39,325

A fine oversized early Marklin tinplate horsedrawn hansom cab, the cast lead white and black horse on wheels pulls a beautiful hand-painted two-wheel hansom cab, with opening front doors and high cabby seat at the rear, 28in. long overall. (Christie's)   £10,285

Marklin 75mm. gauge steam, 'Wurttemberg', circa 1912, fitted with electric light and battery compartment under tender.
(Christie's)   £29,700

J. P. Hartmann 3¾in. gauge painted metal CIWL teak sleeping car, circa 1921, with external body and chassis details, fully fitted and beautifully executed interior, electrically-operated automaton figures en deshabille, compartment lighting, and removable roof and side, 132cm. long.
(Christie's)   £13,200

A rare Marklin hand painted District Railway twin bogie passenger coach, with side opening sliding doors, in original paintwork, circa 1902.
(Christie's)   £4,400

Marklin, Grand Station, with track canopy, interior and exterior fittings, working clocks and electric lighting, circa 1909, 92cm. wide, 54cm. high.
(Christie's)   £16,500

A rare and early Marklin gauge 1 clockwork model of the Central London Railway
'Steeplecab' 0-4-0 electric locomotive, in original green and dark green paintwork, black
chassis, orange and pale green lining, circa 1901.
(Christie's S. Ken)
                £2,200

A rake of three very rare gauge 1 Central London Railway four wheel passenger coaches,
all with opening side doors and roofs, to reveal benches, by Marklin, circa 1903.
(Christie's S. Ken)
                £6,050

A Carette lithographed four seat open tourer, German, 1905-10, cream body lined red and gold, with embossed and lithographed buttoned seats, black wheel arches, red painted spoked wheels with white rubber tyres, lamps, hand-painted driver, male front passenger, and two female rear seat passengers in grey cape coats and yellow hats, clockwork motor driving rear wheels, 12¼in. long. (Sotheby's)   £4,620

A Carette lithographed tinplate limousine, German, circa 1911, lithographed green and black lined yellow, with red surrounds to windows, black wheel arches, hinged rear doors, bevelled glass to windscreen and rear windows, orange painted spoked wheels with white rubber tyres, handbrake, headlamps and spotlamps, adjustable front wheels, restored luggage rack, hand-painted driver in brown uniform and cap, clockwork motor driving rear wheels, 15¾in. long. (Sotheby's)   £4,180

An early hand enamelled four seater open tourer, No. 3358/21, by Carette, circa 1911, 21cm. long, with clockwork mechanism driving rear axle, operating brake, adjustable front metal spoke wheels, white rubber tyres and composition painted chauffeur. (Christie's S. Ken)   £3,080

An extraordinary Marklin tinplate fire set, circa 1919, consisting of three keywind matched fire trucks, each hand-painted in.red, black and yellow with rubber tyres, all three bear the Marklin metal embossed shield on the front panel. The fire pumper has working gears that pump water and a chain drive; the fire patrol wagon consists of an overhead ladder and hose, with seating for six firemen; the ladder truck has chain gears that extend the ladders. All three vehicles are housed in their own hand-painted tinplate curved-roof firehouse of simulated stone. (Christie's)   £43,560

A large Bing tinplate keywind transitional open Phaeton, circa 1902, hand-painted in yellow with maroon piping, leather removable seats, steering, brake, springs, wire wheels, rubber tyres and large cowl lamps, 13¾in. long.
(Christie's)   £13,310

A rare Marklin pull-along automotive water tanker, circa 1912, consisting of a large water reservoir with indicator showing depth of water, tap for regulating or shutting off flow and solid rubber tyred wheels, 22½in. long. (Christie's)   £10,890

A Whitanco lithographed tinplate bus, English, 1920's, finished in maroon lined gold, with white roof, pressed tin wheels, single deck, with rear stair access and interior seats, clockwork motor driving rear wheels, adjustable front wheels, lettered Toyland Playthings Fairyland, 37cm. long.
(Sotheby's)   £1,760

A Chad Valley lithographed double deck Carr's biscuit tin bus, finished in red, as a number 25 London bus, with detachable grey roof, hollow tin wheels, clockwork motor to rear wheels, 10in. long.
(Sotheby's)   £990

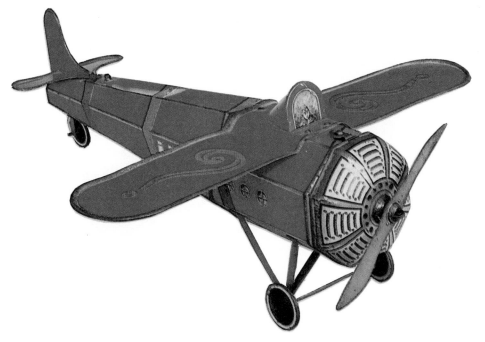

French biscuit tin, lithographed tin plate, circa 1920, 78.5cm. long.
(Christie's) £3,080

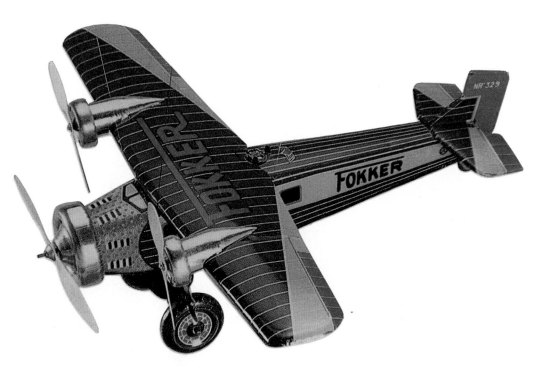

A Nomura Toys lithographed tinplate Fokker tri-motor aeroplane, Japanese, 1930's, the body finished in blue lined silver, with yellow central band, red and silver 'fishscale' effect to nose, numbered 329, with three chromed engines, hollow metal wheels, clockwork motor, 14½in. long overall.
(Sotheby's) £3,190

A number "7" American national pedal car, circa 1910, of tin, wood and brass, finished predominately in red with cream and green rectangular striping, yellow accents and leather button-tufted seats, 42in. long.
(Christie's)   £5,445

A Lincoln pedal car, circa 1935, finished in lime green with forest green mudguards, running boards, features include chrome plate steering wheel, split window windshield with side panes and electric lights, 45in. long.
(Christie's)   £4,840

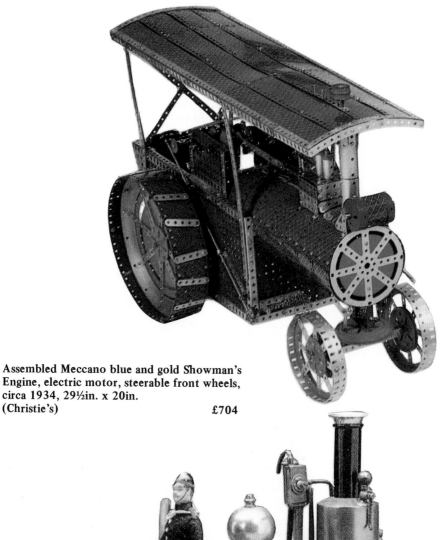

Assembled Meccano blue and gold Showman's
Engine, electric motor, steerable front wheels,
circa 1934, 29½in. x 20in.
(Christie's)   £704

A fine Marklin live steam tinplate and cast-iron fire pumper, circa 1900, featuring a
hand-painted cast chassis and wheels, an ornate brass steam dome, pump mechanism,
fire hose and original burner, 11 x 9½in., (replaced parts, hose reel, side lantern and
hose). (Christie's)   £6,050

A good 'A' series Jules Steiner Bebe, with fair mohair wig, fixed blue glass eyes, feathered brows, pierced ears and closed mouth, on a jointed wood and composition body, dressed in original deep red silk frock and bonnet, all contained within original trunk, 11in. high. (Bonham's) £1,700

A fine J. D. Kestner bisque head 'Googly' eyed character doll, with brown hair wig, weighted blue eyes and closed 'watermelon' mouth, on a jointed wood and composition toddler body dressed in original primrose-yellow gauze frock, hat and shoes, 16in. high. (Bonham's) £3,800

AMUSEMENT MACHINES

In the last few years there has been an enormous upsurge of interest in vintage amusement machines. These are a far cry from the electronic flashing-light horrors which one finds now herded into amusement arcades, and were to be found rather on seaside piers or railway platforms. Many are really quite elegantly housed in wood, while the Art Deco lines of some 30s models make them very distinctive. One of the few drawbacks to collecting amusement machines is finding the space to house them. Few are small, most are obtrusive (designed that way, of course, to attract the customer) and even a small collection can soon take over an average size house. It is not everyone who really wants a 'Matrimonial Bureau' in the bathroom, though real enthusiasts are unlikely to be discouraged by such minor discomforts!

As they become an ever more lucrative collector's field, fakes and reproductions have begun to appear, and buyers should make sure that their prospective purchases are exactly what they seem.

'Tommy', pin ball machine, made by Stoner Bros., U.S.A., circa 1938.   £450

'War Eagle' produced by Mills in the U.S.A., circa 1932.   £1,200

Conveyor, manufactured by Stevenson & Lovett, 1947.   £150

1930's Aeroplane Allwin.   £175

'Rol-a-top' produced by Watling with twin jackpot, made in the U.S.A., circa 1936.   £2,000

The Clown by Jentsch & Meerz, Leipzig, circa 1915.   £275

Try Your Grip, by the Mechanical Trading Company, circa 1895.   £1,000

33

'Playball' Allwin with seven winning chutes, in oak case, circa 1920, 27½in. high.
£150

Auto Stereoscope in oak casing with coin slot, circa 1930, 22½in. high.
£300

Ahrens stereoscopic viewer in oak cabinet, circa 1925, 68in. high.
£850

'Test Your Strength' amusement machine with iron grip handle, circa 1925, 50in. high.
£700

Early Genco pinball bagatelle table with glass top, circa 1935, 39in. long.
£550

'Pussy' Shooter, amusement machine, circa 1935, 76in. high.
£500

American coin-operated muto-scope 'Death Dive', circa 1915, 50in. high.
£600

White City 'Screen Stars' gambling machine in oak casing, circa 1940, 26½in. high.
£175

34

'The Drunkard's Dream', coin-operated automaton, 66½in. high, circa 1935.   £750

'The Burglar', coin-operated automaton, circa 1935, 67in. high.   £500

Caillie Brothers grip-test amusement machine in green-painted case, circa 1910, 59in. high.   £850

'Great Race' game, coin-operated, in oak casing, 47in. wide, circa 1925.   £850

Ahrens '22-Man Football' game, coin-operated, in oak casing, circa 1930, 43¾in. wide. £750

Green Ray 'Television' amusement machine, circa 1945, 75in. high.   £300

Arhens 'Test Your Strength' amusement machine in painted wooden case, circa 1922, 79in. high.   £850

'Zodiac' coin-operated fortune-teller, circa 1940, 24½in. high.   £250

'The Haunted House', coin-operated automaton, circa 1935, 70½in. high.   £650

'Haunted Churchyard' automaton in mahogany case, circa 1912, 72in. high. £750

'The Night Watchman', coin-operated automaton by The British Automatic Co. Ltd., circa 1935, 66½in. high.
£700

'Laughing Sailor', amusement machine, coin-operated bearing Ruffler & Walker plaque, 68½in. high, circa 1935.   £800

'Haunted House' automaton in wooden case with glazed window, circa 1935, 70in. high.   £400

Allwin 'Peerless de Luxe' with seven winning chutes, circa 1925, 29½in. high.
£175

Mutoscope by the International Reel Co., circa 1905, 74in. high.
£750

Brooklands Totalisator bandit with coin slot, circa 1939, 24in. high.
£200

A 'Stars of the Silver Screen' machine, circa 1935, 27in. high. £400

Rare Prohibition gambling machine with metal body, circa 1930, 6in. high. £200

Gottlieb & Co. 'World Fair' pinball table with glass top, 51in. long. £300

Caille gambling machine with five coin slots, circa 1910, 25½in. high. £300

An Aeroplane Allwin-type machine, circa 1940, 33in. high. £175

Coin operated mechanical football game, manufactured by The Baker Novelty Co., circa 1933, 17½in. high. £225

'Pussy' Shooter, coin-operated amusement machine by British Automatic Co. Ltd., circa 1935. £700

The French Execution Coin-slot Automaton, circa 1935, 84in. high. £700

Sapphire, Allwin type 'reserve' machine of French manufacture, 1920's. (Brian Bates)
£175

1950's All Sport two-player game by Bryans. (Nic Costa)
£175

Gipsy Fortune by Bolland, 1950's. (Nic Costa) £150

Personality 'Love Test Meter' manufactured by Oliver Whales, Redcar, circa 1950. (Brian Bates) £140

Mid 1930's, Mutoscope 'Adam & Eve', manufactured in the U.S.A. (Nic Costa) £500

1930's, Allwin nine cup. (Nic Costa) £175

Fruit Bowl by Bryans, circa 1963. (Nic Costa) £150

Reel 21 gaming machine by Groetchen, U.S.A., 1930's. (Brian Bates) £200

Matrimonial Bureau, 'Correct photo of your future husband, wife or baby,' by Bolland, 1930's. (Brian Bates) £250

DOLLS & TOYS

A large Football machine, circa 1935, 64in. high. £750

Jennings Tic-Tac-Toe slot machine in chrome case, 28in. high.   £750

A Little Stockbroker machine, circa 1935, 26in. high.   £250

A six-sided Allwin Column, circa 1925, 66½in. high. £700

Caille 'The New Century' Detroit five-cent upright single-wheel slot machine, circa 1900.   £3,750

A Bryants All-Square Merchantmen Crane in stained oak casing, circa 1930, 84in. high.   £500

American 'twenty-one' gambling machine, circa 1930, 13½in. wide.   £150

An Art Deco style Mills 5c coin operated slot machine. £750

Coin operated mechanical sweepstakes game, manufactured by RMC, trademark Rock-Ola, circa 1930?, 12in. high.   £450

Elevenses, circa 1955, U.K. £250

Le Mille, circa 1935, France. £400

Circle Skill, circa 1928, Made in Saxony. £300

Beromat, circa 1959, Germany. £225

Gretna Green, The Smithy, circa 1930, U.K. £350

Plentywin, circa 1955, U.K. £250

Bullion, circa 1960, Bryans of Kegworth. £180

Columbus, Ball Chewing Gum Vendor, circa 1932, U.S.A. £100
(Nic Costa/Brian Bates)

Dutchboy, circa 1930, U.S.A. £500

DOLLS & TOYS

Grip Tester, circa 1930, U.K. £175

Like A Flash, Cigarette Vendor, circa 1935, U.K. £125

Super Steer-A-Ball, circa 1950, U.K. £400

Clucking Hen, circa 1900, Germany. £3,000

Sky Jump, circa 1948, U.K. £220

Dr. Bone's X-Ray machine, circa 1950, U.K. £200

Extraordinary, circa 1933, U.S.A. £500

Mystery, Chinese Crystal Gazer, circa 1930, U.K. £2,000

Three Gun Bomb Dropper, circa 1914, U.K. £1,000

(Nic Costa/Brian Bates)

French early 20th century
Decamps chamois-covered
walking pig, 15in. long.
£700

**A clockwork lithographed dog
with two puppies finished in
brown and white with red
collars, 17cm.
(Phillips)** £86

American six-piece carved wooden
polar bear with socket head, by
Schoenhut of Philadelphia.
£200

Italian cloth comic figure
in tan felt, by Lenci Tor-
ino, circa 1955, 11in. high.
£175

**A flock covered Carton Boston
terrier, with chain pull growl,
moving lower jaw and glass eyes,
21in. long, French.
(Christie's S. Ken)** £374

**A jointed all-bisque monkey with
moulded face and hands, dressed
in original crochet suit and hat,
2½in. high.
(Christie's S. Ken)** £55

Felix the cat with toothy
grin, circa 1928, 16in.
high. £750

Painted composition cat squeak
toy, America, late 19th century,
painted white with orange and
black markings seated on a
bellows base, 7¾in. high.
(Skinner Inc.) £620

An English leaping clock-
work hare. £75

A clockwork German cow finished in brown and cream, the mechanism causing the animal to walk and nod, 18.5cm. long.   £150

French 'walking pussy cat' toy with white fur covering, circa 1930, 30cm. long.   £200

Late 19th/early 20th century fur-covered papier mache polar bear, 16½in. long.£250

A rare felt-covered Flip The Frog with Dean's Rag Book Co. Ltd., logo on one foot, *Made In England* on the other, 8in. high. (Christie's S. Ken)   £418

The Three Bears, a set of miniature all bisque teddy bears jointed at shoulder and hip wearing original crochet clothes, 2¼in.-1¼in. high.   £400

A clockwork fur covered giraffe with clown rider, 31cm. high, and an HK, Fipps, clockwork nodding puppy.   £85

An unusual Decamps walking terrier, French, circa 1900, 12in. long.   £450

A Steiff fox, plushed covered, button in ear, circa 1912. (Woolley & Wallis)   £410

Six-piece carved wooden leopard, by Schoenhut of Philadelphia, 7in.   £200

DOLLS & TOYS

The most famous 18th century maker of automata was Vaucanson, who is best remembered for what might be termed a 'digestive duck' which voided the food it had first eaten! His finest piece was perhaps a figure playing an instrument which was presented at the Academie des Sciences in 1738.

This inspired many imitations. The greatest acclaim was given to Jacquet Droz, who brought out his Lady Musician in 1773, and this became famous at all European courts.

By the 19th century automata were becoming more and more complex, with acrobats and dancing dolls, monkey orchestras and shoecleaners, while in America walking dolls became popular.

They were powered in various ingenious ways, such as compressed air, water, sand, mercury or steam. It was however the coiled spring which was to prove the most popular and efficient means of power.

It was the Victorian period which saw the heyday of the sophisticated automaton. One late 19th century maker was Gustave Vichy whose work is often characterised by its height, many of his models standing over 30 inches high. His Negro figures with musical instruments have particularly fine leather faces with expressive facial movements even to the lips.

By the end of the 19th century, toymakers, particularly in Germany had recognised the possibilities of mass-producing automatic toys, and the tinplate toy industry began to boom. The machine-produced results, were cheap and rudimentary, and thereafter mechanical toys came to be associated mainly with children.

A 19th century French musical clock diorama featuring a village scene on the banks of a river, signed Hy Marl, 37¾in. x 26¾in. £2,500

A coin-in-the-slot ship automaton featuring a three masted vessel at full sail set in a choppy sea, contained in a fret-cut mahogany glazed case, 42¾in. wide. (Bearnes) £1,550

A picture automaton, the timepiece in the church facade activates the clock-work mechanism, probably French, 35in. long. £1,750

A hand-operated musical automaton toy of a village scene, depicting a train travelling through tunnels, circa 1900 Erzegebirge, 12¼in. wide. (Christie's S. Ken) £660

A boxed clockwork toy, of two composition headed dolls swinging and dancing before a mirror, 11in. wide, circa 1870. (Christie's S. Ken) £660

Die Sud-Nord-Eisenbahn bei Erlangen, a coloured lithograph sand toy, depicting a river scene with a train crossing a viaduct, 10½in. wide, Studio of Godefrey Engelmann, Alsace circa 1830. (Christie's S. Ken) £1,705

Late 19th century French musical landscape automaton with numerous moving figures and animals, on an ebonised base with bun feet, 22in. high. £1,500

A mid 19th century German portable barrel organ automaton with numerous articulated figures, contained in a carved oak case with ormolu decoration, 52cm. wide. £8,000

Unnamed and hitherto unknown musical automat, with 5 tunes, 15cm. metal cylinders with complete 57 tooth tone comb, 2 part spring winding and two mechanical dolls, in wooden case with wall attachment, circa 1890. (Auction Team Koln) £15,668

A French musical manivelle of a 'Mouse Tea-Party', each animal having glass eyes and fur covered body.
(Phillips)   £750

A clockwork fur covered rabbit automaton, emerging from a green cotton covered cabbage, 7½in. high, French, circa 1900. (Christie's) £330

'Monkey Cobbler', automaton with papier-mâché head, glass eyes, and articulated jaw, seated on a box.
(Phillips)   £650

An Austrian rabbit-in-the-lettuce, musical automaton, the rotating white fur-covered rabbit emerging from the painted fabric lettuce, 10in. high.
(Christie's)   £550

A German hand-operated musical automaton, of three wooden fur-covered cats, having a tea party, 19th century, ¼in. wide.
(Christie's)   £715

An R.D. France drinking bear, dark brown and white rabbit fur, glass eyes, electrical, 1930's, 14½in. high. £600

A coin-operated monkey pianist automaton, with the mechanism contained in the oak base, probably French, late 19th century, 16in. high.   £5,000

A clockwork automaton figure of a standing bear drummer, with moving lower jaw and front paws, 27in. high, probably Decamps, 1880. (Christie's)
£1,100

A Pussy Band Printed Paper automaton, circa 1910, 18in. high. £400

AUTOMATONS
ANIMALS

Early 20th century German clockwork musical bear of golden mohair with movable limbs and head, 7¼in. high. **£200**

A German cat picture automaton, depicting a singing master with his choristers, of polychrome painted and lithographed card, framed and glazed, 10½ x 14in., circa 1900. (Phillips) **£750**

A clockwork cabbage automaton containing a white rabbit, French, circa 1900, 6½in. high. **£450**

'Little Mocking Bird' painted tinplate clockwork musical box, with eccentric-driven bellows and rotating songbird, circa 1900, 4½in. wide. (Christie's S. Ken) **£605**

A fine automaton monkey duo comprising a photographer and seated lady, the subject, each with papier-mâché head, glass eyes, articulated kid-covered jaw revealing painted teeth, 26in. base to apex; probably J. Phalibois, late 19th century. (Phillips) **£2,900**

A painted tinplate toy of a monkey on a four-wheel musical carriage, German, circa 1903, 7½in. long. **£350**

A clockwork musical automaton of a white rabbit in a rose, with brown glass eyes and movements to body, head and ears, 8in. high, by Roullet & Decamps. (Christie's S. Ken) **£770**

A hand-operated musical automaton, of a cat and dog with composition heads and glass eyes, playing instruments, in original clothes, 12in. wide. (Christie's S. Ken) **£605**

A Roullet et Decamps 'Cat Ironing' musical automaton, the fur covered body with glass eye (one missing), long tail and carved hands. (Phillips) **£400**

A musical conjuror
automaton, probably
Decamps, French 1880,
overall height 17in.
£7,000

A 19th century bisque-
headed Magicienne automa-
ton.   £7,500

A musical automaton doll in
the form of a magician linking
together a long chain of brass
rings, wearing an exotic
costume in the Turkish style,
15¼in. high. (Bearne's) £940

Automaton magician, 52½in.
high, 36½in. wide.   £2,000

A musical conjuror automaton by
Lambert, the bisque head impressed (Depose Tete Jumeau 4),
overall height 19½in. French,
circa 1880.   £3,500

A musical conjuror automaton
standing at her magic box,
French, circa 1880, 18in. high
by 12in. wide.   £6,000

A musical automaton of a
conjuror, probably by L.
Lambert, French, circa
1880, 16in. high.   £2,000

Swiss automaton music
box, circa 1900, of a
magician, 23in. high.
                          £4,000

A lady conjuror automaton,
lavishly dressed in pink silk,
mounted on square plinth,
probably French, circa
1905, 26in. high.   £3,500

AUTOMATONS
DOLLS

French musical automaton of a girl seated smelling flowers, by Leopold Lambert, circa 1880, 19¾in. high.   £3,000

A French Bebe automaton in original silk dress and underclothes, early 20th century.   £3,500

French bisque automaton doll, in original blue taffeta gown, circa 1880, height 19in.   £7,500

An Armand Marseille bisque headed musical poupard, with blonde mohair wig, fixed blue glass eyes and open mouth, 38.5cm. long overall.(Henry Spencer)   £400

German bisque automaton, dolls by Armand Marseille, circa 1890, 12in. high.   £1,500

German bisque automaton 'The Imhof Walking Doll', 1898-1909, 12in. high, with key-wind mechanism.   £850

French musical automaton, the bisque head stamped Depose Tete Jumeau Bte. S.G.D.G.4, circa 1880, 18in. high.   £4,000

A crying Jumeau musical automaton by Lambert, the bisque head impressed 211 and (Depose Tete Jumeau 4) French, circa 1890, height 20½in.   £4,000

A bisque headed musical automaton, modelled as a standing child holding a covered basket, 19in. high, by Lambert, the head stamped Tete Jumeau. (Christie's)   £2,640

49

A Leopold Lambert musical automaton doll, 'The Flower Seller', the Jumeau bisque head impressed 4, 19½in. high. £5,000

An S.F.B.J. bisque doll and ball automaton, circa 1910, French, height 13in. £700

An Armand Marseille musical/dancing bisque headed puppet doll, impressed 70·20,5. £850

A musical automaton of a doll cradling her baby, probably German, circa 1890, 23in. high. £800

A 19th century clockwork lady knitting automaton, Germany, 21in. high. £2,000

French bisque automaton by Emile Jumeau, circa 1890, 19in. high overall. £3,500

French ballerina automaton with bisque head impressed S.F.B.J. 801, Paris, circa 1900. £3,500

A cane birdcage automaton with bisque doll, German, circa 1915, overall size 13in. £1,500

A bisque-headed automaton standing figure modelled as a child, 20in. high, the key marked L.B.4. £2,500

French bisque automaton by Leopold Lambert, circa 1900, 20in. high.
£3,000

Early 20th century mother rocking baby automaton, German, the oak base contains the mechanism.
£1,000

A Leopold Lambert musical automaton of a flower girl, the Jumeau bisque head with fair mohair wig over cork pate, 18½in. high. (Phillips)   £3,400

French type bisque automaton, 18in. high, circa 1890.
£2,000

A musical automaton of a bisque headed doll beside a dressing table, marked Simon & Halbig S & H 6, the doll 15in. high.
£3,000

French bisque automaton fashion doll, probably Vichy, circa 1875, 15in. high.
£2,250

A bisque headed automaton, the German head impressed 5/0, probably French, circa 1900, 18in. high.   £850

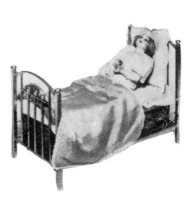

A sleeping doll automaton, the doll lying in a brass bedstead, probably French, circa 1910, 14in.
£2,250

A 19th century French automaton figure, head stamped Depose Tete Jumeau, 47cm. high.
£3,500

A bisque headed automaton with Armand Marseille head, probably German, circa 1900, 14½in. high. £750

A clockwork wheeled toy of a bisque swivel headed ballerina of Parisienne type, French, circa 1880, 17in. high. £2,000

A musical automaton by Lambert, in pale green silk dress and shoes, French, 1885, height 19½in. £5,000

A clockwork musical automaton of a papier mache headed Japanese girl carrying tray and parasol, 33in. high, probably by Vichy. (Christie's) £4,950

A clockwork automaton toy of a bisque headed doll pulling a wooden two-wheeled cart with driver, 13in. long. £2,000

A musical automaton, the bisque head impressed (Depose Tete Jumeau Bte. S.G.D.G. 4), French, late 19th century, height 20in. £3,500

French/German bisque automaton, doll by Simon & Halbig, circa 1890. 21in. high. £6,000

The Reaper, a bisque headed clockwork musical automaton, modelled as a child in original red waistcoat, 17in. high, by Vichy, the head stamped in red Tete Jumeau. (Christie's) £3,080

Two Schoenau & Hoffmeister automaton dolls dressed as Pulchinelles, German, late 19th century, 21in. high by 12½in. £2,500

A musical automaton of a dancing couple by Vichy, French, circa 1860, 13½in. high.   £1,500

German automaton with bisque dolls, circa 1890, 26in. wide, with ten mechanical actions.   £7,000

Late 19th century French clockwork musical automaton of two dancing figures, 13½in. high.   £5,000

A late 19th century Ives 'Dancing Negroes' automaton, each black painted doll with papier-mâché head, within a wooden box, 10½in. high. (Phillips)   £400

A French automaton dancing couple by Theroude, on velvet lined circular base, 12in. high.   £1,500

A coloured lithographic boxed sand toy, depicting Pierrot climbing up to a lady on a balcony with Harlequin preventing him with a stick, 8½in. high, published by Carre-Michels circa 1840. (Christie's S. Ken)   £770

A printed paper on wood automaton toy of a house on fire, with two figures working a pump at the side, 10in. high, German. (Christie's)   £330

A hand-operated automaton of a garden tea party, German late 19th century, approx. 12½in. high by 11½in. wide.   £4,000

'The Old Nurse', an Excelsior mechanical toy of a seated Negro nurse with ward, when activated, mechanism causes nurse to lean backwards, raising the child in the air. (Phillips)   £850

An advertising display automaton on oak base, circa
1930, 25in. wide. £1,500

A bisque headed clockwork
clown standing on his hands
dressed in original outfit,
16in. high. (Christie's) £350

19th century wooden
and papier-mache auto-
maton, 36in. high.
£1,000

A very rare early 20th century
French electrically-operated life-
size black boy magician
automaton, in painted papier-
mâché, 53¹/₂in. high excluding
associated top hat, with Cressall
speed control.
(Tennants) £4,800

French bisque automaton,
probably Farkas, circa
1920, 12in. high.
£1,000

A composition headed auto-
maton modelled as a standing
Chinese man, 30in. high,
French 1880. £7,500

An automaton figure of a
clown with painted composition face and black and white
costume, 18in. high, with
glass dome. £2,000

A novelty automaton electric-
driven watch maker, with
illuminated sign to the front and
lamp to his desk, 8in. high.
(Christie's S. Ken) £660

A papier mache automaton
of a clown, the head inset
with fixed blue glass eyes,
18in. high. £1,000

AUTOMATONS
MALE FIGURES

An electric operated advertising automaton with moving arms, eyes, head and eyebrows, on painted wood base, 30in. high. (Anderson & Garland) £240

A Chinese automaton, of a nobleman in original silk robes and elaborate saddle cloth and harness, sitting astride a white silk covered horse, 19in. high. (Christie's S. Ken) £330

A bisque headed, hand operated automaton of a jester ringing handbells, dressed in original outfit, with musical movement, 15in. high. (Christie's) £490

Clown Equilibriste, a composition-headed musical automaton, modelled standing on a chair, with green and red wool wig, by Vichy, 21in. high. (Christie's S. Ken.) £5,500

A carved wooded headed electric automaton, modelled as a man reading The Complete Car Modeller, inscribed David Secrett, 18½in. long. (Christie's S. Ken.) £385

Rare drinking musical automaton, probably by Vichy, circa 1890, slightly damaged, 29½in. high. £7,500

Mid 19th century papier mache two-faced clockwork musical automaton figure, 18in. high. £750

A papier mache ginger jar musical automaton, French, late 19th century, the hinged cover opening to reveal a chinaman drinking tea, 12in. high.(Christie's) £1,726

Late 19th century 'Boy Feeding Pig' automaton, the bisque head marked Jumeau SGDG 4, 18¾in. high. £2,500

AUTOMATONS
MUSICIANS

A very fine Gustav Vichy musical automaton of a young woman playing the guitar, circa 1870. (Phillips)   £7,200

A French Manivelle automaton of a piano player and dancing couple, the pianist seated before a wooden piano, 8¹/₂in. high. (Phillips)   £600

French musical automaton piano player, head impressed SFBJ 301 Paris, circa 1910, 13in. high.   £800

A barrel organ grinder automaton, probably French, circa 1900, 17in. high.   £800

A bisque headed clockwork musical automaton pianist, with closed smiling mouth and fixed blue eyes, by Phalibois, circa 1885, 24in. high, with label giving the airs. (Christie's S. Ken)   £3,300

A black composition headed musical automaton, modelled as a smiling man seated on a stool strumming a banjo, by G. Vichy, circa 1900, 24in. high. (Christie's S. Ken.)   £4,400

A painted tinplate clockwork musical Puss-in-Boots playing cello, the mechanism operating bowing right arm, probably Martin (one ear missing, spike loose), 9in. high. (Christie's S. Ken.)   £770

A German musical automaton, 'Musical Troupe' with seven bisque dolls, circa 1880, dolls 7in. high.   £3,000

A clockwork musical automaton of a papier mache headed North African girl, sitting on a stool inset with paste jewels and playing a lyre, 29in. high. (Christie's)   £4,180

56

AUTOMATONS
MUSICIANS

A German 19th century automaton of an organ grinder with miniature dancers, on a garden stage.
£3,000

SFBJ bisque headed automaton doll seated playing a piano, the doll impressed SFBJ 60 Paris, with brown hair and fixed brown glass eyes, 13½in. wide. (Hobbs & Chambers)
£400

A musical monkey harpist automaton, probably by Vichy, French, circa 1870, 19in. high.
£6,000

A hand operated musical automaton of a violin player, the bisque head with light brown wool wig, in original red and white suit with wood hands, feet and violin, 7½in. high. (Christie's S. Ken)
£418

Late 19th century German tinplate automaton featuring a violinist and harpist who are activated when the handle is turned on the musical box, 9¾in. wide.
£750

An automaton mandolin player, with musical movement in base, stamped G. Vichy, Paris, 25½in. high.
£2,250

French musical automaton of a piano player, circa 1915.
£1,500

An automaton of a young girl seated at an upright piano, the French bisque head marked 4, 41cm. high.
£4,000

A fine Leopold Lambert musical automaton 'Clown Playing the Mandolin', the composition heads with painted insects, blue glass eyes, protruding tongue, with white and red mohair wig. (Phillips)
£3,600

French musical bird-in-cage automaton, late 19th century, feathered figure with mechanical beak, tail and head, 11in. high. (Robt. W. Skinner Inc.) £400

Celluloid singing bird in a painted tinplate cage, with clockwork mechanism in base of cage, 4¼in. high, German, 1920's. (Christie's)   £400

A singing bird automaton, the domed brass cage with hinged door, French, circa 1900, 21½in. high. £1,250

A singing bird automaton with clock, Swiss, probably by Jacquet Droz, circa 1785, 20in. high.   £35,000

Mid 19th century Swiss musical automaton of singing birds, on oval base, 60cm. high. (Christie's)   £1,400

A 19th century square section bird cage of wire and turned wood, the base containing a musical box, 17in. high.   £250

Mid 19th century Swiss gilt metal automaton with three singing birds, 21in. high. £3,000

A singing bird automaton, French, last quarter 19th century, the glass case containing a tree with silk leaves and flowers and a total of seven birds and two large beetles. (Tennants)   £950

A 19th century European singing bird automaton, 22in. high.   £1,500

A late 19th century French gilt metal automaton bird in a cage, 8in. high. £350

An early Issmayer small tinplate singing bird in cage, circa 1904, 8in. high. £400

Mid 19th century automaton of a singing bird in a cage, the movement signed Bontems, Paris, 21½in. high. (Christie's) £1,100

A Bontems singing bird automaton with three birds under a cage, French, mid 19th century, 21½in. high. £8,500

A Louis XVI ormolu-mounted Paris porcelain musical automaton clock, playing a selection of six tunes through ten organ pipes, cam-and-rod drive through a composition tree to an automaton bird atop flapping its wings, rotating and opening and shutting its beak, 26$^1/_4$in. high. (Christie's) £11,550

A good French twin singing bird automaton, the brass wire domed cage containing a bird on a perch, with a companion below, 22in. high overall, second half 19th century. (Tennants) £1,800

Brass singing bird automaton, having a pair of feathered model birds on branches under domed cage, 7in. high. (Hobbs & Chambers) £255

Mid 19th century Swiss musical automaton of singing birds, 38in. high. £1,000

A gilt metal and composition bird-cage containing a feathered bird automaton on a perch, 12½in. high. £1,000

AUTOMATONS
SINGING BIRDS

A jewelled 3¾in. rectangular gilt brass singing bird box, with key and case. £900

Late 19th century singing bird music box, Switzerland, with bird-shaped key, 4in. wide. £2,000

A singing bird box, the silver plated case with lid opening to small singing bird, 3¾in. wide. £1,000

A gilt metal and enamel singing bird box, decorated with Watteauesque scenes. £1,000

A 20th century singing bird automaton, Switzerland, box height 1¾in. and 4.1/8in. wide. (Skinner Inc.) £419

Late 19th century French key-wind singing bird automaton, 4in. wide. £750

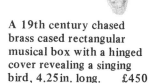

An enamelled gold singing bird box, probably Les Freres Rochat, Geneva, early 19th century, the base, sides and top with blue enamel panels, 9.2cm. long. (Christie's) £21,579

A fine engraved gold singing bird box by Georges Reymond, Geneva, the movement providing song and motions to head, beak and wings of feathered bird, circa 1805–1815, 71mm. long. (Christie's New York) £17,952

A 19th century chased brass cased rectangular musical box with a hinged cover revealing a singing bird, 4.25in. long. £450

Late 19th century Continental singing bird automaton in repousse sterling silver gilt casket, 4¼in. wide. £850

A German silver and enamel singing bird box, struck with English import hallmarks for 1926, 4in. long. £2,500

Early 20th century enamel singing bird automaton, 3¼in. high. £1,000

BABY PLATES

Perhaps the best known series is Doulton's Bunnykins, the original designs for which were inspired by Sister Mary Barbara, who was the daughter of Cuthbert Bailey, general manager at Burslem from 1925. Looking for new designs for nursery ware, his daughter's doodles of rabbits came to mind, and the Barbara Vernon series of characters was born. By 1939 there were 66 different Bunnykins scenes.

German baby plate decorated with a country scene, 7in. diam. £25

Royal Doulton bone china 'Bunnykins'. £15

Royal Doulton baby plate. £10

Late 19th century blue and white miniature plate, 3in. diam. £10

Doulton 'Bunnykins' bowl. £10

Rockwood pottery dish, Cincinnati, Ohio, 1882, signed by Nathaniel J. Hirschfield, diam. 6½in. (Robt. W. Skinner Inc.) £75

'Painted Feelings' rack plate, Behind the Painted Masque Series, 9in. diam., 1982. £20

Saturday Evening Girls pottery motto plate, Mass., 1914, signed S.G. for Sara Galner, 7½in. diam. (Robt. W. Skinner Inc.) £2,750

Wedgwood Beatrix Potter's 'Peter Rabbit'. £10

Royal Doulton bone china 'Bunnykins'. £15

Carrigatine Pottery, 'Winnie the Pooh'. £8

A lithographed Penny Toy of a nodding goose on dark green wheeled undercarriage, 9cm., some rust.
(Phillips) £46

Early 20th century lithographed tin wind-up toy, Japanese 'Chick-Chick', 10in. long. £175

A German painted tinplate clockwork pigeon, with nodding head and call, circa 1910, 21cm. long. (Christie's S. Ken) £200

A tinplate 'Rudy' walking ostrich, the underside marked 'Nifty', 8½in. high, German, circa 1925. £200

A carved wooden paddle toy, modelled as a peacock, 9½in. high. £150

Early 19th century rooster squeak toy, moulded papier mache body on coiled wire legs, 5in. high. £200

Late 19th century cast iron baby chick pull toy, patented 1881, 5in. high. £680

A brass 'Canary songster' photographer's birdie in maker's original box by the Risden Mfg. Co., Naugatuck, U.S.A. (Christie's S. Ken) £528

American carved wooden five-piece goose, with two-part articulated head and throat, by Schoenhut of Philadelphia. £250

BUSES

Many of the finest tin plate toys represented means of transport – trains, ships, cars and buses. They were the first powered by clockwork but as the use of it declined, they were driven by friction motors or battery operated electric motors. Both single and double decker buses were made and they often had interesting advertising along their sides. One Bing model made about 1910 of a vehicle belonging to the United Bus Company Ltd carried a large placard advertising the appearance of Harry Lauder at the Tivoli Theatre. American 'Greyhound' buses were produced by Japanese manufacturers in the 1960s and 70s and trolley buses were made by Brimtoy and Betal. Brimtoy's products are particularly good and rival the German equivalents. When the last Paris trolley bus was taken off the road, a clockwork replica model was made by Joustra and sold well. Triang Minic also included buses in their range.

Model buses range in size from one inch to eight feet in length and prices vary according to condition.

Generally speaking buses are a particularly sought after vehicle group, and command a premium over cars.

Spot-On – 156 Mulliner Luxury Bus (pale blue/silver), (M), boxed.
£450

Gunthermann, post-war tramcar finished in orange, cream and pale yellow.
£100

Crawfords Biscuits Bus OK 3852, with original box, 25.5cm. (Phillips)   £2,400

A Bing clockwork painted and lithographed tinplate 'United Motor Bus Company Ltd' London double-decker bus, circa 1912, 11in. long. (Christie's S. Ken)   £3,850

A Distler lithographed tinplate clockwork London General double decker bus, with moving conductor, circa 1929. (Christie's S. Ken)   £1,100

Distler, open top bus 'Health Virol Strength/Bovril' advertisement, with moving bus conductor, 22.5cm., circa 1929. (Phillips)   £420

'Autobus', a printed and painted tinplate open 'Berlin' type double deck omnibus, by Lehmann, circa 1912, 8in. long. (Christie's)   £770

Wells Brimtoy (Great Britain) tinplate buses and coaches, circa 1950.   Value £40 to £70

Tootsietoy Greyhound Bus (U.S.A.), diecast, circa 1940.   £45

A Lehmann lithographed tinplate EPL No. 590 Autobus, finished in red and yellow, with original price label and tags for securing string handle, in original box with pencil inscription 'Motor Buss'. (Christie's)   £1,980

Triang (Great Britain) prewar and postwar Greenline tinplate coaches.
Value £50 to £80

Copy of a Dinky toy one and a half deck coach by Maruson (Japan), 1950's. £100

Milton Morgan (India) copy of a Dinky coach, 1950's.   £30

1920's fretwork model of a bus.
£250

A Commer Avenger coach, by Chad Valley,
U.K., 1954.   £75

All Metal Toy Co. (U.S.A.), tinplate
coaches, 1940's.   £50

Betall tinplate
trolleybus,
circa 1950,
220mm. long.
£75

Betall (Great Britain)
tinplate trolleybus,
1950's, 175mm. long.
£50

Gunthermann (W. Germany)
tinplate General Bus, 1920's.
£400

Guinness tinplate bottle crate, 1964.
£100

C.I.J. (France) postwar
Renault coach.   £50

C.I.J. (France)
prewar Renault
coach.   £70

A trolleybus, by C.R., France, 1950.   £60

Chad Valley 10005 blue and cream passenger coach, 30cm. (Phillips)   £170

Tinplate coach, by Gunthermann, Germany, map on base, 1948.   £75

Large Bedford coach, by Fun Ho, New Zealand, cast aluminium, 1965.   £30

Guy Arab coach, by Mettoy, U.K. (predecessors of Corgie Toys), diecast, 1950.   £55

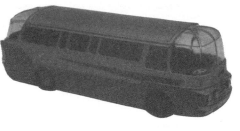

Mulliner Coach, by Spot-On, U.K., 1963. £200

A Gunthermann tinplate and clock-work tramcar, No. 21, 25cm. long. £200

Triang (Great Britain), prewar tinplate bus with white rubber wheels.   £50

A double deck, by Chad Valley, U.K., 1949.
£100

A tramcar, No. 846, by Gunthermann, Germany, 1955.
£85

Chad Valley (Great Britain) double decker Greenline tinplate bus, circa 1930.
£300

Minic Motorways double decker and coach, by Triang, U.K., 1960's.
£30 to £45

A 1950 tinplate Express bus, by Wolverine, U.S.A.
£75

A diecast trolleybus, by Taylor & Barrett, U.K., 1936.
£55

Jitney Bus, Made in Phillipines, 1970's/80's.
£20

Six-wheeled trolleybus, by Joustra, France, tinplate, battery operated lights, 1952. £100

French Dinky — 29f Chausson Coach, circa
1956.   £75
29d Somua Panhard, circa
1951.   £80

Joustra — France — 1950's Ile de France
Tinplate Coach.   £95

Maks — Hong Kong — 1960, Copy in Plastic
of the Dinky Coach.   £8

TN — Japan 1960's Tinplate Greyhound
Lines Coach.   £45

Gamda — Israel, Leyland Worldmaster Diecast
Coach, circa 1950's.   £90

Chad Valley — UK — Tinplate Double Deck
Bus — circa 1949.   £70

Wiking — Germany — Early Plastic Tramcar —
1950's.   £30

Well's Brimtoy — UK — No. 516 Tinplate
Trolleybus, 1950's, Clockwork.   £55

Jye — Spain — 1½ Deck Tinplate Coach, 1950's, Very Rare Model.   £65

C.I.J. — France — 1950's Tinplate Coach.   £65

Guntermann — West Germany — 1930's Tinplate Tram.   £150

Japanese 1960's Tinplate Double Deck Bus.   £45

Tipp & Co — Germany — Circa 1950's Tinplate Bonneted Coach.   £65

Wells Brimtoy Greenline Tinplate Coach, 1950's.   £75

Dinky Toys — UK, 1963 Continental Touring Coach, 1961 School Bus.   £80

HJC — Japan — Tinplate 1950's Greyhound.   £60

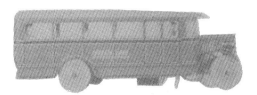

A printed tinplate model of a Green Line bus, German, circa 1925, 11½in. long. £400

Cast iron model of a Leyland Lion single decker bus £800

A handbuilt working model of a 'Freelance' open topped tram. £350

F. G. Taylor — UK — Diecast Trolleybus, Post War Example. £40

Modern Toys — Japan 1960, Battery Operated Old Fashioned Tinplate Bus. £70

Rico(Spain) tramcar with cut out tin figures in the windows, circa 1910. £275

Tootsietoy Greyhound Bus (USA), diecast, circa 1940. £50

A J.E.P. tinplate Paris Bus, lithographed 'Madeleine . . .', French, circa 1925, 10¼in. long. £400

French diecast Dinky toy,
Renault Isobloc, circa 1950.   £85

Joustra — France — 1950's Clockwork
Greyhound Tinplate Coach.   £65

Lesney Model No.12. A horse bus. (David
Lay)   £45

Wells — UK — Tinplate London Bus, circa
1960's.   £65

Bing, English market clockwork tramcar of
'O' gauge proportions, 18.5cm. long.   £500

Spot-On — 145 L.T. Route-master Bus
(transfer Radiator), (M), boxed.   £400

A Gunthermann tinplate and clockwork
six-wheeled general double-decker bus,
35cm. long.   £225

A Gunthermann double-decker bus clockwork activated, German, circa 1930. £400

Trailways Greyhound Eagle, Made in Japan, 1960's tinplates.   £20 — £45

Tinplate coaches by Jaj, Portugal, circa 1960.   £20 — £25

Three plastic Dinky copies of the 1960's, by Maks, Hong Kong. £10 — £15

Johillco (Great Britain)
diecast double decker,
circa 1935.   £100

Johillco (Great Britain)
diecast tram, circa 1935.
                    £150

Chad Valley (Great Britain),
single deck Midland Red
tinplate bus, 1930's.   £250

CIJ Renault coach, diecast, 1953 — £35, a trolley, 1960 and a Solido coach, diecast.
£25 — £40

French tinplate trolleybuses by Joustra, circa 1951.   £150

Tinplate San Francisco trams, Made in Japan, 1950's/1970's.   £20 — £25

Siku (W. Germany) one
and a half deck coach,
circa 1950.   £60

Siku (W. Germany)
Bussing coach,
circa 1950.   £50

Siku (W. Germany)
Riveria coach,
circa 1950.   £35

DOLLS & TOYS

An American carved wood horse, Jumper, the figure with a frightened expression and deeply carved mane, jewelled trappings and saddle with tulips at cantle, 55in. long.
(Christie's East) £991

A carved wood double-sided chariot, with deeply carved depictions of a woman riding a swan adorned with flowers, ribbons and sleeping lion, 54in. long.
(Christie's East) £1,516

A carved wood pig, Jumper, the figure with a corn cob in its mouth and corn stalk flowing from mouth to rear, 49in. long.
(Christie's East) £4,664

A carved wood leaping frog, the figure with whimsical expression and carved saddle, vest and bow tie, 38in. high.
(Christie's East) £9,328

A carved wood rocking chariot, with a deeply carved depiction of a woman holding onto stylised waves amongst carved flowers and jewelled trappings.
(Christie's East) £1,457

A carved wood zebra, Jumper, the figure with short carved mane and looped tail, 43in. long.
(Christie's East) £5,830

An American carved wood horse, Prancer, the figure with expressive face and deeply carved mane, saddle and blanket, 55in. long.
(Christie's East) £4,664

A French carved wood nodding head donkey, Gustave Bayol of Angers, circa 1885, the figure with carved short mane, saddle and tail, 49in. long.
(Christie's East) £3,206

A carved wood cat, the figure in a leaping pose, with a sweet expressive face and deeply carved bow at the neck, 49in. long.
(Christie's East) £10,494

Light brown ram, Stander, the figure with deeply carved horns and fur, a sweet expressive face and carved saddle, 39in. high. (Christie's East) £4,664

A carved wood dog, Jumper, the figure with deeply carved fur and sweet expression, carved collar, chains and saddle with tassels, 53in. long. (Christie's East) £7,579

A carved wood horse, Jumper, the figure with carved mane, saddle and flowing blanket, 49in. long. (Christie's East) £1,632

A carved wood horse, Prancer, the figure in skygazer pose with deeply carved flowing mane and jewelled trappings, 53in. long. (Christie's East) £11,077

A carved wood Uncle Sam chariot, with a deeply carved image of Uncle Sam and an American eagle above an American flag. (Christie's East) £3,789

A carved wood zebra, Jumper, Stargazer pose, the figure with rearing head and carved cropped mane, 42in. long. (Christie's East) £4,664

A carved wood stork, the figure in a striding pose with deeply carved feathers, saddle with a baby at cantle and blanket, 67in. high. (Christie's East) £13,409

A German carved wood pig, Jumper, by Friedrich Heyn, circa 1900, the figure with a sweet expressive face and wagging tongue, 29½in. long. (Christie's East) £496

Multi coloured giraffe, Stander, the figure with carved short cropped mane and sweet expressive face, 59in. high. (Christie's East) £4,956

CARS 1900–1909
BING

Ignaz and Adolf Bing opened their Gebrüder Bing works in Nuremberg in 1863, and they went on to become one of the 'Big Three' German toy manufacturers of the later 19th century, the others being Märklin and Lehmann.

They produced a wide range of clockwork toys, boats, steam-driven models, trains and cars and their work was characterised from the first by the solidity of its construction and by a meticulous attention to detail. The best of their cars were hand painted, had opening doors and bevelled glass.

Up to 1918, Bing products were marked *GBN* (Gebrüder Bing Nuremberg), whereas after 1919 they were marked *BW* (Bing Werke).

BUB

The Karl Bub Company was founded as far back as 1851 in Nuremberg and is most famous for its range of clockwork and electric model trains. It took over the Bing company in 1933, and after the Second World War had a factory in England, although their products are not generally well-known over here. The company ceased trading in 1967.

CARETTE

The Carette company was founded in Nuremberg in 1886 by Georges Carette, and came to be regarded as one of the top toy manufacturers of the period. Quality was paramount and many toys, such as large scale cars, boats and trains, were hand-enamelled. There was also great attention to detail and early Carette cars are unique in having folding windscreens and hand brakes.

Carette closed in 1917 and did not start up again until after the First World War. Their trademarks are *GC* or *GC & Cie.*

A rare 'De Dion', hand enamelled tinplate car, by Bing, circa 1904, finished in white, with maroon seats, black interior, 7¾in. long. (Christie's)   £2,310

Carette, a clockwork four seater Torpedo, hand painted in cream with green lining, lacking lamps, windscreen and two tyres, 32cm. long. (Phillips)   £4,200

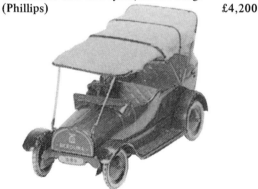

Lehmann, No. 686 clockwork open tourer with hood 'Berolina' finished in blue with gold lining and yellow fabric hood, 10.5cm.   (Phillips)   £943

"Hessmobile", a lithographed and painted tinplate two seater car, with a hand-cranked flywheel mechanism, by Hess, circa 1908, 8¾in. long.   £400

A rare Marklin clockwork four-seat Tourer, German, circa 1909, 9¼in. long.   £6,000

An unusual Marklin small limousine, German, circa 1900, 8¼in. long.   £2,750

A Carette lithographed tinplate and clockwork rear entrance four-seater Tonneau automobile, 12¼in. long, German, circa 1907.   £2,500

A Bing hand-painted open-cab limousine with bevelled glass windows, German, circa 1908, 10½in. long.   £2,750

A live-steam spirit-fired, hand enamelled model of a horseless carriage, probably by Bing, circa 1902, 9in. long.   £1,500

A Carette tinplate Open Tourer, German, circa 1906, 8in. long, together with original cardboard box.   £4,000

A Bing hand-enamelled tinplate model of a De Dion runabout motor car, circa 1905, 7½in. long.   £750

A German hand-painted Bing limousine, circa 1908, 8in.   £1,500

CARS 1910–1919

GUNTHERMANN

Siegfried Gunthermann founded his toymaking firm in Nuremberg in 1877. He died in 1890 and his widow remarried Adolf Wiegel, whose initials were incorporated in Gunthermann toys until 1919, after which time *SG* was used.

Gunthermann are famous for their tinplate horse-drawn vehicles, fire engines and aeroplanes, all of which were of very high quality, while their clockwork cars, dating from the 1930s and 40s, are now among the most collectable of the period.

MÄRKLIN

The firm of Gebrüder Märklin was established in 1859 in Göppingen, in Bavaria. It produced toys that were mainly for the export market, and manufactured trains etc. in styles and liveries according to the taste of the importing country, also altering the names on ships accordingly.

They have remained preeminent in the field of toy production up to the present day.

MOKO

The Moko trademark is that of Moses Kohnstam who set up as a toy distributor and wholesaler in Furth, Germany, in 1875. He was used by many local toy manufacturers to market their toys, which often carried the Kohnstam trademark.

In the 1930s the Kohnstams fled the Nazis and came to England, where Moses' grandson Richard continued to manufacture and also to wholesale the products of small London companies such as Benbros and Lesney. There is also a small range of interesting diecast toys by unknown manufacturers which bear the Kohnstam mark.

A hand painted limousine, by Carette, circa 1912, complete with clockwork mechanism driving rear axle, operating brake (lacks chauffeur and headlamps), 10½in. long. (Christie's)   £1,045

An early hand-enamelled four seater open tourer, No. 3358/21, by Carette, circa 1911, with clockwork mechanism driving rear axle, composition painted chauffeur (very slightly chipped), 21cm. long. (Christie's)   £3,080

A Carette lithographed tinplate clockwork model of a four seater tonneau, with rubber tyred spoked wheels, handbrake, and side lamps, 33cm. long. (Henry Spencer)   £1,900

A repainted tinplate limousine, with clockwork mechansim driving rear axle, possibly by H. Fischer & Co., circa 1912, 13in. long. (Christie's S. Ken)   £242

A printed tinplate model of a 1910 Daimler Voyage limousine, by Carette, 15½in. long.
£1,000

A Bing tinplate and clockwork limousine, 9¾in. long, circa 1910. £2,250

Cast-iron early taxi cab, roofed open driver section, enclosed cab section, circa 1910, 6in. long. £100

A printed tinplate model of a 1910 Daimler Voyage limousine, by Carette, circa 1910, 15½in. long. £2,500

A Bing tinplate De Dion vehicle, the clockwork mechanism driving the rear axle, 6in. long, German, circa 1910. £750

A printed tinplate model of a limousine, by Carette, circa 1910, 15½in. long. £1,750

A Gunthermann tinplate four-seat open tourer and passengers, German, circa 1910, 7½in. long. £3,000

A Carette lithographed limousine, complete with driver, German, circa 1910, 8½in. long.
£2,000

A Bing hand-enamelled Mercedes type open tourer, circa 1912, 15¾in. long.   £5,500

A Moko clockwork six-cylinder saloon, 9½in. long, German, circa 1918-20.   £500

A Gunthermann painted and lithographed four-door limousine with clockwork mechanism, German, circa 1910, 11½in. long. £1,000

A Carette hand-painted four-seat Open Tourer, German, circa 1910, 12½in. long, together with original cardboard box. £7,500

A Carette tinplate and clockwork limousine, circa 1910.   £2,000

A Carette lithograph limousine, with clockwork mechanism, German, circa 1911, 8½in. long.   £1,250

Tinplate clockwork limousine and driver, 15in. long.   £1,500

A painted and lithographed German tinplate toy car, 4in. high.   £450

CARS 1920–1929

C I J

This, the Compagnie Industrielle du Jouet, was a French company founded in the 1920s and based in Paris. They produced high quality, large scale clockwork cars, such as the Alfa Romeo P2, which was almost 22 inches long.

Their products are very sought after, and mint boxed examples of this particular model have fetched over £2,000 at auction.

J E P

JEP (Jouets de Paris) was a subsidiary of the Société Industrielle de Ferblanterie (SIF), which was established in France in 1899. The JEP trademark was used between 1932 and 1965, when the company went out of business.

MARX

Louis Marx established his toy company in New York in 1920.

His products were often aimed at the lower end of the market, being popular, amusing and cheap. A factory was opened in South Wales in the 1930s, but following the Second World War most products were manufactured in the Far East.

TIPP & CO

Tipp & Carstans established a toy manufactory in 1912 in Nuremberg, to which by 1919 Philipp Ullmann had succeeded as sole owner. During the 1930s the company turned out a fine range of large-scale tinplate cars and planes.

The rise of Nazism meant that by 1934 Ullmann was forced to leave Germany. He came to the UK and settled in South Wales, where the company continued to manufacture tinplate toys until 1971.

Their trademark is an intertwined *T.Co* or *Tippco*.

A rare Fischer lithographed and painted tinplate limousine, with clockwork mechanism driving rear axle, German, circa 1927 (roof chipped, slightly damaged), 12½in. long. (Christie's) £550

A fine Distler printed and painted tinplate limousine No. 525, with chauffeur in front compartment, finished in tan over black, German, circa 1927, 6½in. long. (Christie's) £220

Automobile mechanique Andre Citroen, a large clockwork four door saloon, finished in two tone blue with black roof, 53.5cm., 1920's. (Phillips) £1,700

A rare hand painted tinplate four seater open tourer steam car by Doll & Co., circa 1924. (Christie's) £3,080

81

DOLLS & TOYS

A printed tinplate model of a limousine, by Tipp, circa 1920, 15in. long.
£400

An early Bing hand-painted open four-seat Tourer, German, circa 1920, 12¼in. long.
£3,500

A Bub tinplate and clockwork roadster, with tinplate driver, 36cm. long overall.
£1,500

The Buddy 'L', a painted metal push-along model T Ford Coupe, 10½in. long, U.S.A., circa 1924.
£400

A printed and painted tinplate model of a four-door limousine with clockwork mechanism, by Tipp & Co., circa 1928, 8¼in. long.
£600

Gunthermann Fire Car, German, circa 1925, 6¾in. long.
£650

A J.E.P. tinplate Renault Open Tourer, French, circa 1929, 13¼in. long.
£1,000

Turner steel four door sedan, circa 1924, 26½in. long.
£850

METTOY

The Mettoy Company was set up by Philipp Ullmann (of Tipp fame) and one of his erstwhile collaborators in Germany, Arthur Katz, after both men were forced to flee the Nazis in 1934. They took factory space with a firm of Northampton based engineers, where they developed a range of tinplate toys and finally opened their own factory in 1936, launching the Mettoy company in the same year. The first catalogue showed a range of tinplate and pressed metal toys very similar to those which had been made by Tipp. Many had clockwork mechanisms. Among the most sought after examples from this period are the large racing car in red and white and the medium size car and caravan.

After 1942 the factory switched to making armaments and production was not resumed until 1946, when a new catalogue was brought out, featuring many of the prewar lines, with slight variations.

In 1948 they launched a new range of heavy cast metal toys produced exclusively for Marks & Spencer. These were more robust than previous examples, and included coaches, a racing car, a fire engine, a lorry, van and saloons. The 830 racer even featured a clockwork engine, brake lever and steering control. This Heavy Car Mechanical Toys range was in production until 1951.

In 1949 the company opened a new factory in Swansea and it was here that the famous Corgi range of diecast models was made in the 1950s. Pressed tin toys continued to be made until 1960, when production switched entirely to the diecast Corgi products.

A printed and painted saloon, with clockwork mechanism driving rear axle, lady driver with hat and scarf, by Falk, circa 1933, 18in. long. (Christie's)   £715

J.E.P., large painted tinplate Rolls Royce open tourer finished in cream with red mudguards, lithographed 'wooden' running boards, 51cm., repainted, No. 7395 fatigue to driving shaft. (Phillips)   £1,000

Marx spring action two door saloon finished in red, black and brown, 19.5cm. (Phillips)   £50

The American National Company, painted steel model of a Packard finished in red with red and yellow lining, 73cm. long. (Phillips)   £1,200

A Lehmann 'Gala' tinplate limousine, German, circa 1930, 12½in.   £750

A Marx Charlie McCarthy & Mortimer Snerd auto, 1939, lithographed tin, 16in. long.   £550

A Bing lithographed open tourer, the clockwork mechanism driving the rear axle, 12½in. long, German, circa 1930.   £325

A Daimler Sedanca motor car, in the original box.   £400

Mettoy, a large four-door Saloon finished in bright lime-green with cream lining, the interior with chaffeur at the wheel, in box, 35cm. long.   £100

Painted and lithographed tin wind-up sedan, circa 1930, 11½in. long.   £450

Fischer tinplate saloon finished in red and black, German, circa 1935, 12½in. long.   £750

A large and impressive Karl Bub tinplate and clockwork limousine, circa 1932, German, 50cm. long.   £1,250

A Meccano non-constructional car, finished in red and blue, circa 1935, 8¾in. long.
£600

A tinplate limousine by Karl Bub, 14¼in. long, circa 1930.
£500

Pre-war tinplate model of a two-seater tourer car, 9½in. long, and a cardboard model of a 'Daily Mail' pre-war aircraft.
£45

An Ingap four-door limousine with clockwork mechanism, driving rear axle and operating front head lamps, 11¼in. long, circa 1930.
£450

Meccano, No. 2 Constructor Car constructed as a tourer, boxed.
£1,500

A Meccano car constructor kit, complete with clockwork model.
£850

A late 1930's toy sports coupe car with red roof and wings and gold wheels.
£800

A Triang Minic pre-war taxi (M), boxed, with key.
£400

CARS 1940–1970

CHAD VALLEY

By the 1930s and 40s British companies were working hard to compete with Continental tinplate toys. One of the most successful was the Chad Valley Co., which produced many diverse items from rag dolls to board games, but who also at this time produced a range of cars, ships and aeroplanes which were very much cheaper than their German counterparts. Their cars were mainly of the clockwork type, and in the 1930s their racing cars enjoyed a huge success. They are becoming increasingly sought after today.

CORGI

The 'Golden Age' of British toys, in the 1950s, saw the rise of a number of well-known companies. Corgi Toys was founded in 1956 and produced model cars etc. which were both innovative and represented excellent value for money. Their Chipperfield's Circus Gift Set in original box is now worth several hundred pounds. They also skilfully judged the market by launching models based on current crazes, the James Bond 'Goldfinger' Aston Martin DB5, for example, or Chitty Chitty Bang Bang, or even the Avengers Gift Set. Sadly, they too succumbed to the flood of cheap imports from the Far East and went out of business in the 1970s.

ICHIKO

The Ichiko Company set up in post war Japan and produced tin toys, with cars as a speciality. Some have since been reissued, for example a 1960s large scale Mercedes Benz 300 SE was replicated in the 1980s. Collectors should therefore be careful as to the exact dating of any example.

A Distler grey battery-operated tinplate Porsche Electromatic 7500, with instructions, in original box.
(Christie's S. Ken)   £605

A Wells printed and painted tinplate Rolls-Royce 'Coupe de Ville' limousine, with clock-work mechanism, 8¾ in. long, British, circa 1950. (Christie's)
£176

Britains set 1321, large armoured car with swivelling gun, khaki finish with white rubber treaded tyres in original box (E-G, box G)1937.
(Phillips)   £280

Dinky, a rare half dozen trade pack of 106 'The Prisoner' mini-mokes, in original boxes and original cellophane wrapping.
(Christie's S. Ken)   £660

ALPS battery operated Mystery car finished in two tone red and cream, the interior with lithographed detail, 30cm.
(Phillips)   £520

Schuco 5300 Ingenico, the open top saloon car finished in bright red, the interior lithographed in green and chequered seats, 22cm.
(Phillips)   £345

CARS 1940–1970
MATCHBOX

From 1953 the Lesney Company in Essex produced the Matchbox range of contemporary vehicles, their size, as the name suggests, being generally smaller than the average Dinky type. From 1956, they added the Model of Yesteryear Range. Models dating up to 1962 are generally sought after, but prices decline sharply thereafter. The company is still in existence today.

In 1982 Matchbox Toys was formed to replace Lesney products which had sold out to David Yeh of Universal Toys. In 1987 Matchbox purchased the Dinky name and launched a new range of Dinky products. Manufacturing is now done in the Far East, though the research and development departments are based in Enfield.

SOLIDO

Solido is a post war French company making diecast models, the earliest of which date from the early 60s. They are still in business today, but as is the case with Dinky, are no longer the same company, having been subject to a number of takeovers.

SPOT-ON

The Triang Company countered the success of Dinky with their Spot-on range, which were produced between 1959 and 1967. These models were beautifully detailed, with proper suspension and numerous features. The average mint boxed car fetches around £50 while the Bedford 'S' Shell-BP Tanker fetches upwards of £700 and the LT Routemaster Bus almost £500. Many consider them now to be underpriced, so they could be looked on, with caution, as a reasonably good buy. Spot-On closed in 1967, and the dies were shipped overseas.

Corgi, 262, Lincoln Continental, in rare colour scheme, blue/tan. (Phillips West Two) £150

Distler Electro Matic 7500, lithographed and painted battery operated Porsche car, with telesteering control, in original box, circa 1955, 9¾in. long. (Christie's S. Ken) £385

A Schuco Mercedes 190SL Elektro-Phänomenal 5503, with accessories and instructions, in original box, circa 1959. (Christie's S. Ken) £275

A Spot On Ford Zodiac No.100, original factory box. (Hobbs & Chambers) £50

KKK battery operated open top saloon car finished in red with cream interior and working head lights, 21.5cm., boxed. (Phillips) £75

Schuco, clockwork Radio Car 5000 finished in maroon and cream, complete with key and instructions, boxed. (Phillips) £1,800

Corgi Toys, MK1 Jaguar, in yellow trim, 1960-63. £20 − £30

Dinky Toys, XJ Coupe B roadspeed, limited production in the 1970's, no box issued. £5 − £8

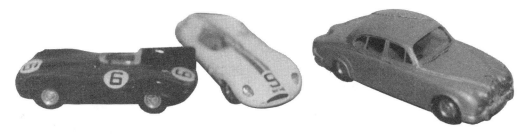

Western Models, D types, (No. 6 Hawthorn's 1955 Le Mans Winner). £20 − £30

Western Models, MK11, 3.8 Jaguar, current model. £30

Burago SS100, well detailed current model showing engine components, exhaust and suspension. £15

Matchbox Series, 3.8 MK11, complete with original box, 1959-67. £7 − £12

Dinky Toys D type Jaguar in light green, complete with original box, 1957-62. £20 − £35

Matchbox Model of Yesteryear, SS100, current model. £5

Solido XJ12's, now ceased production.
£7 – £12

Dinky Toys, SS100 Jaguar, produced 1946-50. £20 – £30

Spot-On Mark X with turning wheel and opening boot, 1963-64. £20 – £35

Dinky Toys, XK120 model, produced 1954-62. £20 – £35

Corgi Toys, Mark X with opening boot and bonnet, 1962-67. £15

Corgi Toys, XJ Coupe, with opening doors and bonnet. £6

Corgi Toys, E type with racer in the foreground, production car behind, 1962-64. £20 – £35

Corgi Toys, Jaguar XJS racer with good detail. £5

A battery-operated four-door Cadillac State Service Car, boxed, 49cm. long. £300

A tin toy car, modelled as two-seater Model A with leather wheels and painted details, 6in. high, 6in. wide, 20in. long. £100

A Hungarian open tourer in blue, 26cm. £100

'Cadillac', a printed and painted tinplate car, with friction-drive mechanism, rubber tyred wheels and tinted windows, by Ichiko, circa 1967, 28in. long. £500

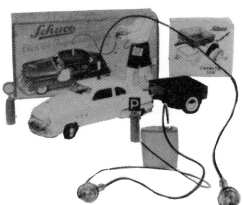

A Schuco Ingenico electric remote control car 5311/56, and a Carreto 5330 trailer, in original boxes. £300

Gama tinplate 300 friction Cadillac in red and black, (M), boxed, 31cm. long. £600

Spot-On, set No. 260, The Royal Presentation Set, in original box. £300

French C.I.J. tinplate Fregate Panhard, French, circa 1955, 12½in. long. £200

Spot-On – 'A' Presentation Set T1, comprising Bentley Saloon, Consul Classic, Triumph TR3, Isetta, Austin A40.   £175

A Marklin Racing Car Set, comprising two cars, drivers, track, layout, transformer and instructions, German, circa 1935.   £600

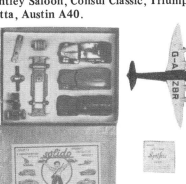

A boxed set of diecast Build-Yourself vehicles, by Solido.   £75

Corgi, Gift Set No. 23, Chipperfields Circus Models, in original presentation box.   £350

Spot-On – 2A Presentation Set.   £800

Spot-On – Presentation Pack of four Sports Cars (E to M), boxed.   £300

Spot-On cars, including No. 256 Jaguar Police car, two No. 215 blue Daimler SP 250 and No. 191/1 Sunbeam Alpine Hardtop, all in original boxes.   £175

CHILDREN'S BOOKS

Books intended specially for children had appeared as early as the late 16th century and it quickly became clear that illustrations were of the first importance if children were to be encouraged to read with pleasure.

As the 19th century progressed, children's books became stratified into certain well-defined types, all of which, however, had the common feature of illustration. Early illustrated educational texts formed one type. Another consisted of thinly disguised moral tracts, where dreadful fates often befell the erring characters. Finally, there were books of pure entertainment, classic tales by such enduring authors as Stevenson, R M Ballantyne and Lewis Carroll. Fairy tales by the Brothers Grimm and Hans Christian Andersen trod the line between the second and third categories.

During the Victorian period, book illustrations achieved the status of an art form and three great illustrators emerged, Walter Crane, Randolph Caldecott and Kate Greenaway. These three were followed by worthy successors such as Arthur Rackham, who carried the tradition forward into the 20th century.

The later 19th century also saw a wealth of ingenuity in book production, with pop-up images, sliding panels, tabs and levers all designed to amuse and appeal.

Another popular childhood book, the annual, actually predates the comics on which so many are now based, with the first, the Xmas Box, appearing in the 1820s. By the 1930s the annual was an indispensible item in many a child's Christmas stocking, and by and large their popularity has lasted to the present day.

'Little Bear And His Friends', 1st Edition, 1921. £18

Diamond Dick, Boy's Best Weekly, 1901. £8

A Primer and Catechisme, and also the notable fayres in the Kalender set forth by the Quenes ma:iestie to be taught unto Children, T. Purfoote, assigned by W. Seres, a remarkable survival of a children's book from the late 16th century. (Lawrence) £4,950

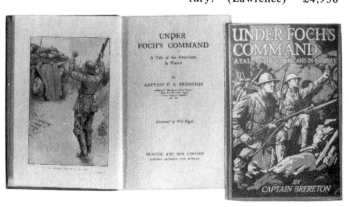

'Under Foch's Command', by Captain Brereton, 1st Edition, 1918. £10

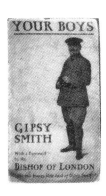

'Alice In Wonderland', Tarrant Illustrations, 1920's.   £5

'Your Boys', by Gipsy Smith, Hodder & Stoughton, 1918.   £4

Fun and Frolic by Louis Wain and Clifton Bingham, a children's poetry book published by Nister, circa 1902. (Phillips)   £140

Sinclair (R), Sir Golly de Wogg, Nursery Portrait Gallery, the artist/author's original illustrated manuscript containing ten tipped in watercolour and black ink illustrations of the Golly pursuing various sports. (Spencer's)   £280

The Magnet, No. 1, New Story Book.   £100

'Chums Annual 1907'. £20

Louis Wain's Annual 1908, a paperback annual published by Bemrose & Sons. (Phillips)   £110

Hans Anderson's Fairy
Tales — ill. Harry Clarke.
£5

'Children's Indoor Games', by G.B.
Crozier, 1910.   £12

'Biggles of the Camel
Squadron', W.E. Johns,
1960's.   £5

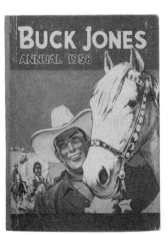

'Buck Jones Annual', 1958.
£10

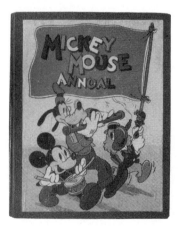

'Walt Disney's Pinocchio', 1940. £20

'Z' Cars Annual 1964'. £5

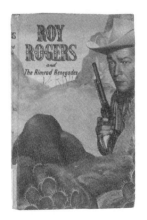

'Roy Rogers', Adprint Ltd.,
1952.   £5

'Mickey Mouse Annual', 1947.
£18

'Ameliaranne and the
Green Umbrella', 1939.
£18

'The Frog Prince', M. L. Attwell Illustrations, 1920's. £15

'The Little Ebony Elephant', by Fitz. £8

'The Adventures of Old Man Coyote', 1945. £5

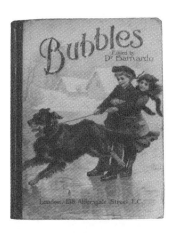

Bubbles, Volume 7. £25

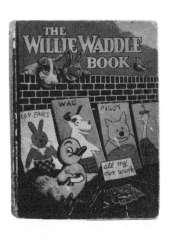

'The Willie Waddle Book', 1930's. £25

The Magic Doorway. £15

'The Brave Little Tailor', 1923. £15

'Diamond Dick', The Boys Best Weekly, 1900. £8

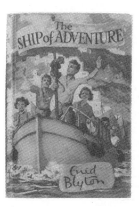

'The Ship of Adventure', Enid Blyton, 1st Edition, 1950. £18

'Jennings Goes to School', Anthony Buckeridge, 1st Edition, 1964.   £5

'The Greyfriars Holiday Annual 1929'.   £20

'Both Sides the Border', G.A. Henty, 1922.   £5

'The Pied Piper of Hamelin', Marspen Library.   £5

'Honours for Heroes', Tuck Painting Book.   £8

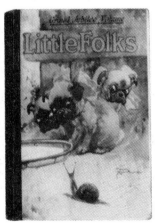

Grand Jubilee Volume of Little Folks 1921.   £10

'Treasure Hunt', Puzzle Book, circa 1940.   £8

'Boys' Cinema Annual 1949'.   £10

'The Mystery of the Spiteful Letters', Enid Blyton, 1949. £6

'Horace and the B.B.C.', by Harry Hemsley. £20

'Alice in Wonderland', Pears Illustrations. £8

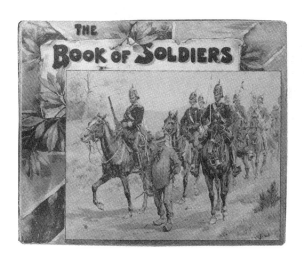

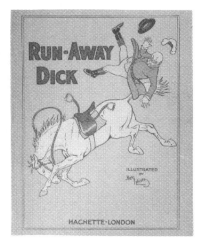

'The Book of Soldiers', E. P. Dutton & Co. £20

'Run-Away Dick', by Harry Eliott, 1936. £12

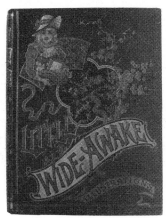

'Some Farm Friends', circa 1900. £20

'Little Wide Awake 1890'. £35

'Merry Hearts 1896'. £45

Lawson Wood's Merry Monkeys.
£12

Master Charlie 1899.   £15

Nister's Holiday Annual.
£25

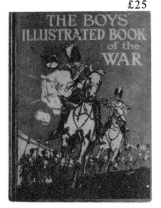

Lawson Wood Nursery Rhyme
Book.   £12

The Bunty Book — published
by G. Heath Robinson & J.
Birch Ltd. Illustrations include
Louis Wain and Gordon Browne.
£25

Sunbeam Annual 1933.
£12

Musical Box Annual.   £7

Boys Illustrated Book of the
War 1917.   £8

Cicely Mary Barker's Flower
Fairy Picture Book. 40 illustrations.   £8

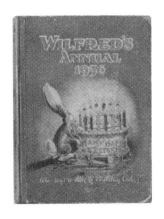

Wilfred's Annual 1936.   £12

Sunbeam's Picture Book 1926.
£5

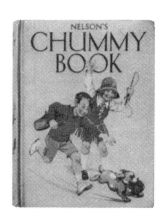

Nelson's Chummy Book 1933.
£14

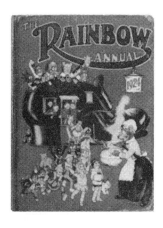

Rainbow Annual 1924.   £15

Adventure Land 1938.   £12

Book of Great Adventurers.
£8

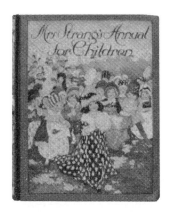

Mrs Strang's Annual for Children 1914.   £20

The Prize for Boys and Girls Volume 66.   £7

Children's Stories from the Poets 1940 — ill. Frank Adams.
£12

'The Golden Seeds', Golden Mill Press, 1950. £6

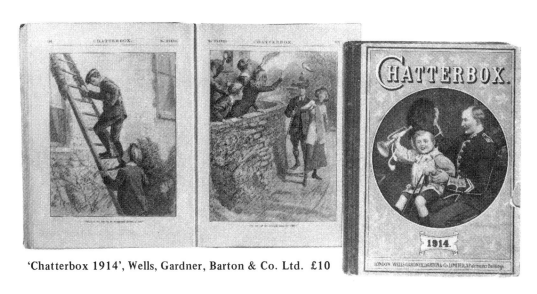

'Chatterbox 1914', Wells, Gardner, Barton & Co. Ltd. £10

'Girl Annual Number 8', 1960. £8

'Dan Dare's Spacebook', 1953. £30

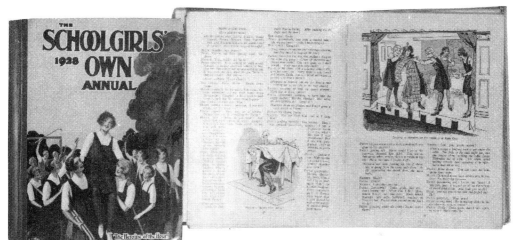

'The Schoolgirls' Own Annual 1928'. £12

'Daily Mirror 'Jimpy' Annual 1952'. £18

Child's Companion Annual
1934. £10

Cassell's Children's Annual
1920 — illustrations include
Anne Anderson, Harry Rountree and C. E. Brock. £15

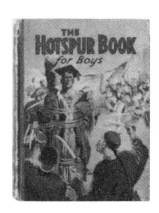

Hotspur Book for Boys 1937.
£12

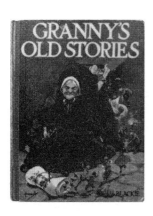

Blackie's Granny's Old Stories
— ill. Hassall 1939. £15

Modern Boy's Book of True
Adventure. £10

Blackie's Girls' Annual
1930. £7

Madge Williams Children's
Annual. £7

Blackie's Children's Annual
1922 — illustrations include
Honor Appleton, H. M. Brock,
Ruth Cobb, A. E. Jackson.
£15

The Jolly Book 1919. £15

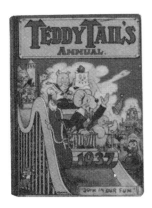

Teddy Tail's Annual 1937.
£12

Peek-a-Boo Japs — ill. Chloe Preston 1916. £20

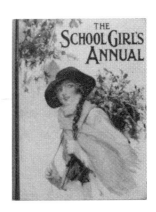

School Girl's Annual volume 3.
£10

Les Vacances de Nane 1924.
— ill. Henry Morin. £8

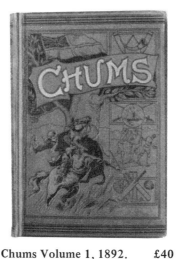

Chums Volume 1, 1892. £40

Noah's Ark Annual 1935.
£8

Pets and Playmates. £12

Tiny Tot's Picture Book 1934
— 80 pages of pictures including Rountree, Beaman and Gordon Robinson. £15

Make Believe Story Book 1924.
£20

'Mickey Mouse Annual 1944'.
£25

'Tales From Scottish Ballads',
1925. £3

'Swift Annual', 1962. £5

'Tintin Destination Moon', 1959.
£10

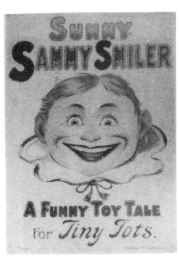

'Sunny Sammy Smiler',
circa 1910. £20

'Rupert' The Daily Express
Annual 1975'. £5

'Rainbow Annual 1957'. £8

'Teddy Tar and the Gipsies',
circa 1960. £3

'Tiger Annual 1961', Fleet-
way Publications. £4

'Archie Andrews Annual
1952'.   £8

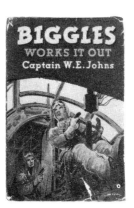

'Biggles Works It Out',
Hodder & Stoughton,
1952.   £4

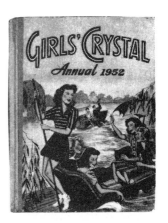

'Girls' Crystal Annual 1952'.
       £8

'The Wizard Book For Boys
1938'.   £20

'Lucie Attwell's Story Book',
circa 1940.   £5

'The Book of Blue Peter 1965'.
       £12

'The Beezer Book 1979'. £5

'The Mickey Mouse Fire Brigade,
1936'.   £40

'Emergency Ward 10' Girls'
Annual'.   £5

'From Many Lands, America', Father Tuck Series, 1904. £25

'The Birds' Alphabet', 1946. £10

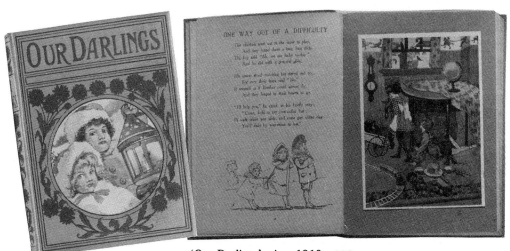

'Our Darlings', circa 1910. £20

'The Tom Merry's Own', 1950. £10

'The Alphabet Book', 1880's. £30

'Under One Flag', Tuck, circa 1900. £8

'The House That Jack Built', George Routledge & Sons. £35

'The Girl's Own Annual 1934'. £20

'The Book of the Teddy Bear', 1964. £15

'Ameliaranne Camps Out', 1st Edition, 1939. £20

Treasure Island 1929 —
illustrated by Rowland
Hilder. £15

Pip and Squeak Annual 1931.
£30

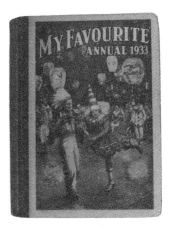

My Favourite Annual 1933.
£15

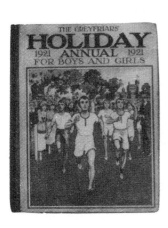

Greyfriars Holiday Annual
1921. £30

Rover Book for Boys 1940.
£15

'Blown to Bits', by R. M.
Ballantyne, 1889. £5

Chatterbox 1907. £12

Peggy and Joan — illustrated
by Honor Appleton. £12

The Oojah Annual. £12

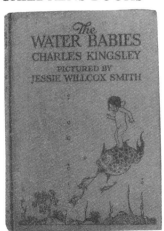

Water Babies 1938 — illustrated by Jessie Wilcox Smith.
£35

My Book of Ships 1913.
£10

Armchair Story Book 1937.
£12

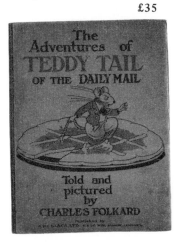

'Teddy Tail of the Daily Mail',   £12

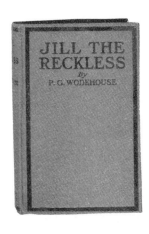

'Jill the Reckless', Eighth Printing, 1928.   £5

'The Splendid Savage', by Conrad H. Sayce.   £5

Big Book of Mother Goose, has revolving disc of hunt scene in cover.   £18

Playbox Annual 1918.
£25

Golden Annual for Girls 1925.   £12

'Children's Outdoor Games', by G.
B. Crozier, 1910.   £12

'My ABC of Nursery Rhyme Friends', Tuck,
circa 1940.   £12

'The Animal ABC', Deans Diploma Series No. 28. £15

'ABC for Little Willie', Daily News Ltd. £10

'Radio Fun Annual', 1957.
     £12

'Boys Who Became Famous', by F.J. Snell, 1924.   £5

'Rosy Cheeks', Nister Untearable. £20

'The Arabian Nights', Hodder & Stoughton, 1949. £30

'Gran'pop's Book of Fun', by Lawson Wood.   £15

'Film Fun Annual', 1941. £25

'The Big Book for Girls', 1927. £8

'Bunter Keeps It Dark', 1960, 1st Edition. £10

'Noah's Ark', Peepshow Book, by Nancy Spain. £8

'The Adventures of Larry the Lamb', 1940's. £10

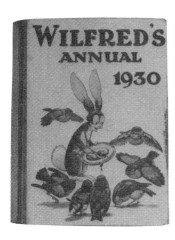

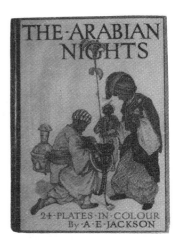

Wilfred's Annual 1930. £25

Peter Pan and Wendy — illustrated by Mabel Lucie Attwell. £30

Arabian Nights — illustrated by A. E. Jackson. £25

'The Gorilla Hunters', by R. M. Ballantyne. £5

'Easy A B C Book', circa 1850. £12

'The Quest for the Perfect Planet', W. E. Johns, 1961. £8

'The Dog Crusoe', by R. M. Ballantyne. £4

'Down at Dinah's Studios', circa 1950. £10

'Billy Bunter's Treasure Hunt', 1961, 1st Edition. £10

'See', by Dorothy Dealtry, 1950. £3

'Andersen's Fairy Tales', Anne Anderson Illustrations, 1930's. £12

'PC49' Eagle Strip Cartoon Book 1950. £15

'With Joffre At Verdun', by Captain Brereton, 1st Edition. £10

Infants Magazine 1903. £12

'The Young Fur Traders', by R.M. Ballantyne. £5

'Under Wellington's Command', by G.A. Henty, 1907. £6

Gulliver's Travels — ill.
John Hassall. £15

'Robinson Crusoe', Nister Publications, circa
1900. £20

'The Lone Ranger Annual 1964'. £8

'Railways For All', 1950's, Painting Book. £8

The Children's Treasury.
£5

'Little Frolic', 1930's. £15

'The Children's Hour', Lilian Rowles. £8

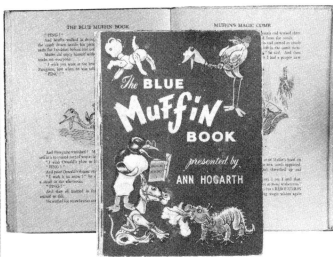

'The Blue Muffin Book', 1951. £10

'The Topper Book', 1958. £10

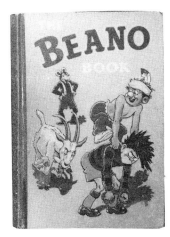

'The Beano Book', D. C.
Thompson.   £15

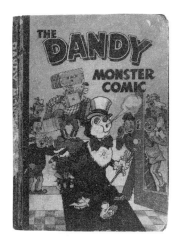

'The Dandy Monster Comic',
1948.   £30

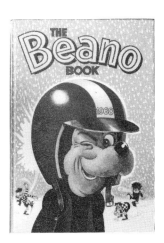

'The Beano Book', 1968.
£10

'Girls' Crystal Annual 1953'.
£8

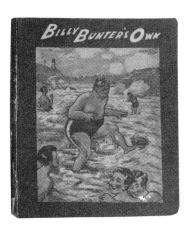

'Billy Bunter's Own'. £8

'The Jolly Gnomes Annual',
1951.   £15

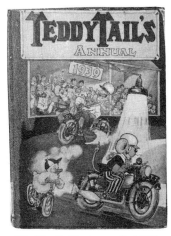

'Teddy Tail's Annual', 1939.
£10

'The Companion Annual',
1924.   £10

'Okay Adventure Annual',
Boardman & Co.   £12

'The Felix Annual', 1930's. £18

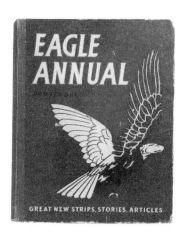

'Eagle Annual Number One', 1952. £20

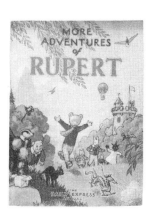

'More Adventures of Rupert', Daily Express 1947. £45

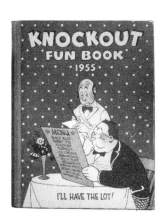

'Knockout Fun Book', 1955. £12

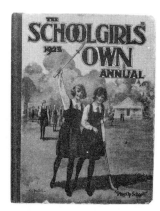

'The Schoolgirls' Own Annual 1923. No. 1'. £15

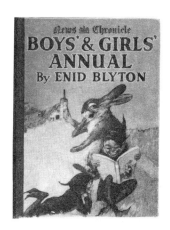

'News and Chronicle Boys' & Girls' Annual', by Enid Blyton. £10

'Nursery Fun', Dean's Picture Book. £3

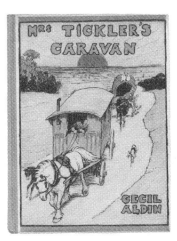

'Mrs Tickler's Caravan', Cecil Aldin, 1931. £20

'Lucie Attwell's Annual.' £10

'The Master Book of Magic', by J.C. Cannell, 1935. £8

'Ethel Graham's Victory', by Mrs H.B. Paul, 1882. £5

'The Dandy's Desperate Dan', 1954. £20

'The Children's Encyclopedia', by Arthur Mee, Set of Ten. £20

'Oscar Danby, V.C.', by Rowland Walker. £5

'Gulliver's Travels', Illustrations by R.R. Russell. £5

CLOCKWORK TOYS

Clockwork toys have their illustrious origins in the ingenious automata which were made in the 17th and 18th centuries for the delight of aristocratic circles and in the 19th for a more general, but still largely adult, public. It was the Germans who first realised the potential for a juvenile market, especially as new inventions made mechanisms and production methods ever cheaper. By the turn of the century the market was flooded with cheap tinplate imports, and these are immensely popular with collectors today. Bing, Carette, Märklin, Günthermann and Lehmann are just some of the names to conjure with, and some of their best products dating from the first thirty years of this century can now fetch well into four figures. Their most popular models were cars, trains, aeroplanes, ships, stationary steam engines and figures as well, all of which were generally very finely painted or printed.

The British companies which entered into competition with these in the 1930s were Wells, Brimtoy and Chad Valley, and their products too are attracting quite a following today. The famous Tri-ang (Lines Bros.) company at this time launched their Minic range, small tinplate commercial vehicles with clockwork mechanisms. Their pre-war cars fitted with lead passengers are particularly rare today. Most early Minics had room for a battery which in turn powered the headlights, or, in the case of the breakdown lorry, the gears and winch of the crane unit.

By the 1950s the Japanese had entered the market and were producing clockwork and battery operated toys in tinplate and plastic which sold very cheaply.

A Hull & Stafford-type tinplate hoop toy, the horses with clockwork mechanism between, American, circa 1871, 9in. diam. £1,000

Britains very rare set 1441, Mammoth Circus Flying Trapeze with clown, female trapeze artiste and original paper sunshade, in original box, 1937.
(Phillips) £1,000

An early hand painted maid, standing at an ironing board, holding an iron and a winged collar, 8in. high, probably by Gunthermann, circa 1903. (Christie's) £550

Late 19th century Connecticut clockwork dancing black couple, 10½in. high. £2,500

A lithographed stand-up American policeman dressed in blue and white uniform, a lever behind enables the figure to raise and lower his arms, 21cm.
(Phillips) £92

A rare humorous composition toy, modelled as a red faced man with startled eyes hanging on to a runaway donkey, 6½in. long, mid 19th century, German. (Christie's) £710

A clockwork wood and papier-mâché head-over-heels figure of a policeman, dressed in navy-blue felt uniform, 9½in. (Phillips)   £100

A rare and early hand enamelled tinplate woman pushing a cart, with caged goose, probably by Gunthermann, circa 1903, 7½in. long. (Christie's)   £475

American composition character automaton, circa 1880, 21in. high.   £400

Carved and painted dancing toy, probably America, 19th century, in the form of a black man wearing a black vest, 11½in. high. (Skinner Inc.)   £859

A German post-war clockwork Boxing match, boxed (no lid).   £100

Lithographed tin balloon man, triple animation, Germany, 1930, 6.5/8in. high.   £400

A tinplate pool player, at a printed and painted tinplate pool table, with clockwork mechanism, 7¼in. long, stamped P.W., German, circa 1912. (Christie's)   £385

A German clockwork Drummer Boy dressed as a soldier in busby, 28cm. high.   £85

Nomura, a tinplate battery operated doll dressmaker seated at her sewing machine, 17cm. high. (Phillips)   £80

An early Japanese lithographed tinplate travelling boy, with clockwork mechanism, 1930's, 8in. high. (Christie's)　£440

A painted tinplate pool player, with clockwork mechanism and seven numbered pockets at far end, probably by Guntermann, circa 1910, 28cm. long. (Christie's S. Ken)　£550

Linemar, battery operated Bubble Blowing Popeye.
£300

A papier mâché headed political toy modelled as Churchill, with frowning expression, remains of cigar, small bowler hat, and red bow tie, 10½in. high, circa 1920s.
(Christie's S. Ken)　£99

Linemar battery operated Busy Secretary, the blond girl wearing spotty blouse and fluted skirt, 19cm. high., boxed.
(Phillips)　£150

A German lithographed clown dressed in yellow chequered trousers, blue jacket with a spinner above his head, 11cm.
(Phillips)　£34

'Popeye the Sailor', No. 268, a printed and painted tinplate toy of the cartoon sailor in a rowing boat, 14in. long, by the Hoge Mfg. Co., Inc., USA., circa 1935.　£1,750

A clockwork painted tinplate horse with seated gentleman rider finished with blue tailed jacket, 15.5cm.
(Phillips)　£220

Marx, clockwork Dagwoods aeroplane boxed.
(Phillips)　£180

George W. Brown clockwork doll pushing hoop bell toy, Connecticut, 1872, 12in. long. **£3,000**

Chein tin roller coaster and car, original paint and stencilling, key wind, 19in. x 9½in. (Du Mouchelles) **£96**

An English J.W.B. mechanical artist toy, contained in original box, circa 1900, 4½in. wide. **£1,000**

A bisque headed moving clown toy, the white face with painted hat and features, the wood and wire body with wooden hands and feet, the head impressed *1720,* German, late 19th century, 10in. high. (Christie's S. Ken) **£440**

A bisque headed clown acrobatic toy, the white face with painted blue and red cap, grey tufts of hair and clown maquillage, impressed *138 3 3,* German, late 19th century, 16½in. high. (Christie's S. Ken) **£440**

A German papier-mâché sailor swallowing fish, the hand operated automaton with moulded painted features, probably Sonneberg, late 19th century. (Phillips) **£700**

Late 19th century painted tin clockwork bowing man, 7½in. high. **£200**

Goodwin clockwork doll and carriage, doll with papier mache head, 11in. high, 9½in. long, 1868. **£750**

Dummy cigar box in which a hand and head pop out when a concealed button is pressed. **£30**

A tinplate mechanical lobster, German, circa 1910, 8½in. wide. £450

Nomura, friction The Great Swanee River Paddle Steamer, colourfully lithographed with deck details and passengers, 27cm.
(Phillips) £85

Fighting boxers, with clockwork mechanism, in original paintwork, by Einfalt, circa · 1935, 9½in. long. (Christie's S. Ken) £242

Marx, clockwork Hi-Yo-The Lone Ranger, boxed. £125

'The Juba Dancers', carved and stained wood mechanical toy, by Ives, U.S.A., circa 1874, 10in. high. £400

A German lithographed Penny Toy of a pram and child within, on four spoked wheels, 6.5cm., some wear and rust.
(Phillips) £92

A lithographed Penny Toy of a jigger dressed in red jacket, with yellow hat and trousers, on green box base, 9cm.
(Phillips) £126

Unique Art tin wind-up Li'l Abner and his Dogpatch Band, America, 1946, 8½in. high. £350

ALPS clockwork lithographed Little Shoemaker dressed in stripy T-shirt and chequered jacket, 15cm., boxed.
(Phillips) £75

'Echo', EPL No. 725, a rare
printed and painted tinplate
motor cyclist, with clockwork
mechanism, 8¾in. long, by
Lehmann, circa 1910.
(Christie's)   £1,870

A Wilhelm Krauss spring
action lithographed AA Road
Services motorcyclist and
sidecar, 18cm. long. (Phillips)
                            £500

Well's Big Chief mechanical
motor cycle, with Indian Chief
rider, clockwork mechanism,
in original box, 1930s, 7½in.
long. (Christie's S. Ken)
                            £550

Unique Art Manufacturing Co.
clockwork 'Kiddy Cyclist', fair
haired young boy on tricycle, the
wheels with lithographed
animals, 23cm.
(Phillips)   £207

'Mac 700', a printed and painted tinplate motorbike and rider
with clockwork mechanism,
causing the rider to hop on and
off, 7¼in. long, by Arnold,
W. Germany, circa 1955. £350

Kellermann, a lithographed
freewheeling negro on a tricycle,
dressed as a clown in stripy
trousers, 10cm. long.
(Phillips)   £240

A. G. Vichy bisque-headed
tri-cyclist automaton, French,
circa 1880, 10½in. long £700

Ingap, clockwork lithographed
motorcycle and rider finished in
bright colours, 13cm.
(Phillips)   £260

An early French mechanical tri-
cyclist, circa 1890, 8¼in. long.
                            £800

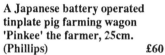

A Japanese battery operated tinplate pig farming wagon 'Pinkee' the farmer, 25cm. (Phillips) £60

A 'Peter Rabbit' chickmobile, hand car, No. 1103, circa 1935. £450

German clockwork automaton of a Chinese mandarin pulling a cart, circa 1900, man impressed Halbig. £1,250

A Gunda-Werke lithograph tinplate motorcycle and sidecar with clockwork mechanism, 6½in. long, circa 1920, and a tinplate monkey moneybox. £1,000

Marx tin wind-up Moon Mullins and Kayo Handcar, America, 1920's, 5½in. high. £300

Ingap, clockwork lithographed Dipsy car with young clown rider finished in red, yellow and pale blue, 12.5cm. (Phillips) £126

A Bell-toy, with plush covered monkey seated on a cloth covered platform with three fretwork metal wheels below, 8in. (Phillips) £340

Lithographed tin Toonerville Trolley, New York, 1922, 6½in. high. £500

An early 20th century stock tin plate clockwork four wheel gocart, driven by a uniformed school boy, 12.75cm. long. (Henry Spencer) £240

A Gustav Stickley spindle-sided baby's crib, no. 919, circa 1907, 56½in. long. (Robt. W. Skinner Inc.)   £833

17th century Dutch or German oak cradle with panelled tapering body, 38½in. wide.   £1,000

Early 18th century Spanish or Venetian parcel gilt and polychrome hanging cradle of navette form, 49½in. wide. (Christie's)   £2,200

A French white painted wickerwork cradle, decorated with spandrels and scrolls, with a swing bed beneath a coronet cresting, 42in. (Christie's)   £770

A rare Napoleon I ormolu-mounted mahogany cradle of slatted boat-shape suspended between two turned uprights, 52in. long.
(Tennants)   **£7,000**

A mahogany and cane cradle with arched top and square frame, the two ends joined by stretchers, first half 19th century. (Lawrence Fine Arts)   £495

A George III painted cradle with ogee-arched hood and cane-filled sides, 41in. long. (Christie's)   £827

A tubular brass child's cot, circa 1910, 3ft. 8in. long.   £750

Late 19th century ebonised Bentwood cradle, Europe, 52in. long. (Robt. W. Skinner Inc.)   £625

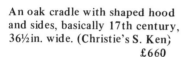

An oak cradle with shaped hood and sides, basically 17th century, 36½in. wide. (Christie's S. Ken) £660

19th century American Victorian walnut cradle on stand with shaped and pierced splats, 36in. high. £200

A 17th century oak cradle with arched hood, 40in. wide. £1,500

An Arts and Crafts oak crib, the cylindrical barrel type rocking body supported by tall triangular rounded plank ends, 1.27m. high x 1.10m. long. (Phillips) £280

An Italian baroque giltwood cradle in the form of a shell carved with flowerheads, each end with a putto, one leaning over the edge, the other seated and holding a garland of flowers, probably Roman, early 18th century, 61in. wide. (Christie's) £10,450

A George III mahogany cradle of rectangular form, the scrolling side panels applied with roundels, 39in. wide.(Christie's) £495

Child's metal cot by Theodore Lambert, 1910, 133cm. long. £600

A Biedermeier walnut cradle, the oval body with detachable tin liner, 52in. wide. (Christie's) £4,104

German gondola shaped cradle cross banded in black, slung between lyre shaped end pieces, on ogee feet, circa 1820. (Kunsthaus am Museum) £2,174

In 1933 Frank Hornby had another good idea when he launched his 'Dinky' range of models. The name meant neat or tiny, and the original intention was to make accessories for train sets, but the range grew to include all kinds of transport.

The first Dinky vehicles were a tank, two sports cars and a tractor, a motor truck and a delivery van. At the time they cost sixpence each, but now, especially if they are painted with contemporary advertising signs, they are worth hundreds. It is important that they should have their original boxes and be in as near mint condition as possible, though worn pre-war models still sell well.

The first models were cast in heavy lead alloy with metal wheels, but by the outbreak of war in 1939 they had become lighter and the wheels had white rubber tyres which perished or went flat – a sure sign of authenticity. Roadsigns, animals and wayside buildings were at this time added to the range.

After the war Dinky vehicles tended to have black rubber tyres, and new lines were brought out each year. Sadly, they went out of business in 1980, but in 1988 started up again. Matchbox who had bought the rights to the name, relaunched the Dinky range. The new products are well made and may well prove to be collectables of the future.

The most valuable Dinky set is the No. 24, which comprises a Vogue saloon, sports tourer 4-seater and 2-seater. Boxed and in good condition, this will fetch up to £5,000.

514 Guy Van, Weetabix, boxed. (Phillips)   £1,400

280C Delivery Van, Shredded Wheat, 2nd Type. (Phillips)   £450

198 Rolls Royce Phantom V, in metallic green and white, boxed. (Phillips)   £95

Studebaker 'Commander', red with tan roof, boxed. (Phillips)   £100

180 Packard Clipper Sedan, orange and grey, boxed. (Phillips)   £95

941 Foden 14 ton Tanker, Mobilgas. (Phillips)   £650

137 Plymouth Fury Convertible, metallic green, boxed. (Phillips)   £110

28N Delivery Van, Meccano 1st Type. (Phillips)   £1,300

The first Dinky boxed set, No. 60, issued in
1934 to 1940. **£400**

Dinky Supertoys No. 923 Big Bedford Van,
advertising 'Heinz Tomato Sauce', in original
box.
(Christie's S. Ken) **£605**

French Dinky Supertoys, Set No. 60, Coffret
Cadeau Avions, in original box.
(Christie's) **£275**

Rare Dinky 920 Guy Warrior Heinz
van, in original box.
(Christie's) **£3,080**

Dinky Gift Set No. 699 Military Vehicles, in
original box.
(Christie's S. Ken) **£264**

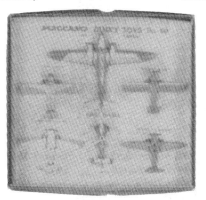

Dinky rare pre-war French Set No. 60 Avions,
including Arc-en-ciel, Potez Type 58, Hanriot
Type 180T, Dewoitine Type 500, Breguet
Type Corsaire and Autogire, in original box,
circa 1937.
(Christie's) **£5,500**

Dinky pre-war Set No. 60 Aeroplanes (2nd
issue), in original box.
(Christie's S. Ken) **£528**

DINKY

42 Set Police Hut, Motor Cycle Patrol and Policemen, boxed. (Phillips)   £520

934 Leyland Octopus Wagon, yellow and green, boxed. (Phillips)   £420

Ships of the British Navy, set no. 50, complete with box. (Phillips)   £200

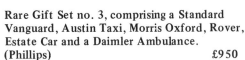

Rare Gift Set no. 3, comprising a Standard Vanguard, Austin Taxi, Morris Oxford, Rover, Estate Car and a Daimler Ambulance. (Phillips)   £950

Pre-war No. 64 Set French Factory Avions comprising a Dewoitine, Bloch, Amiot, Potez 662 and a Potez 63, boxed. (Phillips)   £2,200

No. 24 Set Motor Cars, comprising an Ambulance, Limousine, Town Sedan, Vogue Saloon, Super Streamlined Saloon, Sportsmans Coupe and 2 Sports Tourers, boxed. (Phillips)   £3,000

Rare 675 Ford Sedan Staff Car for U.S. Market. (Phillips)   £280

No. 12 Postal Set comprising a Royal Mail Van, Pillar Box, Pillar Box Airmail, Telephone Box, Telegraph Messenger and Postman, boxed. (Phillips)   £650

299 Post Office Services Gift Set, boxed. (Phillips)   £600

Gift Set no. 4, Racing Cars, comprising a Cooper Bristol, Alfa Romeo, Ferrari, H.W.M. and a Maserati, boxed. (Phillips) £680

A Willeme Tractor and covered Trailer, boxed. (Phillips)   £120

 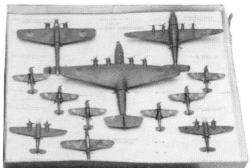

Pre-war No. 68 Set Camouflaged Aeroplanes, comprising an Armstrong Whitworth Whitley Bomber, Frobisher Liner, 3 Hawker Hurricane Fighters, 3 Vickers Supermarine Spitfire Fighters, Armstrong Whitworth Ensign Liner, 2 Bristol Blenheim Bombers and a Fairey Battle Bomber, boxed. (Phillips)   £6,500

998 Bristol Britannia Air Liner, Canadian Pacific, boxed. (Phillips) £140

No. 24 Set of Motor Cars, comprising an Ambulance, Limousine, Town Sedan, Vogue Saloon, Super Streamlined Saloon, Sportsman's Coupe, Sports Tourer 4 Seater, Sports Tourer 2 Seater, boxed. (Phillips) £5,000

DISNEY

With the opening of Disneyland Europe and the re-release of such Disney classics as Snow White and Peter Pan, there has been an upsurge in interest in the myriad objects which comprise Disneyana.

The most popular characters are without doubt Mickey Mouse, Goofy, Snow White and Donald Duck, and representations of these have been made in a wide range of materials, from games made of card to diecast and tinplate figures. There is plenty of plastic too, of course, such as large size figures of Mickey and Minnie Mouse and Donald Duck, and these are of interest to doll collectors.

In the 1950s, several British diecast toy companies made Walt Disney figures, such as a Matchbox series showing various characters riding in Matchbox cars.

With so much about, it is obviously the rarer pieces which attract a premium. One of these is a Britains lead set of Snow White and the Seven Dwarfs, first brought out in 1939, which provoked many later white metal imitations. These, however, are generally given away by the brightness of the colours. Among tinplate collectables, Mickey Mouse mechanical figures or the clockwork Pinocchio toys brought out by Louis Marx before the Second World War are worth looking out for.

Because of the wide range of forms which they take Disneyana objects appeal to a wide range of collectors, and this of course helps increase their value.

A Wadeheath pottery Walt Disney teapot, the body moulded in relief with Grumpy and various woodland animals, 6^1/$_2$ in. high.
(Christie's S. Ken) £198

A Wadeheath pottery Walt Disney series jug, the body moulded in relief with Dopey and various woodland animals, 8in. high.
(Christie's S. Ken) £308

Pelham Puppets, Mickey Mouse and Minnie Mouse.
£100

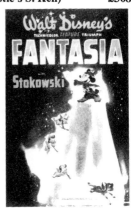

Fantasia, Disney, 1940, one-sheet, linen backed poster, 41 x 27in.
(Christie's East) £3,615

A set of eight Snow White and the Seven Dwarfs hand-painted porcelain toothbrush holders, 6in. and 4^1/$_4$ in. high.
(Christie's S. Ken) £462

A large felt-covered Mickey Mouse with yellow gloves, green shoes, red shorts, a stitched smile and felt eyes, 16^1/$_4$ in. high.
(Christie's S. Ken) £440

One of two original hand paintings on celluloid, from the Walt Disney film Snow White and the Seven Dwarfs, 6½ x 9½in.   £750

Lead model Mickey and Minnie Mouse barrel organ group.   £50

Walt Disney Studios, Snow White and the Seven Dwarfs, 1937 — 'Five Dwarfs in a heap', pencil and coloured crayon animation drawing, 10 x 12in. (Christie's)   £352

A felt-covered Grandmother Duck with wire glasses, wooden broomstick, and original 'Lenci' swing-tag ticket, 20in. high. (Christie's S. Ken)   £1,045

A draylon plush-covered Donald Duck with yellow felt feet and a Daisey Duck with brown felt high-heeled shoes and handbag, with three smaller similarly covered Huey, Duey and Louie toys.
(Christie's S. Ken)   £1,210

A Japanese celluloid clockwork Popeye, with original label *Copyright King Syndicate Inc. 1929*, 8in. high. (Christie's S. Ken)   £176

'Felix the Cat', large plush-covered toy with cloth bow tie, 28½in. high, circa 1930.
£1,000

A painted wooden rocking Mickey Mouse swinging on a stand, made by Triang, circa 1938–9, 32¼in. long.
(Christie's S. Ken)   £385

Glazed earthenware musical jug depicting the 'Three Little Pigs', circa 1935, 10in. high.   £250

Mickey Mouse, Two Gun
Mickey, 1934 – Mickey With
Lasso, a concept drawing,
graphite pencil on paper, 9¼ x
12in.
(Christie's S. Ken)   £605

A plush-covered Minnie Mouse
with felt-covered cardboard-
lined ears, holding a wire and
felt flower, 16in. high, 1930's.
(Christie's S. Ken)   £198

Walt Disney Studios, Snow
White and the Seven Dwarfs,
1937 – 'The Seven Dwarfs',
gouache on full celluloid
applied to a wood veneer background, 10½ x 13¾in.
(Christie's)   £1,650

Dumbo, Disney, 1941, one-sheet,
linen backed poster, 41 x 27in.
(Christie's East)   £2,332

A Mickey Mouse Ingersoll
pocket watch, depicting Mickey
Mouse on the face, the animated
hour and minute-hands shaped
as Mickey's arms and hands,
2½in. high.
(Christie's S. Ken)   £440

Silly Symphony, Disney, 1933,
one-sheet, linen backed poster,
41 x 27in.
(Christie's East)   £3,498

Walt Disney Studios, Sleeping
Beauty, 1959 – 'Briar Rose,
woodland animals, and Prince
Phillip', gouache on celluloid,
a compilation of seven
celluloid pieces stapled onto
paper, 11½ x 13½in. (Christie's)
     £242

Mickey Mouse soft toy by
Deans Rag Book Ltd., 1930's,
6¼in. high.   £150

Walt Disney Studios, Snow
White and the Seven Dwarfs
1937 – 'Five dwarfs peering
into a water trough', gouache
on full celluloid applied to a
wood veneer background,
9½ x 12½in. (Christie's)
     £2,090

Alarm clock, clockface depicting the Three Little Pigs, circa 1935, 6in. high. **£300**

Walt Disney, a polychrome woollen rug depicting Mickey and Minnie Mouse performing in a circus arena, 46¾ x 71in., circa 1930's. (Christie's) **£385**

A rubber inflatable Mickey Mouse 41cm. high. (Phillips) **£28**

Robin Hood, 1973, and the Rescuers 1977 — three celluloids, 'A Vulture', 'A Hen' and 'A Small Child', each gouache on celluloid, stamped 'Walt Disney Productions Certified Original Hand-Painted Movie Film Cel'. (Christie's) **£242**

Mickey Mouse Corporation 'Minnie Mouse' watercolour, pen and ink, initialled W.D.P. with 'Micky Mouse Corporation Produktions-Afdelingen' ink stamp 9¼ x 6¼in. (Christie's) **£176**

Snow White and the Seven Dwarfs, circa 1937 — eight celluloids: 'Doc', 'Sleepy', 'Sneezy', 'Snow White', 'Three Running Dwarfs', 'Happy', 'Grumpy' and 'Woodland Animals', each gouache on celluloid, one inscribed '1936 Walt Disney Productions'. (Christie's) **£385**

Snow White and the Seven Dwarfs, Disney, 1937, one-sheet, linen backed poster, 41 x 27in. (Christie's East) **£4,664**

An Art Deco style Mickey Mouse figure of cast iron finished in gilt, 5¾in. high. (Christie's) **£385**

Der Fuehrer's Face, Disney, 1943, one-sheet, linen backed poster, 41 x 27in. (Christie's East) **£1,749**

'Jiminy Cricket', original Walt Disney celluloid, framed and glazed, 16¼ x 17½in.   **£700**

Back and front of German tinplate Mickey Mouse mechanical bank, circa 1930, 6¾in. high.   **£500**

Pinocchio doll, with clock-work movement within the articulated legs, circa 1942, 7½in. high.   **£350**

Britains extremely rare set 1645, Walt Disney's Mickey Mouse, with Minnie Mouse, Goofy, Clarabelle Cow, Donald Duck and Pluto, 1939. (Phillips)   **£2,200**

'The Moles', a celluloid taken from 'Song of the South', framed and glazed, 12¼ x 10½in.   **£200**

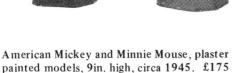

American Mickey and Minnie Mouse, plaster painted models, 9in. high, circa 1945. **£175**

American Mickey and Minnie Mouse, two Fune-Flex painted wooden toys, circa 1931, 6¾in. high. £300

Walt Disney's 'Alice in Wonderland' Punch-Out Book, 1955. £20

Walt Disney rug in tufted cotton, showing characters from his films, 1950's, 104 x 70in. £350

'The Three Caballeros', three plaster figures of Disney characters, circa 1950. £175

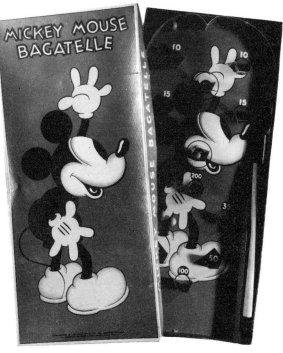

Mickey Mouse Bagatelle by Chad Valley Co. Ltd. £40

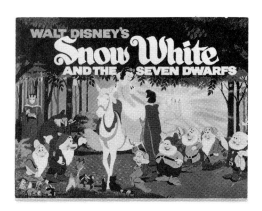

Walt Disney's Snow White and the Seven Dwarfs. £3

Four Disney stuffed figures, comprising a velveteen Mickey Mouse and Pluto; two corduroy 'Widgets', late 1930's-40's. £400

A Mickey Mouse wicker and coloured plastic cane hand bag, 25½ in. high. (David Lay) £180

Child Guidance Products Inc., 126 cartridge 'Mick-A-Matic Deluxe' novelty camera in maker's original box. (Christie's) £55

American composition character doll of Pinocchio made by Ideal Novelty & Toy Co., circa 1935, 12in. high. £140

Eight polychrome moulded terracotta figures of Snow White and the Seven Dwarfs: Sneezy, Sleepy, Bashful, Doc, Grumpy, Dopey and Happy, 10in. and 6in. high. (Christie's) £99

Walt Disney's 'The Jungle Book' souvenir brochure, 1967. £4

Unusual tinplate and composition Minnie Mouse and pram, probably by Wells, 7½in. long, circa 1933.   £1,750

'The Three Caballeros', an original Walt Disney celluloid, signed, 18 x 16in., framed and glazed.   £2,000

'Mickey Mouse Organ Grinder', tinplate toy with clockwork and musical mechanisms, by Distler, circa 1930, 6in. long.   £750

Marx tin wind-up Merry Makers, 1930, 9in. high.   £250

Marx, Walt Disney's Donald Duck Duet, boxed.   £300

A set of Chad Valley Snow White and the seven dwarfs, 17in. high, the dwarfs 9½in. high. £308

Seven Walt Disney opaque glass ornaments, circa 1935, 4½in. to 7in.   £800

Walt Disney Studios – Peter Pan, 1953, 'Peter Pan and Wendy flying', gouache on full celluloid, framed and glazed, 12½ x 15in.(Christie's) £660

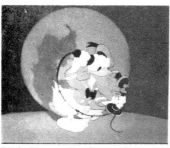

Walt Disney Studios – Der Fuehrer's Face, 'Donald Duck speaking into a telephone', gouache on celluloid, stamped 'Original WDP', 7½ x 9in. (Christie's)   £5,340

Walt Disney Studios – Snow White and the Seven Dwarfs, 1937, gouache on celluloid, 10½ x 13¾in. (Christie's S. Ken)   £1,100

A piece of Cunard White Star RMS Queen Elizabeth headed paper illustrated with a pencil drawing of Mickey Mouse, signed and inscribed *Best Wishes, Walt Disney*, 17.4 x 13.7cm. (Christie's S. Ken) £3,080

Eight hand-painted Wadeware figures of Snow White and the Seven Dwarfs, largest 7in. high. (Christie's)   £385

Bambi, Disney, 1942, one-sheet, cond. A, linen backed, 41 x 27in. (Christie's East)   £1,049

Walt Disney Studios – Snow White and the Seven Dwarfs, 1937, 'Dopey and Animals', gouache on celluloid with air-brush background, 5¾ x 5½in. (Christie's)   £2,420

A Wadeheath pottery Walt Disney series novelty musical jug, the handle modelled as the Big Bad Wolf, printed factory mark and original paper label, 10in. high. (Christie's S. Ken)   £495

Walt Disney Studios – Sleeping Beauty, 1959, 'Malificent with Crow', gouache on celluloid, 8 x 10in., window mounted and Walt Disney production label on reverse. (Christie's)   £1,760

DOLLS

Goss doll (No.31) child with real hair, glass eyes, china arms and stuffed legs. £500

Max lithographed tin Amos and Andy, N.Y., 1930, 11½in. high. £600

A bisque headed doll's house doll modelled as a man with a black-painted moustache and hair, 7in. high. £132

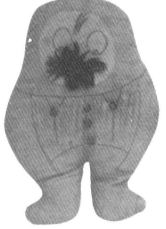

A shoulder bisque marotte, with blond mohair curly wig, fixed blue glass eyes, painted features and open mouth, 35cm. high overall. (Henry Spencer) £160

Old Bill 'Humpty Dumpty' shape cloth doll with no arms, 18cm. high. £80

A marotte with three dancing children with bisque heads and wooden bodies in original clothing, 11in. high (music needs attention). (Christie's) £410

A cloth doll with black button eyes, painted facial features and stuffed body, in Highland dress, 10in. (Lawrence Fine Arts) £33

A small early 20th century Goss doll with real hair, glass eyes and original clothes. £400

Late 19th century German hanging automaton contained in a mahogany glazed case featuring a boy who moves with the music, 44in. high. £800

DOLLS

Pedigree Coronation doll
in original clothes, 14in.
high.   £22

A cloth doll painted in oils
with grey eyes and blonde
painted short hair, 23in. high.
£200

19th century porcelain
doll, circa 1850, 17in.
high, in green silk gown.
£390

**A brown bisque-headed child
doll, with brown sleeping eyes,
pierced ears and jointed body,
29in. high.
(Christie's S. Ken)   £935**

An all bisque child doll, with
closed mouth, blue eyes,
blonde wig and moulded shoes
and socks, wearing contemporary red and white dress,
6¼in. high. (Christie's S. Ken)
£143

A shoulder composition doll,
with closed mouth, fixed blue
glass eyes, fair wig, dressed as
a parlour maid. (Lawrence
Fine Arts)   £110

A bisque shoulder headed
doll, the stuffed body with
bisque limbs, 11½in. high,
circa 1860. (Christie's)
£715

**A china shoulder-headed doll,
the moulded black hair swept
into a loop over each ear and
into a plaited bun at the nape,
22in. high, circa 1860.
(Christie's S. Ken)   £770**

Japanese bisque character
doll, with French type composition and wooden join-
ted body, circa 1910. 13in.
high.   £240

A bisque-headed character child doll with brown sleeping eyes, 24in. high. £500

A bisque headed character baby doll moulded as an Oriental, 9¼in. high, marked 3/0. £418

A china-headed autoperipatetikos with moulded black ringlets, 10½in. high. £400

A bisque headed doll with tinted complexion and kid covered body, 21in. high. £250

A bisque two-faced doll with original blonde wig and with jointed composition body, 11in. high. £900

A bisque headed autoperipatetikos doll with painted blue eyes and brown kid arms, 10in. high. £200

A bisque shoulder headed doll with fixed blue eyes, marked Goss 18, 17in. high. £400

A bisque flange-necked fashionable doll, with unusual construction allowing the head to turn only 90 degrees, 14¹/₂in. high, circa 1870. (Christie's S. Ken) £715

A bisque swivel headed doll, with fixed blue eyes, pierced ears, blonde wig and cloth body, 15½in. high. (Christie's) £440

DOLLS

A 20th century bisque headed doll with brown hair and jointed limbs, 22in. (Anderson & Garland) £100

Early 20th century ventriloquist's dummy in a military coat. £200

A bisque-headed child doll, label reading Gekleidete Puppe no. 9052, circa 1880. £750

An 18th century group of Italian creche figures, six average height 9in., four average height 11½in., and two at 14½in. £2,250

A ventriloquist's dummy modelled as a school girl with moving eyes and lower jaw, in original gym slip and skirt, 34in. high. (Christie's) £110

A pair of advertising dolls modelled as the 'Bisto Kids', designed by Will Owen, 11in. high, circa 1948. (Christie's) £209

A composition character headed doll modelled as Lord Kitchener, in original clothes with Sam Browne hat and puttees, 19in. high. (Christie's) £164

DOLLS

A pink china shoulder headed doll, the kid body with wooden limbs, 15in. high, circa 1840. (Christie's) £330

Queenie, a bisque headed doll with blue lashed sleeping eyes, moulded brows and brown wig, blue leather shoes, marked *ABG*, 26in. high. (Christie's S. Ken) £715

A bisque shoulder headed doll with closed mouth, solid pate and kid body with bisque arms, 14½in. high. £352

A bisque headed character doll with a quantity of other items, including bedding, shoes, a parasol, a box of washing items and twenty-three changes of clothes, 14½in. high, marked F.S. and Co., 1272/352 Deponiert. £935

A flesh tinted china shoulder head with dark brown mohair wig, 19in. high. (Christie's) £1,870

Pair of cloth character dolls, made by Norah Wellings, England, circa 1930, each 11in. high. £245

19th century all china doll in one piece, circa 1885, 12in. high. £200

A white bisque-headed clown doll with fixed blue eyes, marked 157 3, 11in. high. £250

An Edwardian 'Austrian' porcelain doll with fixed eyes, 8½in. high. £100

A china doll of an Irish gentleman, with gusseted kid body and china lower limbs, 13in. high. £120

A painted felt-headed child doll, in original Royal Air Force tunic and flying suit, 28in. high, by Norah Wellings, with original Harry the Hawk R.A.F. comforts fund swing ticket. (Christie's S. Ken) £770

A bisque figure of a seated naked woman with moulded black bobbed hair, 3in. high. £99

A celluloid headed teddy doll with plush covered body, beige felt hands and feet, moulded hair and painted features, circa 1908, 16in. high. £125

A composition headed Japanese doll with closed mouth, inset eyes and black hair wig, 16½in. high. £165

A bisque headed bebe, with fixed blue eyes, a wedding dress, petticoat, underclothes, shoes and socks, 12½in. high. (Christie's S. Ken) £990

A bisque shoulder headed doll with brown sleeping eyes, marked 309,5, 17in. high. £200

DOLLS

A bisque-headed clock-
work walking talking doll,
14in. high.   £350

Early 19th century Eng-
lish composition articul-
ated toy modelled as an
old woman, 13in. high.
£380

A 19th century porcelain
doll with slight pink tinted
complexion, 14in. high.
£150

A Scottish boy doll in
Highland dress, with bisque
head, in original box marked 'Kelly Boy 306', 12in.
high.   £110

A large Festival doll of a seated
samurai in armour, with cloth
covered kabuto, and an atten-
dant figure with jingasa similarly dressed the figures 19th
century with 18th century
brocade, 96cm. and 54cm. high
respectively. (Christie's) £7,700

A bisque headed character
doll modelled as an Oriental,
with fixed brown eyes, wearing pink silk trousers and
printed blue silk kimono,
10¼in. high. (Christie's S. Ken)
£220

A terracotta headed creche figure
modelled as a Turk with moustache
and pigtail, painted wooden hands
and feet, 19in. high.   £330

A bisque headed child doll
with auburn wig and jointed
composition body, 32in.
high.   £400

19th century porcelain
doll with black moulded
hair, 12in. high.   £530

AMERICAN CHARACTER DOLLS

The Americans were great importers of European dolls in the late 19th and early 20th century.

Of the companies who originally imported European products, many went on to manufacture their own. One such was the Amberg Co., which by 1910 had become one of the first to manufacture on a large scale dolls made entirely in the US.

Amberg employed such artists as Grace G Drayton and Jeno Juszko, who contributed the Baby Beautiful range and the New Born Babe, a two day old infant which first appeared in 1914.

Otto Ernst Denivelle worked for Amberg at the beginning of his career and designed new dolls and production methods, such as the introduction of collapsible moulds for cold press composition dolls' heads. He also held some copyrights for dolls.

George Borgfeldt was one of those distributors who grew to be the largest in the country and added American manufacturers to his list of suppliers. One of the most famous Borgfeldt products was the Kewpie doll, created by Joseph Kallus from Rose O'Neill's drawings.

Another major importer turned manufacturer was Fleischaker & Baum, established in 1910 in New York. They used the trademark Effanbee and made a wide range of composition and composition and cloth dolls. These usually had sleeping eyes, either of celluloid or metal rather than glass. One of their most famous was the Baby Grumpy model, registered in 1914 and reproduced in a smaller version in 1927 as Grumpykins.

American composition character doll of Shirley Temple, circa 1935, 13in. high. £280

German all bisque character doll of Kewpie, Rose O'Neill's fantasy creature, circa 1910, 11in. high. £275

A pair of all-bisque Kewpie dolls, with jointed arms, 5½in. high, impressed O'Neill on the feet, in original boxes. (Christie's S. Ken) £770

American plastic character doll, with soft head, circa 1962, 12in. high. £200

An American 'Shirley Temple' personality doll, 21in. high, circa 1935. £475

AMERICAN CHARACTER DOLLS

American composition character doll, produced by Cameo, circa 1926, 17in. high. £270

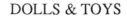

American composition character doll, 14in. high, circa 1940, in original clothes. £250

American cloth child doll, styling indicative of Art Fabric Mills, circa 1895, 13in. high. £200

American artist all bisque doll in one piece by Jeanne Orsini, New York, 1920, 7in. high. £450

American composition character baby, contained in its original cardboard trunk, 10in. high. £200

A composition doll, modelled as Shirley Temple, the straight limbed composition body dressed in outfit from the film "Miss Annie Roonie", 15in. high. (Christie's S. Ken) £99

American plastic lady doll, New York, circa 1975, 21in. high. £450

American plastic Lissy-faced character doll, circa late 1950's, 12in. high. £400

Late 19th century American cloth Folk Art doll, 23in. high in original plaid dress. £250

AMERICAN CHARACTER DOLLS

American composition character doll of Mortimer Snerd, circa 1940, 13in. high.   £350

American composition personality doll by the Reliable Toy Co., circa 1935, 17in. high.   £200

A painted cloth character doll with jointed velvet body, 17in. high.   £250

American composition character doll of Jiminy Cricket, by the Knickerbocker Toy Co., circa 1935, 10in. high.   £160

A cloth and leather figural grouping, Lucy Hiller Lambert Cleveland, Salem, Massachusetts, 1840, 15in. high. (Robt. W. Skinner Inc.)   £1,704

American composition character doll 'Bobbie-Mae', circa 1940, 12in. high, in original box.   £200

American composition character doll of Aunt Jemima, by Tony Sarg, circa 1925, 18in. high.   £350

American artist all bisque doll 'Miss Muffet', 1981, on purple tuffet, 7in. high.   £150

American plastic character doll with bendable knees, circa 1965, 7½in. high.   £400

AMERICAN
CHARACTER DOLLS

American artist all bisque doll 'Little Bo Peep', 1981, 10in. high.   £225

A roly-poly Santa, Germany, probably early 20th century, 10in. high.   £115

American cloth character doll, by Marjorie H. Buell, circa 1944, 14in. high.   £245

American composition artist doll, designed by Dewees Cochrane in 1938, 14in. high.   £700

Pair of American composition character dolls by Pat Burnell, 1976, 14in. high.   £100

A composition shoulder headed doll, by Joel Ellis of the Cooperative Doll Co., 11in. high.   £200

American composition child doll, with mohair wig, circa 1940, 21in. high.   £175

American cloth character doll, made by Georgene Novelties Inc., circa 1940, 13in. high.   £250

A bisque headed child doll with blue sleeping eyes, blonde wig and jointed body, 23in. high, probably Alt Beck & Gosschalk. (Christie's)   £605

AMERICAN CHARACTER DOLLS

American cloth child doll, New York, circa 1900, 22in. high.
£450

American plaster character Buddha-like figure, by Rose O'Neill, 5½in. high.
£30

American plastic character doll, by Terri Lee, circa 1965, 16in. high. £155

American composition character doll by Effanbee, circa 1940, 17in. high, dressed in formal wear. £350

An autoperipatetikos cloth-headed doll, stamped Patented July 1862: also Europe 20 Dec. 1862, American, circa 1862, 9in. high. £375

Composition child doll by the American Doll Co., New York, circa 1940, in riding clothes, 13in. high. £350

American wooden character doll of Mr Peanut, 8in. high. £70

American cloth character doll by Charlene Kinser, 25in. high.
£70

American papier-mache and plush character doll, circa 1909, 13in. high.
£200

AMERICAN INDIAN DOLLS

Most primitive cultures have doll figures for various purposes, and a particularly rich tradition exists among some American Indian tribes, whose products fetch astonishing sums today.

The best known are perhaps the kachina models of the Hopi and Zuni Indians. These are made of dry cottonwood root and are painted in exact imitation of the masks worn by tribesmen who impersonate kachinas, or supernatural beings, at their annual tribal ceremonies. A huge variety of kachinas exist representing such various features as warm rain, rainbow or sun gods.

It is often difficult to tell Hopi and Zuni kachinas apart, although the Zuni versions tend to be taller and more slender than their Hopi counterparts. Their rich decoration of beads and feathers make them very popular with collectors, and many are now made especially for sale.

Originally, however, after the ceremonies it was forbidden for the kachinas to leave the village, and some were hung on the walls of houses or given to the children, who would thus gain familiarity with the rituals and traditions of the tribe.

Other types of primitive dolls commonly relate to the female life pattern, and can be carried in the hope of promoting fertility, or to ward off evil. The Ojibwa Indians, for example, had 'unlucky' figures representing a dead child. By caring for one of these, the bereaved mother could believe that she was assisting her child's passage into the next world.

Plains polychrome and fringed hide doll, Northern, 1880's, 18½in. high. £1,011

Plains beaded and fringed hide doll, Northern, 1880's, 13½in. high. £898

Late 19th century Hopi polychrome wood Kachina doll, possibly 'Qoia', a Navajo singer, 16½in. high. £2,247

Yuma polychromed female figure with traditional horsehair coiffure, inscribed 'Yuma, Arizona Indian 1931', 8in. high. £255

Southwestern polychrome male figure, Yuma, attached card reads 'Bought 1892 Albuquerque, New Mexico', 8¾in. high. £475

A Hopi wood Kachina doll, 'Mahuu' (locust), with black, mustard and rose decoration over a white painted body, 15¾in. high. £816

BRU DOLLS

The doll making factory of Bru Jne & Cie was established in 1866 by Casimer Bru. He remained with the company until 1883. It then passed through a series of directorships before amalgamating with a number of other French firms to form the Société Française de Fabrication de Bébés et Jouets (SFBJ) in 1899. Bru dolls, though less costly than their Jumeau counterparts, were luxury items, with bisque heads and composition, wood or kid bodies. Casimer was a great experimenter, and he invented many mechanical devices.

His designs were many and varied and included crying dolls, feeding dolls and two-faced dolls, which showed a happy and a crying or sleeping face.

With regard to bodies, Bru designed types in jointed wood, gusseted and jointed kid and combinations of composition and kid. Early models had bisque shoulder-heads or swivel heads mounted on gusseted kid bodies, and were often adult in shape. These Bru lady dolls tend to have smiling faces with strikingly upturned mouths. The eyes are usually of glass, fringed by long, densely painted lashes.

In 1872 the Bébé Bru line was introduced often with open moulded mouths revealing teeth and tongue.

Like other manufacturers of the time, Bru made dolls representing different nationalities. Wigs were made of various materials, not only the conventional mohair on canvas, but also from lambswool or animal fur on the original skin backing. Bébé Bru models continued to be made until the 1950s.

The most common Bru mark is *Bru J^{ne} R*.

A bisque headed clockwork walking, talking bebe petit pas, marked BRU Jne R 11, 24in. high. £2,500

A bisque headed bebe with closed mouth, pierced ears and fixed blue yeux fibres, 10in. high. (Christie's) £1,320

A bisque swivel-headed fashionable doll, with closed smiling mouth, narrow grey eyes and kid body in contemporary cream trained dress and underclothes, 12in. high, impressed *B*, probably by Bru. (Christie's S. Ken) £1,485

A fine bisque swivel-headed bébé, with closed mouth, fixed brown yeux fibres outlined in black with pink shaded lids, 20in. high, impressed *BRU Jne 7*, circa 1880. (Christie's S. Ken) £12,100

A 'walking/crying' Bru Jeune R bisque doll, French, circa 1895, 24½in. high, in original Bebe Bru Marchant No. 9 box. £3,300

A bisque headed bébé, with brown yeux fibres, pierced ears, fair mohair wig and jointed wood and composition body, 28in. high, impressed *1907 13*. (Christie's S. Ken) £770

A bisque swivel headed bebe with closed mouth, brown paperweight eyes, moulded feathered brows, pierced ears, 18½in. high, marked BRU Jne 6 (one finger damaged).
(Christie's)   £9,900

Bisque Bebe, incised as follows: head, Bru Jne 9, left shoulder-Bru, right shoulder-N9, shoes marked Bru. Wardrobe consists of corset cover, bloomers, 1/2 slip and two dresses. Paperweight eyes, closed mouth, and human hair wig, kid body with label: Bebe Brevete S.G.D. Tout Contre facteur sera saisi et Poursuivi conforme menta la loi, and bisque arms, height 24in.
(Butterfield & Butterfield)   £13,238

BRU DOLLS

A rare bisque headed bebe, with closed mouth, fixed blue eyes, pierced ears, cork pate and painted wooden body, 16in. high, marked 1 by Bru. (Christie's)   £9,350

A bisque-headed bebe impressed Bru Jne 8 and Bru Jne Paris, with closed mouth, brown paperweight eyes and original clothes, 18½in. high. (Christie's S. Ken)   £14,300

A bisque shoulder headed fashion doll, possibly by Bru, French, circa 1880, 12in. high.   £990

A bisque headed bebe with jointed wood and composition body, marked BRU Jner 4, 13in. high. £1,800

A bisque headed bebe with five upper teeth, fixed brown eyes and pierced ears, 18½in. high.   £800

A Bru Teteur bisque doll, French, circa 1875, 19in. high. (Lawrence Fine Art) £4,400

A rare early bisque shoulder-headed Parisienne, with short blonde mohair curls, unpierced ears and kid over wood jointed body, 10½in. high, possibly by Bru, circa 1870. (Christie's S. Ken)   £1,540

A Bru Jeune bisque headed doll with original sheepskin wig, blue paperweight eyes and pierced ears, 19in. high. (Phillips)   £15,000

French bisque child doll, marked Bru Jne R9, says 'Mama' when legs move, 1895.   £2,420

A bisque swivel headed Parisienne, wearing original peacock green silk dress with matching sleeveless jerkin, marked on head and shoulder D, by Bru, circa 1862, 15in. high. (Christie's S. Ken) £1,650

French Bru Jeune bisque doll in original silk dress and bonnet, 16½in. high, circa 1875.   £4,000

CHAD VALLEY DOLLS

The British toy firm Chad Valley, founded in the district of that name in Birmingham in 1860, started making dolls in 1920. They produced only soft dolls, the heads heat moulded under pressure and made of buckram, canvas or felt. Some dolls' heads were also stiffened with starch or shellac and provided with openings in which glass eyes could be inserted from the inside. It was claimed that they were virtually indestructible.

One of Chad Valley's most famous lines was based on the drawings of Mabel Lucie Attwell, and included a soldier doll, a coloured doll and a boy in morning dress. These came in a special 'Bed-Bye' box.

One of Chad Valley's famous designers was Nora Wellings, who worked for them for seven years, before setting up on her own. Early Chad Valley dolls are now quite rare, as the fabric faces were very prone to discoloration, and they were then often thrown away. They are usually marked with labels sewn under the feet.

English cloth character doll with velvet head, probably Chad Valley, circa 1935, 20in. high.
£175

English cloth character doll by Chad Valley, 18in. high, with mohair plaited wig.
£450

A Chad Valley doll of Winston Churchill, the moulded rubber head with painted facial features, 14in. (Lawrence Fine Arts)
£55

A good Chad Valley 'Princess Elizabeth' character doll with pressed felt head having mohair wig, 17in. (Phillips)
£360

A 'Chad Valley' boxed set of Snow White and the Seven Dwarfs in original clothes, Snow White with painted pressed felt face, jointed velvet body, the blue velvet bodice with pale blue and pink slashed sleeves and short cape, 17in. high, the Dwarfs 9½in. high.
£2,860

DEAN'S DOLLS

Samuel Dean launched his toy making enterprise in 1903 with the laudably realistic purpose of making playthings for children who 'wear their food and eat their clothes'.

Soft toys were introduced shortly after rag books in the same year. The company produced comparatively few designs but those they had were durable and the same figures were still being issued as late as 1936. The first were in sheet form. From 1906 clothes were sometimes included on the sheet, and separate costume sheets were introduced in 1925.

After the First World War the True to Life range was introduced. These could be either moulded or flat printed, and included a range of character dolls, including Charlie Chaplin and Popeye. Dean's worked hard to keep ahead of German and US rivals. Their A1 label was introduced in 1923, and under this they marketed some beautifully dressed dolls, including a Two faced Bo-peep.

Velvet faced dolls with glass eyes were launched in 1926, some very like those designed by Norah Wellings, and Dancing Dolls followed in 1928.

'Minnie Mouse', stuffed toy by Dean's Rag Book Ltd., circa 1930, 7in. high. £300

A painted cloth doll made for Oxo Ltd. by Deans Rag-book Co. Ltd., 17in. high. £300

Betty Oxo, a cloth doll with painted features, blue side-glancing eyes, smiling mouth and blonde mohair wig, 17in. high, marked with Dean's Rag Book label, especially made for Oxo Ltd. (Christie's S. Ken) £495

A gollywog, with cloth face, hands and shoes, comical eyes and mohair hair, with Deans Rag Book Co. stamp on bottom of foot, 13¹/₂in. high. (Christie's S. Ken) £176

A painted cloth character doll with blue shaded eyes, ginger wool wig and jointed legs, 18in. high, with Deans Rag Book Co. Ltd. circa 1926. £200

Mickey Mouse, stuffed toy by Dean's Rag Book Ltd., circa 1930, 6¼in. high. £350

English cloth character doll, by Dean's Rag Book Co. Ltd., of Lupino Lane, 13in. high. £206

A bisque headed doll's house doll modelled as a man with cloth body and bisque hands, 6in. high. £143

An all bisque doll's house doll, marked 253 12 on the head and body, 5¼in. high, and an all bisque standing character boy, 3¼in. high. £100

A bisque headed child doll with closed mouth, fixed blue eyes, blonde wig and composition body, 7in. high, marked 16. £110

A bisque headed doll jointed at neck, shoulder, thigh and knee, 7in. high, marked 199 2/0. £165

A pair of all bisque doll's house dolls modelled as roguish girls, jointed at neck, shoulder and hip, 3½in. high. £462

A bisque headed doll's house doll modelled as a man, 6½in. high. £198

A bisque headed doll's house doll modelled as a man with full beard and hair, 6½in. high. £209

Two all bisque doll's house dolls with fixed blue eyes, blonde wigs and moulded socks and shoes in original national costume, 4in. high. £110

A china doll's house doll with painted features, in seated position, in a dressed metal high-chair, 3in. high. (Christie's) £231

DOLLS & TOYS

French bisque child doll
with blonde human hair
wig, marked 137, 14in.
high.   £694

Rabery and Delphieu bisque
doll with jointed body, in
ivory satin dress, 28in. high.
                          £325

French bisque child
doll, circa 1880, in
original dress and bon-
net, 9½in. high.
                     £550

French bisque child
doll, circa 1870, in
original muslin dress
and bonnet, 13in.
high.   £450

A bisque-headed bebe, the
fixed wrist jointed composition body dressed in blue,
impressed SteA.1, 16in.
high.   £1,870

French bisque novelty doll,
torso forming sweet con-
tainer, 18in. high, circa
1890.   £750

A black bisque doll impressed 34-24, with jointed
wood and composition
body in original pink dress,
probably French, circa
1910, 14¼in. high. £1,320

A bisque headed Pulchin-
elle puppet, impressed 2,
French, circa 1870, 24in.
high.   £1,210

Huret bisque doll with sock-
eted head and jointed body,
circa 1860, 17½in. high.
                    £7,500

French bisque child doll, by E. Denamur, circa 1885, 11in. high. £635

Large French bisque bride doll with kid body, 26½in. high, circa 1875. £3,000

French bisque headed child doll, circa 1935, 11½in. high. £400

Rare French shoulder bisque Oriental doll in original clothes, circa 1860, 13in. high. £5,000

French bisque child doll, marked Mon Cheri, by Lanternier Et Cie, circa 1915, 18in. high. £280

A bisque-headed bebe, the jointed body dressed in pink, 19in. high, marked on the head 8 and with the Schmitt of Paris shield mark on bottom. £2,090

French bisque lady doll, circa 1870, 19in. high, with kid and wooden body, £1,500

French bisque character doll with mohair wig, by A. Marque, early 20th century, 22in. high. £25,000

A French mechanical walking doll, the bisque head with blonde mohair wig, 38cm. high. £680

French bisque child doll, circa 1875, 20in. high. £1,500

A French bisque shoulder-headed fashion doll with a kid-covered wooden body, 45cm. high. £3,000

Rare negro bisque doll, probably French, circa 1870-85, 16in. high. £2,500

A swivel-head shoulder-bisque doll, with kid body, French, circa 1860, 13in. high, together with a cream chintz bag, circa 1880. £825

Danel et Cie bisque headed doll impressed E5D Depose with fixed blue glass eyes, painted mouth, fair hair wig, 16in. high. (Hobbs & Chambers) £450

French all bisque miniature doll, circa 1880, in 'Jester' costume, 6in. high. £400

French cloth character doll, by Poupees Gerbs, circa 1924, 28in. high. £173

A French bisque headed doll with cork pate, the leather shoes impressed with a number 11, a bee and a Paris Depose, 25in. high. £1,350

French bisque doll with jointed wood and composition body, circa 1895, 21½in. high. £350

FRENCH DOLLS

Unusual French bisque doll, circa 1870, 17in. high, in original shot-silk dress. **£400**

A swivel-head bisque doll, French, circa 1850, 15½in. high. **£770**

A bisque-headed bebe, with string pulls for voice box marked Jullien 10, 24½in. high. **£1,600**

French bisque lady doll, circa 1875, 18in. high, with wooden body. **£2,000**

A clockwork musical dancing doll, with waxed papier mâché head, wired composition arms and tiered organdie skirt hiding the mechanism, 11in. high, with A. Theroude's stamps, circa 1850.
(Christie's S. Ken) **£748**

French bisque lady doll with wooden articulated body, circa 1870, 31in. high. **£3,855**

An F. Martin 'Le Gai Violiniste', in original clothes, French, circa 1920, 7¾in. high. **£400**

Rohmer china head doll with wooden joints, circa 1866, 14in. high. **£2,000**

A Simonne bisque shoulder-headed fashion doll, French, circa 1870, 17½in. high. **£1,980**

GAULTIER DOLLS

Fernand Gaultier was a French manufacturer of porcelain dolls' heads and dolls who won a silver medal at the Paris Exposition of 1878. Other medals followed, and in 1889 the company became Gaultier Frères when he went into partnership with his brother François.

Gaultier products vary widely in quality, though the basic modelling was generally well done. Their heads are often found on bodies by other manufacturers, including Jumeau, and are marked *FG*. There have, however been many reproductions and forgeries of these.

Gaultier's fame as a doll manufacturer lay mainly in the manufacture of lady dolls in the Parisienne style, but they also made some very attractive child dolls with huge eyes and rather petulant expressions. There are much rarer than the lady dolls, and attract very much higher prices.

In 1899, Gaultier was one of those who amalgamated to become the SFBJ, in an attempt of counter the threat posed to the French doll making industry from German manufacturers.

A François Gaultier bisque shoulder head marotte with fixed blue glass eyes, pierced ears and closed mouth, 7in., marked *FIG*. (Phillips) £180

French FG bisque fashion doll in original blue dress, 16in. high circa 1875. £1,000

Pair of French bisque shell dolls, probably by F. Gaultier, circa 1875, 10½in. high. £2,000

A bisque swivel shoulder-headed Parisienne, with blue eyes, feathered brows, pierced ears, the stuffed body with kid arms and individually stitched fingers, 11in. high, probably by Gaultier. (Christie's S. Ken) £418

French bisque lady doll, Ferdinand Gaultier's Parisienne with Gesland stockinette body, circa 1870, 23in. high. £2,065

Pair of French bisque adult dolls by Ferdinand Gaultier circa 1890, 13in. high. £1,000

A bisque swivel headed Parisienne, with closed mouth, pale blue bulbous eyes and rigid kid body, by Gaultier, 11in. high. (Christie's S. Ken) £440

DOLLS & TOYS

A bisque headed doll, c1912, by Franz Schmidt, 12½in. high. £310

German porcelain half doll, by Dressel & Kister, circa 1900, 6in. high. £190

Heubach Koppelsdorf bisque headed doll, 20½in. high. £220

A German Marotte doll, the circular wood body containing the musical mechanism, circa 1890, 12in. high. £300

Set of six late 19th century all bisque dolls, German, mounted in candy box, inscribed on cover 'found in the nursery of a ruined old chateau — Verdun, France — 1917', 4in. high. £393

A German porcelain half doll, 'Pierrette', circa 1920, 9½in. high. £750

Late 19th century Heubach 12-Koppelsdorf bisque headed doll, impressed AWW, Germany, 32in. high. £568

A Hebe bisque headed doll, marks indistinct, with open mouth and upper teeth, sleeping blue eyes and long fair plaited hair, 24in. high. £187

A Franz Schmidt bebe doll with sleeping brown eyes, open mouth and composition body, 9in. high. £125

German all bisque
novelty doll, circa
1900, 2¼in. high.
£150

German porcelain half doll of an
adult nude woman, by Dressel
& Kister, circa 1910, 6in. high.
£763

Late 19th century German
bisque headed novelty doll,
13in. high.   £325

A bisque-headed three-faced
doll, the faces crying, sleeping
and smiling, wearing tucked
frock with lace insertions, 16in.
high, stamped *CB* in a circle for
Carl Bergner.
(Christie's S. Ken)   £1,155

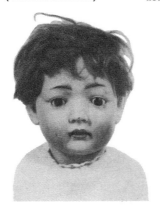

A pair of black composition
character china dolls, with
brown sleeping flirting eyes,
smiling mouths and toddler
bodies, 16½in. high, impressed
K & W 134 12/0, by Konig &
Wernicke.
(Christie's S. Ken)   £396

A composition headed
Motschmann type baby doll
with dark inset eyes, painted
curls and floating hands and
feet, 8in. high, circa 1850.
(Christie's)   £418

A German 'Frozen Charlotte',
the pink tinted china body with
black painted and brushstroked
head, 16in.
(Phillips)   £260

A bisque headed character
baby doll, marked K & W
13, Konig and Wernicke,
24in. high.   £380

A German bisque head doll,
marked Heubach-Koppelsdorf,
250-4, 25¾in. high.   £260

DOLLS & TOYS

German porcelain half doll, circa 1920, 4in. high. £100

German bisque headed character baby doll, circa 1925, 10in. high. £400

Bisque headed German doll marked 'Mignon', 22in. high. £275

A bisque headed doll with composition body, marked Porzellan Fabrik Burggrub Das lachende Baby, 1930/3/ Made in Germany DRGM, 18in. high. £430

A bisque shoulder-headed doll in the French taste, with solid pate, closed mouth, the stuffed body with bisque arms wearing white lawn frock, 13½in. high, German circa 1880. (Christie's S. Ken) £1,155

A china-headed doll, the cardboard and stuffed body with squeaker and china lower limbs, German, circa 1860, 15in. high. £880

A shoulder-bisque doll with fixed blue glass eyes, German, circa 1890, 17in. high. £264

A German bisque head doll, marked 283/297, Max Handwerck, 24¾in. high. £260

German bisque child doll with wooden body, circa 1915, 18in. high. £750

German all bisque char-
acter doll, circa 1915,
3½in. high.   £150

German bisque character
doll with composition bent
limb baby body, by Kley &
Hahn, circa 1915, 13in. high.
£380

A German bisque charac-
ter doll with toddler body
and 'tremble' tongue,
circa 1915, 30in. high.
£2,250

A Bahr & Proschild bisque
doll, impressed B & P
320.12 de, in white brod-
erie-anglaise dress, German,
circa 1885, 21in. high.
£990

Four German all bisque character
dolls, depicting characters from 'Our
Gang', 2in. to 3½in. high, together
with a book, 1929.   £104

German bisque character
doll, the wooden ball-
jointed body with 'walker'
mechanism, circa 1910,
27in. high.   £820

A bisque headed doll with open
mouth, sleeping eyes and brown
hair, stamped with a monogram
'GW', Germany, 16in. (Anderson & Garland)   £195

German celluloid character
doll, wearing original outfit,
marked Kecsa, 16in. high.
£120

A large shoulder-china doll
with kid body in original
dress, German, circa 1860,
20in. high.   £175

German bisque half doll, incised marks suggest Mettlach production, circa 1910, 4in. tall.
£400

Early 20th century German bisque bathing belle, resting on one hand, the other raised shielding her eyes, 3½in. high.   **£330**

German bisque headed doll with original blue knitted frock and hat, 13in. high.
£680

German bisque character doll, by Kley & Hahn, circa 1915, 28in. high.
£629

Two German all bisque miniature dolls, 5in. high, circa 1900, with mohair wigs.   **£300**

A shoulder-china doll, the long face with painted features, German, circa 1860, 15½in. high.   **£400**

A bisque headed doll with open mouth, blonde hair and sleeping eyes, stamped '21, Germany, R6/OP', 14in. (Anderson & Garland)   **£70**

German bisque novelty figure of a young boy, circa 1910, 3½in. high.
£100

German all bisque figure doll, circa 1915, 18½in. high.   **£700**

German porcelain half doll with painted facial features, circa 1910.
£150

Early 20th century German bisque bathing belle with painted facial feature and auburn wig held in a net cap, 3in. high. £264

German bisque Oriental doll with five-piece composition body, circa 1910, 10½in. high.
£450

German bisque character doll with blonde mohair wig, the kid body labelled 'Dainty Dorothy', circa 1911, 25in. high.
£550

Two dolls, one impressed with a clover leaf 5, the other W.D. 5, with fixed brown glass paperweight eyes, German, circa 1900, 13½in. high. £880

German bisque miniature doll, circa 1920, with papier-mache body, 6½in. high. £200

German bisque character doll with wooden ball jointed body in white wool snowsuit, 19in. high. £750

German bisque character baby doll, by Kley & Hahn, circa 1915, 17in. high.
£570

German bisque character doll with brown moulded hair, circa 1920, 13in. high. £2,500

GOOGLY EYED DOLLS

'Googly eyes' are side glancing eyes, either fixed or painted and are also known as 'roguish'. 'Googly' has now come to refer to a doll with such eyes, the better ones having eyes that move by lever action. They were produced by most 20th century doll manufacturers and are extremely popular at present among collectors.

A composition mask faced googly-eyed doll, with smiling watermelon mouth, wearing pinafore and bonnet, 9in. high. £200

A bisque headed googly-eyed doll, with water melon mouth, brown mohair wig, and painted shoes and socks, 7in. high. (Christie's) £528

German bisque character doll with 'googly' eyes, by Strobel & Wilkens, 12in. high.£1,750

A bisque group of two googly-eyed figures in original hats, by William Goebel, 3½in. high. £308

A composition mask faced googly-eyed doll, with smiling watermelon mouth, 13in. high, Hug Me Kiddies, circa 1914. (Christie's) £264

A composition mask faced googly-eyed doll, with smiling watermelon mouth, wearing spotted dress, 10½in. high. (Christie's) £330

An all-bisque googly-eyed doll's house doll with smiling water-melon closed mouth, 4in. high. £220

'Googly-eyed' bisque doll by JDK Ges. Gesch, 11in. high, in knitted pullover and cap. £1,500

GEBRÜDER HEUBACH DOLLS

Gebrüder Heubach opened in 1840 as a porcelain factory in Lichte, near Wallendorf, Thuringia, and later in Sonneberg. They are principally noted for the superb quality of their heads, and they produced an astonishing range of character examples. These are fashioned with great sympathy for the subject and are characterised by their intaglio eyes, which were incised in the moulding before being painted and highlighted. The faces have well defined features, and lightly moulded hair is also common.

Unfortunately, the company tended to mount these on very inferior composition bodies. Many examples were made for export, and Heubach produced heads for many other companies, perhaps even for Jumeau.

Gebrüder Heubach used two marks. The earlier was a rising sun design, registered in 1882, while the later square mark is much more common.

German bisque character doll by Heubach, circa 1915, 9in. high, with 'googly eyes'. £450

A bisque figure of a seated fat baby, marked 95 and the Heubach square mark, stamped in green 68, 5in. high, together with two child dolls. £99

Trio, German all bisque miniatures, by Gebruder Heubach, circa 1900, each about 5in. high. £600

A bisque-headed whistling doll, marked with the square Heubach mark, 11½in. high. £525

A Gebruder Heubach bisque socket head baby boy doll, with moulded hair line, painted features and composition body, 36.5cm. tall.
(Spencer's) £480

German bisque character doll with papier-mache body, 8in. high, by Heubach, circa 1915. £200

A bisque laughing walking doll with the walking talking mechanism concealed under original outfit of blue and cream lace, 9in. high, marked with Gebruder Heubach Square.
(Christie's) £264

A bisque-headed character doll, modelled as a laughing child, with open/closed mouth, 12½in. high, impressed 4 the Gebruder Heubach sunburst 41. (Christie's S. Ken) **£770**

A bisque figure of a chubby baby, impressed No. 9902, 4½in. high, and a bisque figure of a baby playing with his toes, 5½in. long, impressed Gebruder Heubach. **£500**

A rare bisque-headed character doll, modelled as a laughing baby, with open/closed mouth with upper and lower teeth, impressed Gebruder Heubach square mark, 11½in. high. (Christie's S. Ken.) **£825**

A bisque figure of a seated boy, wearing a cream and orange bathing cap, 11½in. high, impressed with the Gebruder Heubach Sunburst and 4859. (Christie's) **£660**

German bisque character doll by Heubach, circa 1915, 10in. high. **£400**

Heubach mechanical rocking doll with original clothes and hair. **£500**

Heubach bisque head doll, Germany, circa 1900, 15½in. high, original dress and hat. **£300**

Pair of German all bisque novelty dolls, possibly by Gebruder Heubach, circa 1900, 4in. high. **£175**

20th century Heubach dusky bisque character doll, with glass eyes, 6¾in. long. **£150**

PIERRE JUMEAU DOLLS

Pierre Jumeau opened his family doll making enterprise in Paris in 1842. They had a factory complex at Montreuil-sous-Bois where they made not only the wood and kid bodies, but also the clothes, and in 1873 kilns were opened, enabling the manufacture of heads as well. The company continued until 1899, when it became part of the SFBJ. After that time the SFBJ continued to produce Jumeau dolls, reissuing them as late as the 1950s.

Initially, Jumeau used heads by other manufacturers, such as Simon & Halbig. Original bodies were shaped kid or jointed wood, but after 1870 these were made also of composition, and it was then too that bébé-type dolls began to be made. (Though bébé refers to representations of children from babyhood to about 6 years, most Jumeau examples are of the older type.)

Jumeau dolls were very much at the top end of the quality scale, and won many international awards in the 1880s and 90s. The eyes are often particularly fine, while other characteristics include rather heavily drawn eyebrows and somewhat chunky bodies.

In addition to lady and child dolls, many character dolls were produced, perhaps modelled on real children. Two-faced dolls and those representing other nationalities were also made, together with a few mechanical types. Jumeau were very skilful at marketing their dolls, which were displayed with accessories in the Paris showroom. Exhibitions specially devoted to them were also held at venues as far flung as Melbourne, London and New York.

A Jumeau bisque doll, French, circa 1880, 15in. high. £1,320

Bisque child doll by Emile Jumeau, France, circa 1880, 17½in. high. £3,000

A pressed bisque swivel headed lady doll, the fixed sky blue eyes with shaded lids and grey brows, the kid body wearing original novice's habit of the Augustinian order, Jumeau, circa 1875, 31in. high, with original stand. (Christie's S. Ken) £3,520

A long-faced bisque headed bebe with closed mouth, pierced and applied ears, blue paperweight eyes, 19½in. high, head impressed 9, body marked with blue Jumeau Medaille d'Or stamp. (Christie's) £8,250

French bisque child doll by Emile Jumeau, France, circa 1880, 15in. high. £2,500

Jumeau phonograph bisque doll in original dress and straw bonnet, circa 1895, 24in. high. £3,000

A Jumeau bisque doll
with real auburn hair wig,
French, circa 1880,
20½in. high.   £1,320

A Henri Lioret phonograph
Jumeau doll, impressed 11,
French, circa 1893, 25in.
high.   £1,870

Bisque headed bebe, marked
1907, with sticker printed
Bebe Jumeau, 24in. high.
                     £720

A bisque-headed bébé, with
closed mouth, fixed brown eyes,
pierced ears and jointed wood
and composition body, 25in.
high, stamped in red *Dépose Tête
Jumeau 11.*
(Christie's S. Ken)   £2,090

A bisque-headed bébé, with blue
yeux fibres, heavy brows,
pierced ears, brown wig and
jointed wood and composition
body, 18in. high, stamped in red
Tete Jumeau.
(Christie's S. Ken)   £1,430

A bisque-headed bébé, with
closed mouth, fixed blue eyes,
pierced ears and jointed wood
and composition body, 23in.
high, stamped in red *Déposé Tête
Jumeau.*
(Christie's S. Ken)   £3,300

A bisque-headed bebe with
jointed composition body,
mark 7 stamped in blue on
the body Bebe Jumeau
Depose, 15in. high.
                £1,045

A Dep Tete Jumeau bisque
headed doll, impressed DEP
8, with jointed wood and
composition body, 19in.
high.   £350

French bisque child
doll by Emile Jumeau,
circa 1895, 13in. high.
                £1,500

JUMEAU DOLLS

An Emile Jumeau bisque 'talking' doll, circa 1880, 19in. high, together with clothing. **£5,000**

A French Jumeau bisque doll, circa 1880, 30in. high, together with twenty pieces of clothing. **£3,300**

A fine French bisque headed doll by Emile Jumeau, circa 1885, 15in. high. **£1,500**

A bisque headed bébé, with closed mouth, fixed blue eyes, blonde wig, and composition body, 14in. high, stamped in red, *Déposé Tête Jumeau Bte.* (Christie's S. Ken) **£2,640**

A bisque headed bebe with fixed blue yeux fibres and pierced ears, 15in. high, impressed 6 body stamped Jumeau Medaille d'or Paris. **£1,155**

A bisque-headed bébé, with closed mouth, fixed brown eyes, blonde mohair wig and fixed wrist , wood and papier mâché body, 12in. high, impressed *DEPOSE E 4 J* and the shoes marked *E. JUMEAU MED. OR 1878 PARIS.* (Christie's S. Ken) **£4,180**

French bisque child doll by Emile Jumeau, circa 1900, 17½in. high. **£2,000**

French bisque child doll by Emile Jumeau, circa 1890, 10in. high. **£1,500**

French bisque child doll by Emile Jumeau, circa 1875, 14½in. high. **£3,000**

A bisque headed bebe with fixed brown eyes, closed mouth, pierced ears and blonde wig, 19in. high, stamped in red Depose Tete Jumeau. (Christie's) £2,860

A bisque-headed bebe with closed mouth, marked E. J. A 10, 1878 Paris, 25in. high. £5,000

A bisque-headed bebe, stamped Tete Jumeau and body Bebe 'Le Parisien' Medaille d'Or Paris, 23in. high. £900

A bisque headed bebe, the pressed head with closed mouth, fixed brown eyes, pierced applied cars and blonde wool wig, impressed *7 EJ*, 1880s, 19in. high. (Christie's S. Ken) £4,400

20th century Jumeau doll with bisque head and body. £5,000

French bisque child doll, stamped Jumeau Medaille d'Or Paris, circa 1890, 13in. high. £1,500

A pressed bisque headed bebe, with fixed pale blue eyes outlined in dark blue, shaded lids, closed mouth and pierced ears, by Emile Jumeau, 1880s, 16½in. high. (Christie's S. Ken) £4,950

A bisque headed bebe, with fixed blue eyes, heavy brows, closed mouth, pierced ears and blonde hair wig, stamped in red *Depose Tete Jumeau 12,* 26in. high. (Christie's S. Ken) £1,760

Percy, a bisque headed bebe with fixed brown eyes, closed mouth, pierced ears and short light brown wig, stamped on the body *Jumeau,* 18in. high. (Christie's S. Ken) £2,200

KÄMMER & REINHARDT DOLLS

The firm of Kämmer & Reinhardt was established at Waltershausen in 1886 by a designer and modeller, Ernst Kämmer, and a business man Franz Reinhardt. They did not actually manufacture dolls, but organised the assembly of components brought in from a number of other sources. They were, however, responsible for the design of a great number of their end products, and held the relevant copyrights and patents.

Until 1909 they copyrighted several dolls, such as Mein Liebling, The Flirt, Der Schelm, and others. In that year, however they launched a completely new concept in doll production when they produced their first Charakterpuppe, and thus gave these dolls the generic name they have borne ever since.

The original Charakter-puppe, no. 100, represents a baby of about six weeks, and succeeding moulds were numbered on from there, representing children of varying ages and expressions. These were all named, and among the most famous are Hans or Gretchen, no. 114, (the sex depending on the wig which was supplied) which was widely exported, and Max & Moritz (113 and 114) two naughty boys who were much copied by other manufacturers.

Many Kämmer & Reinhardt designs were produced in bisque by Simon & Halbig and in celluloid by the Rheinische Celluloid und Gummi Fabrik. They also produced dolls in rubber, wood, wax and felt and, in addition to the character dolls, made normal pretty-faced dolls, mechanical dolls and dolls representing various occupations.

Bisque character doll by Kammer & Reinhardt, circa 1915, in sailor's costume, 18in. high. **£800**

A bisque headed character child doll with closed pouting mouth, painted blue eyes and blonde mohair wig, marked K*R. (Christie's) **£715**

A Kammer and Reinhardt bisque headed character doll, the jointed composition body dressed in red cotton dress, 12½in. high. (Phillips) **£1,000**

A bisque-headed character doll, with closed mouth, grey painted eyes and jointed composition body, 15½in. high, impressed *K * R 114 43*. (Christie's S. Ken) **£1,760**

German bisque character doll, by Kammer & Reinhardt, circa 1915, 8½in. high. **£1,500**

German bisque walking child doll, by Kammer & Reinhardt, circa 1910, 25in. high. **£500**

German bisque charac-
ter doll by Kammer &
Reinhardt, circa 1915,
28in. high.　£4,500

German bisque character baby
by Kammer & Reinhardt,
circa 1915, 12in. high.　£325

German bisque charac-
ter doll by Kammer &
Reinhardt, circa 1915
27in. high.　£2,500

A bisque headed character
doll with closed mouth, blue
painted eyes, blonde wig and
jointed composition body,
18in. high, marked K*R 114.46.
　　　　　　　　　£2,420

A pair of bisque-headed baby
dolls, with open/closed mouths,
grey painted eyes and baby's
bodies, 15in. high, impressed 36
K * R 100.
(Christie's S. Ken)　£935

A bisque-headed character
doll, with closed mouth,
dressed as a boy in smock
and breeches, 18in. high,
impressed K*R.
(Christie's)　　£2,420

A Kammer & Reinhardt
bisque-headed doll with
composition body, 46cm.
high.　　　　£3,000

Kammer & Reinhardt char-
acter bisque doll, 15in. high,
head repaired, in white
cotton dress.　　£750

German bisque child doll
with brown head and body,
by Kammer & Reinhardt,
circa 1915, 22in. high.
　　　　　　　£1,000

One of the earliest and most prolific of 'modern' German doll manufacturers was the firm of Kestner, which was established as early as 1805 in Waltershausen by Johannes Daniel Kestner and turned out papier-mâché heads and wooden bodies. These were known as Täuflinge (a Taufling is a child to be presented for baptism). These bodies were carved and painted but the name has come to refer to all dolls made at Waltershausen. By the middle of the century bodies of kid, fabric, and wax over composition heads were also being made.

In 1860 the company, under the direction of Johannes Daniel Kestner Jr., acquired a porcelain factory at Ohrdruf, and began to make china and bisque heads. The production of these continued until the late 1930s. Kestner are known for the fine quality of their bisque and in fact dolls with a bisque head and shoulders over a leather body are often known as 'Kestners'.

Kestner's output included lady, toddler and child dolls, and character dolls with a very wide range of expressions. Celluloid dolls with heads by Rheinische Gummi were also produced, as were all-bisque and dolls' house-size dolls.

The Kestner mark was registered in 1896 as a crown with streamers, though later the simple initials *JDK* were used. Kestner executed many commissions, particularly for American designers. For Borgfeldt in particular they made bisque versions of such well-known dolls as Kewpie, Bye-lo Baby and the Natural Baby. They also produced versions of popular cartoon characters of the day.

A bisque headed character baby doll, 9in. high, marked 142 2/0 by Kestner. £200

A bisque headed character baby doll with open closed mouth, marked 211 J.D.K., 17in. high. £380

A pair of all bisque character dolls modelled as Max and Moritz, with painted black and ginger hair, by J. D. Kestner, 5in. high. (Christie's S. Ken) £1,320

A Kestner 'Googly' eyed bisque head character doll, with large blue eyes, on a jointed wood and composition toddler body, 17in., marked *Made in Germany*. (Phillips) £3,000

A bisque-headed child doll, with blue sleeping eyes, and fixed wrist jointed composition body dressed as Little Red Riding Hood, 13in. high, impressed *192 2*, by Kestner. (Christie's S. Ken) £462

An all bisque googlie eyed doll, with blue painted eyes glancing to the left, closed watermelon mouth and **moulded** blue socks and black shoes, by Kestner, 5½in. high. (Christie's S. Ken) £330

German all bisque minia-
ture doll, 7in. high, by
Kestner, circa 1910. £250

German bisque character
baby doll by Kestner,
circa 1915, 15in. high.
£525

German all bisque minia-
ture doll, probably by
Kestner, 8in. high.
£300

German all bisque
miniature doll, pro-
bably by Kestner,
circa 1890, 8in.
high. £400

Bisque character doll by J. D.
Kestner, Germany, circa 1915,
15in. high. £450

German all bisque minia-
ture doll, probably by
Kestner, made for Strobel
& Wilken, circa 1900, 8in.
high. £138

German all bisque character
doll with 'googly' eyes, probably by Kestner, circa 1915,
4½in. high. £300

A fine German character doll
by Kestner, with original
clothes, 13in. high, circa 1915.
£1,500

German all bisque minia-
ture doll with blue glass
eyes, by Kestner, circa
1900, 5in. high. £200

German all bisque
miniature doll by
Kestner, circa 1900,
9½in. high.   £300

A bisque-headed charac-
ter baby doll with brown
sleeping eyes, marked
JDK 257, 17½in. high.
       £350

German bisque character
doll by Kestner, circa
1900, with olive tinted
skin, 13in. high.   £3,500

All bisque character doll by J. D.
Kestner, circa 1915, 'Our Baby',
10in. high.   £350

An all bisque child doll, with
closed mouth, fixed brown
eyes and moulded socks and
grey tasselled boots, by J. D.
Kestner, 6in. high. (Christie's
S. Ken)   £352

J. D. Kestner bisque headed
'Hilda' doll, with combed hair,
open mouth and upper moulded teeth, 20½in. long.
(Hobbs & Chambers)   £1,300

A bisque-headed character
boy doll, impressed 7
3072 and with JDK sticker
on the body, 20in. high.
       £605

German bisque character
doll by J. D. Kestner, circa
1910, 14in. high.   £920

German bisque char-
acter doll by Kestner,
circa 1910, with papier-
mache body, 8in. high.
       £550

Bisque adult lady doll by Kestner, circa 1900, in excellent condition, 10in. high. £700

A bisque swivel-headed child doll, with blonde mohair wig arranged in elaborate plaits, and jointed body in original Hungarian costume, 22in. high, impressed *H 12 129*, by J.D. Kestner.
(Christie's S. Ken) £550

German bisque miniature doll by J.D. Kestner, circa 1900, in crocheted dress, 8in. high. £450

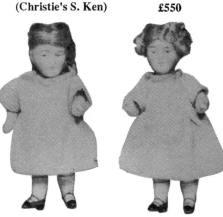

German bisque headed character doll with 'googly' eyes, by J. D. Kestner, circa 1910, 16in. high. £2,870

A pair of all bisque doll's house dolls with blue painted eyes, 5in. high, marked 1503 and 1603 on the legs, by Kestner, circa 1910. £200

Kestner lady doll with articulated arms and legs, 24in. tall. £350

An all bisque character doll with side glancing googlie eyes, watermelon mouth and blonde mohair wig, marked *Kestner*, 5½in. high. (Christie's S. Ken) £198

Large Kestner bisque head doll, circa 1900, 32in. long, with sleeping glass eyes. £600

An all bisque googlie eyed doll, with open/closed watermelon mouth, brown sleeping eyes glancing to the side, marked *222 28,* by Kestner, 11in. high, and a quantity of doll's clothes. (Christie's S. Ken) £1,650

KÄTHE KRUSE DOLLS

The dolls created by Käthe Kruse were the result of her dissatisfaction with the products available for her own children in the early years of this century. The wife of the sculptor Max Kruse, she decided to create her own, more realistic, dolls made of cloth. These designs were based on real people and given their names, and by 1910, Frau Kruse was making then for other people also, with hand painted, reverse treated muslin heads and stockinet bodies.

Her baby dolls were extremely realistic. They were sometimes even made to the actual size and weighted with sand to feel like a real baby, and were complete in every detail, even down to a lump for the tummy button! Perhaps such a degree of realism was too much for some tastes, for it was her toddler types which proved the most popular.

Her company, situated between Nürnberg and Munich, still produces dolls today in the original style, though modern examples have vinyl heads. New ranges have also been introduced, including an inexpensive terry towelling type.

Kathe Kruse boy doll, Germany, in original clothes, circa 1920, 17.3/8in. high. £1,500

German composition character doll by Kathe Kruse, circa 1920, 36in. high. £2,500

Early 20th century German character doll by Kathe Kruse, 17in. high. £300

A Kathe Kruse fabric boy doll with short wig, dressed in red cotton shorts, white shirt and raincoat, 20in. high. (Phillips) £580

A cloth character doll, the head in five sections, 16in. high, by Kathe Kruse, and The Katy Kruse dolly book, published 1927. £1,045

A painted cloth doll with brown painted hair, the stuffed body jointed at hip and shoulder, by Kathe Kruse, 17in. high. £360

An early Kathe Kruse cloth doll with swivel joints at hips, German, circa 1911, 17in. high. £935

LENCI DOLLS

Lenci is the tradename of a Turin based company founded in 1920, and it comes from the nickname of the wife of the proprietor, Enrico Scavini.

A remarkable range of figures was produced, from a 'Mozart' to a 'Madonna and Child', and it was claimed that each doll was studio designed by an Italian artist, and painted by hand.

Lenci dolls are made of felt, individually modelled on real children, and are often known as 'art' dolls. The faces were pressed in moulds, and had no disfiguring seam. All the bodies were articulated, and small dolls were given real hair. The eyes are painted, with highlights, glancing to the side, and the facial expression is often sulky. A further characteristic of Lenci dolls is the fact that the middle fingers of each hand are joined.

Great attention was paid to detail and also to costume, and these dolls are much in demand today. The Lenci company is still in business, and from time to time produces re-issues of their popular 1920s and 30s designs.

A painted felt doll modelled as a young girl, marked on the feet Lenci, 25in. high.
£170

Italian all cloth doll with felt face, by Lenci, circa 1925, 17in. high.   £450

A painted felt doll, the felt body jointed at shoulders and hips, dressed in purple silk gown trimmed with organdie and felt, 15in. high, marked Lenci. (Christie's)   £220

A Lenci fabric boy doll with short fair mohair wig, painted brown eyes and features, 14in. high. (Phillips)   £440

A painted felt doll dressed in the costume of Sicily, 15in. high, marked on foot, by Lenci, circa 1941. (Christie's)
£187

A large Lenci Oriental cloth doll, 23in. high, circa 1925, together with a late 19th century Chinese silk tunic. £475

Italian cloth doll by Madame Lenci, circa 1930, 24in. high, in original cardboard box.
£700

Italian cloth character Lenci doll, by Madame di Scavini, circa 1930, 19in. high. £170

A Lenci pressed felt head doll with side glancing brown eyes and 'pursed' lips, 18½in. (Phillips) £299

Italian cloth character doll by Lenci, 1927, 22in. high. £2,500

William, a felt headed character doll, with side glancing eyes, fair mohair wig, the felt body dressed as a boy, Lenci 300 Series, circa 1930, 16in. high. (Christie's S. Ken) £1,320

A good Lenci cloth doll, Italian circa 1930, the stiffened felt head with painted features, eyes looking to the right and blonde short curly mohair wig, 56cm. high. (Henry Spencer)

Italian Lenci cloth character doll, by Madame di Scavini, circa 1925, 17in. high. £315

Italian cloth character doll, Lenci, by Madame di Scavini, circa 1925, 21in. high. £280

A Lenci fabric boy doll with fair mohair wig and painted brown eyes looking right, 18in. high. (Phillips) £600

Lenci doll in provincial costume, circa 1930, 19in. high. £230

187

A painted cloth Lenci-type doll wearing original Red Indian costume, 16in. high.   £350

A Lenci fabric girl doll with fair mohair wig and painted brown eyes looking left, 12in. high. (Phillips)   £380

Italian all cloth character doll with felt swivel head, by Lenci, circa 1925, 19in. high. £2,000

A Lenci pressed felt girl doll, circa 1930, with moulded and painted facial features and blonde wig, 49cm. high. (Osmond Tricks)   £220

A painted felt child doll, with blue eyes, blonde wig and original green and white frilled organdie dress, marked on the soles *Lenci*, circa 1930, 14in. high. (Christie's S. Ken) £550

A painted felt doll, wearing original organdie frock decorated with felt flowers, 17¹/₂in. high, 300 Series by Lenci.
(Christie's S. Ken)   £418

A painted head doll with blue eyes, the felt body in original, clothes, 16in. high, marked Lenci, circa 1930.   £121

Lenci girl, dressed in cerise felt dress, hat and shoes, 1930's, 16in. high.   £100

Italian Lenci cloth character doll, by Madame di Scavini, 13in. high. £138

MADAME ALEXANDER DOLLS

Mme Alexander was a second generation US immigrant who, as a girl, helped her parents run their dolls' hospital and toyshop in the early years of this century. During the First World War she created a Red Cross figure, which was followed in the 1920s by a whole series, including some baby dolls with sleeping eyes. Most of the dolls represent characters, such as those from Dickens or Alice in Wonderland or contemporary celebrities, such as the Dionne quins. She painted the heads herself, and the hair was made of wool.

The dolls were produced in large numbers, and many went for export so they are still quite plentiful today.

American plastic character doll by Madame Alexander, circa 1958, 8in. high.   £1,000

Vinyl character doll by the Alexander Doll Co., circa 1965, 13in. high.   £500

A set of composition dolls representing the Dionne quintuplets with doctor and nurse, 7½in. high, the adults 13in. high, by Madame Alexander.   £418

American plastic character doll, 'Prince Charming', by Madame Alexander, circa 1950, 18in. high.   £400

American plastic character doll by Madame Alexander, 1975, 22in. high.   £255

American plastic character doll by Madame Alexander, circa 1961, 14in. high.   £250

American plastic character doll by by Madame Alexander, New York, circa 1966-68, 8in. high.   £400

ARMAND MARSEILLE DOLLS

Despite the undeniably French ring of the name, the firm of Armand Marseille was in fact founded in 1885 in Köppelsdorf in Thuringia, where they became one of the largest manufacturers of bisque dolls' heads.

Marseille created all sorts of dolls, the majority being of the straightforward pretty variety, with happy smiling faces, as these proved to be the best sellers. However, they also produced character dolls, and the marks sometimes vary to denote this. The usual mark is *AM* together with the Company's name and *Germany* or *Made in Germany*, and the mould no. *390*. This mould represented a pretty, socket head, which was made between c. 1900–c. 1938.

Another variation introduced in 1925 was the word *Ellar*, and mould *355* for an oriental type bisque head, and other mould numbers around this figure represent variations on this type, while *Fany* was used on a rather chubby child's head, issued with either moulded hair or a wig.

Marseille created many dolls for other companies and to specific designs, some of which were requested by US importers such as Borgfeldt, Wolf and Amberg. Armand Marseille made their own technological advances and were, moreover, quick to take advantage of new techniques pioneered by others, such as sleeping, flirty or intaglio eyes, national dolls and dolls with a variety of bodies, composition, kid or celluloid, together with the occasional use of rubber for hands. Marseille produced dolls in a wide quality range, with some designed to be within the reach of the poorest child.

An Armand Marseille bisque-headed 'dollie', wood and composition ball jointed body, 24in. high.   £170

A bisque-headed googlie-eyed doll, with brown sleeping side-glancing eyes, smiling closed mouth and composition baby's body, 8½in. high, impressed *323 A 5/0 M.*
(Christie's S. Ken)   £440

Bisque headed character doll by Armand Marseille, circa 1920, 12in. high, in excellent condition.   £750

German bisque character doll, by Armand Marseille, circa 1920, 24in. high.   £431

A bisque shoulder-headed doll, with brown sleeping eyes, blonde wig and stuffed body with composition arms, wearing contemporary farm labourer's costume, 23in. high, impressed *370 AM 2½ DEP.*(Christie's S. Ken)   £363

German bisque character doll with five-piece papier mache body, by Armand Marseille, circa 1925, 7in. high.   £280

ARMAND MARSEILLE DOLLS

Armand Marseille doll, fully jointed body and limbs, clothed and in glazed wooden case.
£150

A bisque headed doll with jointed composition body, marked Armand Marseille, Germany A9M, 24in. high.
£190

Bisque character doll by Armand Marseille, circa 1920, 7in. high, in original Dutch costume.
£400

An Armand Marseille bisque socket head girl doll, with painted features, blue glass closing eyes and with a white cotton dress with floral whitework hem. (Henry Spencer)
£260

A brown bisque-headed baby doll with brown composition baby's body, 14½in. high, marked AM341/ 2.5K.
£220

An Armand Marseille 'Googly'-eyed bisque head character doll with light brown mohair wig, 13½in., marked *Germany 323 AOM.*
(Phillips)
£650

German bisque headed character doll, Fany by Armand Marseille, circa 1915, 14in. high.
£3,000

An Armand Marseille bisque socket head girl doll with painted features, closing blue glass eyes with hair eyelashes, open mouth with four upper teeth, 59cm. high. (Henry Spencer)
£170

German bisque child doll with composition and wooden ball jointed brown body, by Armand Marseille, circa 1895, 13in. high. **£312**

ARMAND MARSEILLE
DOLLS

Early 20th century Armand Marseille bisque headed Floradora doll, 14in. high. £130

A bisque-headed character baby doll, marked AM353/4K, 17in. high. £900

A bisque headed doll with blue sleeping eyes, blonde wig and jointed body, 17in. high, marked '390 A ½ M', in original box stamped 'Toyland, Hull'. (Christie's) £330

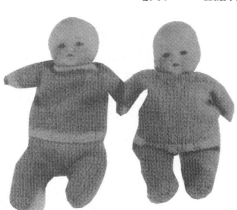

A bisque headed doll with moving eyes, marked on head A.M. 4DEP, Made in Germany, 19in. high. £180

Pair of Armand Marseille bisque headed dolls. £300

A bisque headed character child doll, marked 231 DRMR 248 FANY A2/0M, 14in. high. £2,420

An Armand Marseille bisque doll, with sleeping blue eyes, brown wig and cream apron and hat, 10in. high. (Lawrence Fine Arts) £61

An Armand Marseille '980' bisque headed doll with open and shut eyes, dressed, 22in. high. £180

German bisque child doll wearing an original Shaker costume, by Armand Marseille, circa 1925, 16in. high. £208

PAPER DOLLS

The earliest paper dolls were made as costume studies and were very popular in the 18th century. The commonest method was to have a painted dummy figure some 5 or 6 inches high with an assortment of paper dresses to fit on to it. Ladies amused themselves by making these as drawing room accomplishments.

Flat paper and card dolls became popular in Europe around 1790 and were sold in sheet form. Some represented trades or professions as well as simply showing off elegant costumes, and were popular with children and adults alike.

The idea was still in vogue during the Regency period, when books were published, notably by F C Westley of Piccadilly and S & J Fuller of the Temple of Fancy, in which cut-out figures replaced the illustrations or could be placed against background scenes to more or less act out the story. They could be dressed in successive layers, e.g. shirt, then jacket etc.

These are very much on the borderline between childrens' books and dolls, and Continental makers appear to have adhered much more closely to the traditional paper doll style. Interestingly, in their offerings of the period, the costumes often include the arms in a variety of positions rather than having them showing on the basic model as has latterly become more popular. The dummies were usually dressed in a low necked petticoat and the dresses, which had backs as well as fronts, fitted on over the shoulders.

In both England and America, manufacturers such as Sunlight Soap, also used paper dolls as a give-away advertising gimmick.

'We're All In It, Mummy Puts On Uniform'. £10

Psyche, a double sided hand coloured paper doll in her petticoat, with twenty-one double sided changes including wedding dress, ermine trimmed jacket, evening and day dresses and hats, 7in. high.
(Christie's)   £400

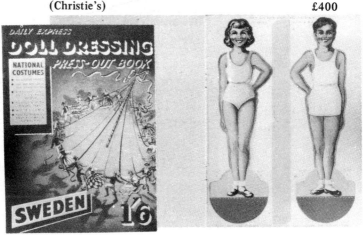

Daily Express Doll Dressing Press-Out Book, 'Sweden'. £8

Set of four articulated paper dolls, circa 1890, each 9in. high. £75

Set of lithographed paper dolls on heavy cardboard, depicting Hansel and Gretel, printed in Germany, circa 1890, 7½in. high. £25

Group of various paper dolls, including Miss Ida Rehan, 14in. high, by Raphael Tuck & Sons, 1894. £355

'The History of Little Fanny', exemplified in a series of figures, printed by S & J Fuller consisting of a number of paper dolls with an assortment of dresses and accessories with accompanying text, circa 1810. £100

PAPIER MÂCHÉ DOLLS

Papier mâché dolls began to be made in the 18th century, and became really popular in the Regency period, when hairstyles lent themselves to a moulded treatment. A few, however, do have hair wigs, and these are particularly rare and sought after.

Most models were made by pressing pulp into metal or plaster moulds, and the rough cast result then covered by an even layer of gesso or plaster to provide a sound base for painting.

The shoulder heads were glued on to fabric, leather or wood bodies which were filled with sawdust and stiffened by wire.

In the 19th century German papier mâché head manufacturers were paramount, though French bodies were generally used.

Later in the century design improved, with simple, everyday hairstyles and these were the forerunners of attempts to create childlike figures.

Throughout the later part of the 19th century experiments were being carried out to find an alternative substance which was both strong and could be successfully moulded. As a result of these experiments later papier mâché heads are of a much denser mixture, with so much plaster that they can be very easily scraped away. This type or debased papier mâché came to be known as 'composition'.

From about 1855, therefore, the era of true papier mâché had passed and even the later sales literature referred to the debased mixture as being 'similar to china', by which, with wax, it was finally superseded.

The painting was usually skilfully done and the finished face then lightly varnished.

A papier-mache shoulder-headed doll, Sonneburg, circa 1840, 25in. high.
£550

A papier-mache headed autoperipatetikos with brown painted eyes, 10in. high. £350

A papier-mache headed doll with moulded ringlets, the stuffed body with wooden limbs, 11in. high, circa 1840. (Christie's) £286

A papier mache headed doll, the moulded black hair arranged in a loose bun at the nape, 9in. high, circa 1840. (Christie's) £110

A Biedermeier shoulder-papier-mache doll with painted face, circa 1825, 10½in. high. £330

19th century miniature papier-mache doll with kid body, circa 1850, 7½in. high. £250

An early papier-mache headed doll with painted features, circa 1840, 11in. high.   £220

German papier-mache novelty doll, circa 1880, 11in. high, in the form of a witch.   £65

German black papier-mache doll with fixed black enamel eyes, circa 1860, 7½in. high.   £330

19th century miniature papier-mache doll with kid body, circa 1850, 7½in. high.   £250

A pair of papier-mache shoulder head dolls, each with black-painted and brushstroked pate enamel eyes, painted lashes, brows and open mouth, probably French, circa 1840. (Phillips)   £480

An early shoulder-papier-mache doll in original clothes, French, circa 1840, 11½in. high. £385

A 19th century papier-mache doll, circa 1850, 7½in. high.   £200

A papier mache mask faced doll with turquoise blue eyes, the cloth and wood body in original Central European costume, 15½ in. high, circa 1860. (Christie's)   £198

A large shoulder-papier-mache doll with kid body and wooden lower limbs, German, circa 1830, 24in. high.   £660

PARISIENNES

Parisienne is the name given to the intensely fashionable lady dolls which were particularly popular between 1860–85. They came with amazingly elaborate wardrobes and accessories and manufacturers encouraged a fierce spirit of competition among their customers as to who could have the best and most perfectly dressed doll. By and large, the clothes were considered to be of more importance than the quality of modelling.

A bisque shoulder-headed Parisienne doll, circa 1870, 15½in. high.   £400

A white bisque shoulder-headed Parisienne doll, French, 13in. high. £450

A bisque swivel headed Parisienne with blue fixed eyes, pierced ears, fair mohair wig with cork pate, 16½in. high, with Cremer, 210 Regent Street stamp on body.(Christie's)   £1,100

A bisque swivel headed Parisienne with closed mouth, fixed blue eyes and Geslard body with bisque limbs, 14in. high. (Christie's) £1,760

A bisque swivel headed Parisienne, 17½in. high without stand, the head marked 3. (Christie's)   £3,600

A bisque swivel headed Parisienne with blue fixed eyes, feathered brows and sheepskin wig, 16in. high, probably by Jumeau. (Christie's)   £1,320

A swivel headed clockwork musical walking doll, with a Parisienne type head, 21in. high.   £1,000

A bisque swivel headed Parisienne modelled as a child with blue eyes, pierced ears and blonde mohair wig, 9½in. high. (Christie's)   £1,100

197

PEDLAR DOLLS

Pedlar dolls are usually considered as a purely English phenomenon though some are featured in German catalogues dating from the turn of the century, and wax street vendors were made until quite recently in Mexico. The real thing, however, dates principally from the Regency and early Victorian periods. Pedlar dolls were not made as playthings, but as ornaments for adults, many having glass shades which not only protected them from dust but also from prying little fingers.

Fake pedlar dolls abound, and great care must be taken. Fakes are most often of the wooden type, though battered wax dolls can also be equipped with spurious items such as knitted gloves, hats and purses (these knitted on dressmaker's pins), eked out with some bits and pieces from old dolls' houses. Sprayed with dust, they can look quite effective, and potential buyers should look carefully for fading and warping.

It is dolls dating from the early 19th century which are the most sought after, and the pins used to hold the wares in place, or even those on sale, can provide useful clues to age and authenticity. In the early 19th century the Tudor method of making a pin from two pieces of brass wire, one coiled into a brass head, was still being used. This was superseded by a one-piece construction, retaining the coiled head. Then in 1830 solid headed pins began to be made by Taylor & Co. Reels of cotton would also be out of place on a genuine doll of the period, since at that time thread would still have been sold in hanks. The genuine article usually has a very 'settled' appearance, acquired over a hundred years or so.

A 19th century pedlar doll standing beside a table cluttered with her wares.
£1,400

A wax over composition headed pedlar doll, 12in. wide, under glass dome.
£650

A papier mâché shoulder-headed pedlar doll, with painted features, brown wig and stuffed body, wearing a flower-sprigged dress, red cloak and brown bonnet, circa 1840, 12in. high. (Christie's)
£825

A china-headed pedlar doll, dressed in original striped and printed cotton frock, 10in. high, late 19th century, under dome. (Christie's S. Ken)
£528

A good Edwardian pedlar doll on ebonised stand under glass dome, the wax covered boy sailor standing on his one leg. (David Lay)
£260

An English mid 19th century vendor doll of wood and cloth, under glass dome with turned walnut base, 16in. high. (Robt. W. Skinner Inc.)
£2,112

PORTRAIT DOLLS

There are various definitions of 'portrait dolls'. The most accurate is a doll modelled on a known person, such as Queen Alexandra or Lord Roberts. However the term has also been used to describe various bisque or porcelain heads which bear a passing resemblance to such beauties of the time as Jenny Lind.

The situation is further confused by the fact that American collectors sometimes refer to early almond-eyed Jumeau dolls as 'portrait Jumeaus', while English collectors also use the description for later dolls that resemble actual children.

A set of Madame Alexander Dionne Quins, in original romper suits, bonnets, shoes and socks, 7in. high, marked Alexander. (Christie's) £495

A composition portrait doll modelled as Shirley Temple, 13½in. high, marked S.T. 5/0 CB Germany. £242

A Chad Valley painted felt portrait doll modelled as the Princess Elizabeth, circa 1938, 18in. high. (Christie's) £308

Three Martha Thompson bisque portrait models of The Queen, Prince Charles and Princess Anne. £400

English cloth portrait doll of Edward VIII, circa 1930, 15in. high. £350

A pair of poured wax portrait dolls, modelled as Edward VII and Queen Alexandra, 21in. high, by Pierotti. (Christie's) £1,100

A painted felt portrait doll modelled as HRH The Princess Elizabeth, with original pink frilled rayon dress, 17½in. high, by Chad Valley. £198

Two composition dolls, modelled as Shirley Temple, with green eyes and curly blonde mohair wigs, 24 and 21in. high. (Christie's S. Ken) £462

BRUNO SCHMIDT DOLLS

The firm of Bruno Schmidt was one of those active in Waltershausen where it was established in 1900. They produced bisque, composition and celluloid dolls in varying designs which included baby, oriental and character varieties. Schmidt acquired Bähr and Pröschild's porcelain factory at Ohrdruf in 1918.

Their main trademark was based on a heart shape.

SCHOENAU & HOFFMEISTER DOLLS

It is often possible for the novice to confuse dolls made by Schoenau and Hoffmeister with Simon & Halbig, since the initials are of course the same. The Schoenau & Hoffmeister mark is SPBH with the initials PB (Porzellanfabrik Burggrub) enclosed in a five-pointed star.

In general, although some of their products display great delicacy of feature, they are inferior to their Simon & Halbig counterparts. Among the best models turned out by Schoenau & Hoffmeister are their Oriental girl doll and some of their closed mouth bébés. They also made baby heads marked only Porzellanfabrik Burggrub. These are often untinted, and there is a tradition that some of these dolls were intended as clowns, to have their faces decorated by the purchaser. Some still bear traces of commercial spray-on paint colour.

Many Schoenau & Hoffmeister dolls carry numbers on the back of their heads which seem to be the year of production, such as 1909, but the same models continued to be used for many years. The much rarer shoulder heads are marked with an 1800 sequence.

Rare late 19th century Bruno Schmidt bisque Oriental doll, Germany, 16in. high, in original dress. £1,500

Rare Jumeau 19th century. Bruno Schmidt bisque Oriental doll, Germany, 16in. high, in original dress. £2,000

A Schoenau & Hoffmeister shoulder-bisque Marotte doll, German, circa 1900, 15in. high. £350

Schoenau and Hoffmeister 'Princess Elizabeth' bisque headed doll impressed Porzellanfabrik Burggrub Princess Elizabeth 6½ Made in Germany, 23in. high. (Hobbs & Chambers) £480

A Schoenau & Hoffmeister 'Princess Elizabeth' bisque doll, circa 1938, 16in. high. £1,000

Schoenau and Hoffmeister doll with blue eyes, 26in. tall, circa 1909. £300

SCHOENHUT DOLLS

Names are nothing to go by when guessing the nationality of doll makers and Schoenhut is no exception. The company was established in Philadelphia in 1872 and made all-wood dolls and toys, such as the Humpty Dumpty Circus. The wooden dolls all had carved heads with moulded hair and their bodies were fully jointed. They could moreover be easily positioned, for the joints were metal springs and the feet drilled with holes to fit onto a small stand.

Wooden character doll by Schoenhut, Philadelphia, 12in. high, circa 1915.
£230

American wooden character doll by Albert Schoenhut, circa 1915, 18in. high.
£300

American wooden character doll with intaglio brown eyes, by Schoenhut of Philadelphia, circa 1911, 15in. high.   £243

American carved wooden doll and animal, 'Milkmaid and Cow', by Schoenhut of Philadelphia, each 8in.   £416

A wooden character doll with carved and painted features, in pink velvet and organza dress and original underwear, 14½in. high, by Schoenhut. (Christie's)   £418

American wooden character doll by Schoenhut, circa 1911, 16in. high.   £750

American carved wooden character doll with brown intaglio eyes, by Schoenhut of Philadelphia, circa 1911, 15in. high.   £312

American wooden character doll, by Schoenhut of Philadelphia, circa 1911, 16in. high.   £420

S.F.B.J. DOLLS

The Société Française de Fabrication de Bébés et Jouets was set up in 1899 to assist French makers in their struggle to compete with the increasing flood of German imports, many of which were of better quality and less expensive than their French counterparts. About ten companies amalgamated under the association, which ironically came under the leadership of Saloman Fleischmann of Fleischmann & Bloedel. Each of these donated the rights to one of its designs, usually of the bébé type, and those companies which had porcelain manufactories leased them for head production.

In addition to this bank of existing designs, SFBJ also launched many new ones, and produced a wide range of different dolls. Their initials were adopted as their trademark in 1905. Reissues of popular lines, such as Bébé Bru and Bébé Jumeau occurred at intervals right up to the 1950s.

SFBJ products could vary enormously in quality. The better ones are very good indeed, but there are many which are poorly modelled and badly decorated. Thickly moulded brows, pierced ears and well modelled teeth are characteristic of the better type.

A bisque headed character baby doll, 27in. high, marked SFBJ252 Paris 12.   £1,540

French bisque character doll by SFBJ, Paris, circa 1915, 19in. high.   £690

French bisque child doll by SFBJ, Paris, circa 1915, 30in. high.   £1,700

A bisque-headed character doll, marked SFBJ236 Paris 6 and embossed 21, 14in. high.   £550

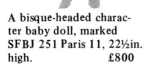

A bisque-headed character baby doll, marked SFBJ 251 Paris 11, 22½in. high.   £800

A bisque-headed doll with composition body, 17in. high, impressed SFBJ60 Paris O.   £200

Early 20th century bisque-head character boy doll, SFBJ France, 18in. high.   £1,500

A rare bisque-headed googly-eyed character doll, marked SFBJ 245 Paris 4, 13½in. high. £3,000

S.F.B.J. bisque headed doll in lace-trimmed dress, 45cm. high.£225

Early 20th century bisque-head character boy doll, impressed SFBJ 238 Paris 4, France, 17¾in. high. £2,750

An SFBJ bisque character boy doll, impressed 237 8, with jointed composition body in navy sailor suit, French, circa 1910, 23in. high. £1,430

A bisque headed child doll, marked SFBJ Paris 14, 32in. high, original box marked Bebe Francais. £800

A bisque headed doll with glass eyes, open mouth and composition body, marked S.F.B.J. 60 Paris, 18in. high. £110

A bisque headed doll, impressed SFBJ 236 Paris 12, with composition toddler body, circa 1910, 24in. high. (Hobbs & Chambers) £600

French bisque character doll, SFBJ, circa 1915, 12in. high. £2,240

A bisque-headed character baby doll, with open/closed mouth, blue sleeping eyes and baby's body, 18½in. high, impressed R S. F.B.J. 236 PARIS 10. (Christie's S. Ken) £605

SIMON & HALBIG DOLLS

The Simon & Halbig porcelain factory was established at Ohrdruf, Gräfenhain, in 1869 and made many other products apart from dolls' heads. Their head output, however, was exceeded only perhaps by Marseille and they made for many other companies, both French and German. They appear to have made heads specifically to order, for each head is marked with a mould number and each number was used by only one company.

In particular, Simon and Halbig worked closely with Kämmer & Reinhardt on their 100 series of character dolls. They in fact became part of K & R in 1920, and thus part of the Bing empire, which had taken over K & R some two years before.

The quality of Simon & Halbig's bisque was excellent and they were also expert modellers and painters. They produced baby, child and lady dolls. Their lady dolls were often of the double-jointed type, very delicately constructed and most attractive. Their open-mouth types were not generally so pleasant as the sweeter-faced closed-mouth examples. They also produced many large-size dolls, which often seem to make more money on the size alone.

Coloured and oriental dolls were produced, sometimes from the same moulds, and simply in a different coloured bisque, though they did have some special moulds for these which allowed for greater accuracy or representation.

Simon & Halbig trademarks vary; early examples generally only have the initials *SH*, which was revised to *S&H* in 1905. Sometimes the name is written in full, and the mould numbers are usually included.

A Simon & Halbig bisque headed doll with composition ball jointed body, 24in. high. £340

Simon & Halbig walking/talking doll with jointed body, 20in. high. £450

Early 20th century 'Googly' doll by Simon & Halbig. £2,500

Simon and Halbig bisque headed doll, having brown sleeping eyes, open mouth with two moulded upper teeth, 23½in. high. (Hobbs & Chambers) £300

A bisque-headed child doll, with blue lashed sleeping eyes, pierced ears and blonde mohair wig, 21in. high, marked *Simon & Halbig K*R 53*. (Christie's S. Ken) £660

A bisque headed child doll with blue sleeping eyes, pierced ears and fair mohair wig, 17in. high, marked Simon & Halbig. (Christie's) £440

DOLLS & TOYS

A bisque-headed charac-
ter toddler doll, marked
Simon & Halbig, 26in.
high.   £600

A Simon & Halbig bisque
'walking' doll, German,
circa 1890, 13in. high.
                         £450

Late 19th century Simon &
Halbig bisque Oriental doll,
12in. high.   £1,250

A Simon and Halbig bisque head
Indian character doll with black
mohair wig, feathered brows,
fixed brown glass eyes, 13½in.,
marked *1368*.
(Phillips)   £280

A Simon & Halbig bisque
headed Jutta character doll,
impressed 'Jutta 1914 12',
circa 1920, 21in. high.
(Hobbs & Chambers)
                         £440

A bisque-headed character doll,
modelled as an Oriental, with
sleeping slanting brown eyes,
and yellow jointed wood and
composition body, 15in. high,
impressed *S H 1199 DEP 6½*.
(Christie's S. Ken)   £1,210

A bisque-headed
character doll, marked
1488 Simon & Halbig
4, 12½in. high.
                       £1,650

Simon and Halbig bisque
headed child doll made for
Luno and Otto Dresall, right
shoulder with red Dresall stamp
of a winged helmet, circa 1910,
21in. (G. A. Key)   £300

Bisque child doll by
Simon & Halbig,
Germany, circa 1900,
41in. high.   £450

Japanese doll by
Simon and Halbig.
£1,250

A Simon & Halbig mulatto
bisque doll, with open mouth
and upper teeth, 10in. high.
(Lawrence Fine Arts)

£165

German bisque character
doll by Simon & Halbig,
21in. high. £800

A Simon & Halbig bisque doll,
impressed 1079, in original
crocheted underclothes, German, circa 1890, 13in. high.
£330

A bisque headed child doll, with
blue sleeping eyes, pierced ears
and blonde wig, the composition
jointed body wearing robe with
lace insertions, marked *Simon &
Halbig K,* 19in. high. (Christie's
S. Ken) £550

A Simon & Halbig bisque
doll impressed 1079, with
jointed wood and compos-
ition body, German, circa
1890, 28in., together with
a pair of kid doll's gloves.
£550

German bisque child doll by
Simon & Halbig, circa 1920,
13in. high. £800

Simon & Halbig bisque
headed doll, Germany,
circa 1880, 12½in. high.
£750

Simon & Halbig bisque
child doll with clockwork
mechanism, circa 1890,
22in. high. £670

SIMON & HALBIG DOLLS

German bisque child doll by Simon & Halbig, circa 1920, 14in. high.   £600

A bisque-headed character child doll, 23in. high, marked K*R Simon and Halbig 117n58, and a boy doll, 22in. high.   £935

A German bisque walking doll by Simon & Halbig, circa 1890, 16½in. high.   £1,500

A bisque headed child doll, with brown lashed sleeping eyes, pierced ears and jointed body, 12½in. high, marked S&H. (Christie's)   £550

A clockwork toy of a bisque headed doll pulling a two-wheeled cart, marked 1079 Halbig S & H 7½, by Toullet Decamps.   £550

A bisque headed child doll with fixed brown eyes and blonde wig, 10in. high, marked 1079 DEP S&H.   £250

A Simon & Halbig bisque lady doll, with open mouth and upper teeth, German, circa 1910, 27in. high.   £1,320

Very rare late 19th century black bisque doll, impressed 7 1302 Dep S & H, 19½in. high.   £6,000

Bisque lady doll by Simon & Halbig, circa 1880, 10½in. high, with unusual swivel neck.   £700

Simon & Halbig kneeling doll with porcelain head, cloth body and bisque arms. £600

German bisque character doll in the shape of an American Indian, by Simon & Halbig, circa 1900, 22in. high. £3,250

A bisque-headed child doll, 22in. high, marked Handwerck 109-11 Halbig on the shoes, NAPAUD 32 rue du 4 Septembre. £825

A bisque swivel headed doll, with closed mouth, blue sleeping eyes, pierced ears and gusseted cloth body with bisque arms, wearing provincial costume, marked *S 5 H 719DEP* 14½in. high. (Christie's S. Ken) £715

German bisque child doll by Simon & Halbig, circa 1900, 21in. high, with original clothes. £650

Simon & Halbig bisque character doll, wooden ball-jointed body with adult modelling, circa 1900, 27in. high. £10,450

Simon & Halbig version of the Gibson Girl, circa 1900, 25in. high. £675

A bisque-headed character child doll, 23in. high, marked K*R Simon and Halbig 117n58, and a boy doll, 22in. high. £935

A bisque headed child doll, 8½in. high, marked 1078 S&H. £264

SIMON & HALBIG /
KAMMER & REINHARDT

Kammer & Reinhardt/
Simon & Halbig bisque
doll with jointed body,
26in. high.   £500

Simon & Halbig/Kammer &
Reinhardt bisque-headed
doll, 1914-27, 26in. high.
(Hobbs & Chambers)
£470

Kammer & Reinhardt/Simon
& Halbig 'My Darling' doll
with jointed body, 22in. high.
£2,000

A Kammer & Reinhardt/
Simon & Halbig bisque
character doll impressed
126 24, German, circa
1910, 11in. high.   £264

One of two bisque headed doll's
house dolls with blue sleeping
eyes, one with brown wig, 5½in.
high, one marked Halbig K*R 13.
£286

A Kammer & Reinhardt/
Simon & Halbig bisque
character doll, impressed
121 42, German, circa
1910, 17in. high.   £460

A bisque headed character
child doll with blue sleeping
eyes, marked K*R SH115/A
42, 16½in. high.   £2,300

Kammer and Reinhardt/Simon
and Halbig bisque headed character doll, with brown glass
sleeping eyes, moulded closed
mouth, 21¼in. high. (Hobbs
& Chambers)   £2,800

A bisque headed child doll
with blue lashed sleeping
eyes, pierced ears and blonde
mohair wig, 20in. high, marked
S & H K*R 50. (Christie's)
£660

STEINER DOLLS

The firm of Jules Nicholas Steiner was established in France in 1855. They produced all kinds of dolls, from the bébé variety to lady dolls, but are perhaps best known for their mechanical examples, which could often both walk and talk and in addition were most elegantly dressed.

The moulding of the head is usually very fine, and many early examples have a double row of teeth, cast in the moulded head. Steiner also produced coloured dolls of different races, and some representing different occupations, such as clowns.

A bisque headed bebe, marked J. Steiner Paris, SreA.3, 11in. high. £800

A Steiner Motschmann-type bisque doll, France, circa 1860, with fixed glass eyes, 12¾in. high. £1,307

A bisque swivel shoulder-headed doll, with blue yeux fibres, feathered brows, upper and lower teeth, 15in. high, by Jules Nicholas Steiner, circa 1880. (Christie's S. Ken) £1,210

A bisque headed bebe with jointed composition and wood body, by Steiner, 12in. high. £1,100

A bisque headed bébé, with blue lever-operated sleeping eyes, pierced ears, two rows of teeth, blonde skin wig and jointed wood composition body, 17in. high, marked *STe A 1*, Steiner, circa 1880. (Christie's S. Ken) £2,860

French bisque automaton by Jules Nicholas Steiner, circa 1890, 20in. high. £1,500

A bisque headed bebe with papier mache jointed body, marked 12 by Steiner, 29in. high. £2,400

Steiner bisque head girl doll with five-piece composition body, Paris, circa 1890, 9in. high. £454

French Jules Steiner Bourgoin bisque doll, circa 1880, 18½in. high. £2,750

Steiner Patent walking bisque doll in original dress and jacket, circa 1860, 15¼in. high. £1,500

French bisque child doll, beautifully dressed, by Jules Steiner, circa 1890, 19½in. high. £1,750

A bisque-headed bebe, marked SteA.2 and written in red Steiner A.S.G.D.G. Paris Bourgoin jeun, and a wig, 18in. high. £1,650

A bisque headed bebe with composition jointed body, marked FTE C 3/0 by Steiner, 10in. high. £1,200

A bisque headed clockwork Bebe Premier Pas with kid upper legs and blonde wig, 17½in. high, by Jules Nicholas Steiner, circa 1890. £1,100

Rare Jules Steiner Bourgoin bisque portrait doll in original suit, circa 1880, 29in. high. £5,000

Steiner Patent walking bisque doll in blue dress with lace overdress, 15in. high circa 1880. £750

A bisque-headed bebe with fixed blue eyes, marked J. Steiner Bte SGDG Paris Fre A9, 10in. high. £675

A bisque shoulder-headed doll, possibly by Steiner, having a Motschmann-type body, 29cm. high. £550

French walking doll by Jules N. Steiner, circa 1880, 15in. high. £600

French bisque child doll, by Jules N. Steiner, circa 1885, 14in. high. £1,250

Steiner talking bisque doll in original lace dress, circa 1880, 17½in. high. £750

Tireur Automate, an extremely rare bisque-headed clockwork toy, modelled as a Zouave soldier with moulded brown moustache, 10in. wide, stamped on the base 'J Steiner'. (Christie's) £3,520

Good Steiner clockwork walking/talking doll with papier-mache and kid body, 18in. high. £700

A Jules Steiner 'Kicking/Crying' automaton, the bisque head having brown mohair wig, fixed blue eyes, feathered brow, pierced ears, open mouth and upper teeth, 21in. high. (Bonhams) £900

A bisque swivel-headed clockwork gliding talking doll, with fixed blue eyes, wire ear loops, moving bisque arms and carton "skirt", 15in. high, by Steiner, circa 1880. (Christie's) £1,320

A bisque-headed bebe, with closed mouth, blue yeux fibres, feathered brows, pierced ears, blonde mohair wig, 10½in. high, marked J Steiner Fre A 3. (Christie's) £1,870

IZANNAH WALKER DOLLS

By the mid nineteenth century dolls made in the United States had come to acquire that rather distinctive homespun character which is typical of so much Americana, and styles had ceased to follow slavishly European influences.

The first notable American doll-maker was probably Izannah Walker of Central Falls, Rhode Island, who was reputedly making rag dolls as early as 1855. She did not, however, take out a patent until 1873, and under patent law it would have been illegal for her to have been producing these before her application in June of that year.

Her dolls have very characteristic hair, with the fashionable corkscrew curls of the time being painted in oil colours. Ears, fingers and other details are notable for the delicacy of their definition.

The dolls were made by stiffening several layers of stockinet which were compressed into moulds. The hardened shells were then sewn together and stuffed.

American cloth character doll, produced by Izannah Walker of Rhode Island, circa 1860, 26in. high. £2,000

American cloth character doll by Izannah Walker with corkscrew curls and painted boots, 18in. tall, circa 1875. £2,500

An Izannah Walker doll with brushed hair and painted boots, circa 1873, 17in. high. £4,365

American cloth character doll by Izannah Walker, circa 1870, 18in. high. £7,875

Izannah Walker cloth character doll with brushed hair, Central Falls, Rhode Island, 18in. tall. £2,750

Ragged cloth doll by Izannah Walker of Rhode Island, circa 1870, 18in. high. £2,000

Izannah Walker doll, Central Falls, Rhode Island, 1870-1880, moulded, painted stockinette figure of a girl with corkscrew curls, 18in. high. (Skinner Inc.) £1,534

WAX DOLLS

Wax composition dolls first became really popular in the Regency period. The composition substance which formed the core of the heads was similar to papier mâché, and the heads were made in two moulds which were then joined with glue and applied with pink watercolour after being dipped in wax.

Eyes could be fixed or sleeping, and the dolls were sometimes given wigs. Bodies were usually of strong cotton, often with leather 'gloves', and filled with sawdust.

A later development was the poured wax doll, which was made by pouring a delicately tinted wax into a mould and allowing it to cool before adding another layer. After removing the mould the eye sockets were cut out and glass eyes inserted. The complexion was then powdered to render it less glossy and hectic. Hair was inserted laboriously into the head, usually by means of a metal gouge and a heated roller to seal.

The major doll-making families in London in the late 19th century were the Pierotti, the Montanari and Lucy Peck. The Pierottis made dolls which tended to be slimmer and more shapely than those produced by the Montanari. The latter's offerings, on the other hand, were very lifelike, and characterised by plump, short necks, with a roll of fat at the front, and attractive violet eyes. They were made for only a short time, and are comparatively rare.

Lucy Peck was another maker of wax dolls at the turn of the century, and she obligingly stamped her dolls with an oval or rectangle on the stomach. She specialised in little girls with thick bodies and limbs, and would insert the owner-to-be's own hair on demand.

A poured-wax child doll with lace edged underclothes, circa 1851, 13in. high. (Christie's) £320

A poured shoulder-wax doll, English, circa 1860, 20in. high. £550

A wax over composition headed doll, with fixed blue eyes and blonde ringlets, carrying a banner embroidered with the message *Forget me not*, mid 19th century, 12in. high, in glazed case. (Christie's S. Ken) £385

A beeswax headed figure of a woman, with bead eyes, cloth body and wax hands, in original embroidered muslin dress decorated with metal braid and blue and white silk tasselled fringe, 11in. high, 1795. (Christie's S. Ken) £990

A poured wax headed doll, with blonde mohair wig, the stuffed body with wax limbs, dressed in contemporary red frock, 21in. high. (Christie's S. Ken) £198

A waxed shoulder-composition doll, circa 1880, 21½in. high, slight cracking to face. £220

A wax composition doll, with sleeping blue eyes, fair wig and stuffed cloth body, 14in. long. (Lawrence Fine Art) £280

A poured-wax child doll with fixed pale blue eyes, 20in. high, in box. (Christie's) £380

Late 1820's wax shoulder-headed doll with painted brown hair, 12in. high. (damaged). £200

Eliza, a wax over composition doll, with wired eye mechanism, brown mohair ringlets, the stuffed body with wax over composition limbs, circa 1845, (wax cracked) 22in. high. (Christie's S. Ken) £495

A wax over papier mache headed doll, the cloth body with pink kid arms with separated fingers, wearing original clothes, mainly 1780-1790, 17½in. high. (Christie's S. Ken) £825

A wax over composition pumpkin headed doll, with dark inset eyes, moulded blonde hair with black band, the stuffed body with squeaker, 12in. high, circa 1860. (Christie's S. Ken) £220

A Pierotti poured shoulder-wax doll, English, 1870, 19½in. high. £420

A wax headed doll, with bead eyes, painted short hair, cloth body and wax arms, circa 1840, 7½in. high. (Christie's S. Ken) £495

A poured shoulder-wax doll with fixed blue glass eyes, English, circa 1880, 18½in. high. £352

A poured-wax child doll with fixed blue eyes, 21in. high.   £500

19th century wax over papier-mache doll, circa 1860, 20in. high.   £220

A poured shoulder-wax doll, English, circa 1860, 23in. high.   £330

Charlotte Norris, a wax-over-composition headed doll with smiling mouth, the stuffed body with pink kid arms, 23in. high, 1840-45. (Christie's)   £308

A waxed composition shoulder head doll with white ringletted wig, on a stuffed cloth body with pink kid forearms, 13in., circa 1840. (Phillips)   £500

A wax over composition headed doll, with fixed blue eyes, long blonde wool wig and stuffed body with waxed limbs, 16in. high, possibly French circa 1865. (Christie's S. Ken)   £440

A shoulder-waxed-composition doll, German, circa 1880, 16in. high, right arm loose.   £150

A poured wax doll, the stuffed body with wax limbs in spotted muslin dress trimmed with lace and pink ribbon, 13½in. high. (Christie's)   £440

A poured wax child doll with fixed blue eyes, the long blonde hair inset in groups into head, 21½in. high, with Lucy Peck oval stamp on body. (Christie's)   £440

DOLLS & TOYS

A poured shoulder-wax male doll, the stuffed body with wax limbs, circa 1860, 18in. high.
£300

A wax over composition shoulder headed doll, the blue eyes wired from the waist. (Christie's)
£300

A wax over composition bonnet headed doll with wooden limbs, 12½in. high.
£250

A wax swivel-headed doll, with blue eyes, blonde mohair wig, the stuffed body with wax shoulder plate, 19in. high, circa 1870s.
(Christie's S. Ken)
£308

A wax over papier mache headed doll, with fixed bright blue eyes and hair wig, the stuffed body with waxed arms, 14in. high, circa 1840, in glazed case. (Christie's S. Ken)
£209

A poured wax headed doll, with blue sleeping eyes, the stuffed body with wax limbs dressed in original fawn silk frock, 22in. high, damage to leg.
(Christie's S. Ken)
£1,045

A shoulder-waxed-composition doll with blonde mohair plaited wig, German, circa 1880, 18in. high.
£308

A wax over composition headed doll with smiling painted face, circa 1878, 7in. high.
£75

A wax figure of a fashionable woman, marked Lafitte Desinat, 1915, 12in. high.
£75

Early wax head swaddling baby, circa 1840, 18in. high. £420

German Motschmann-type waxed composition doll lying in a basket, circa 1860, 9in. long. £300

A wax-headed figure of a fashionable woman, with label reading Meurillon et Cie, Paris, 11½in. high. £150

Late Victorian wax doll in original pink silk dress and leather shoes. £500

Victorian waxed shoulder-papier-mache pumpkin head doll, 20in. high, circa 1860, in box. £300

A waxed shoulder composition doll with painted closed mouth and fixed blue eyes, 30in. high. (Lawrence Fine Art) £310

A waxed shoulder composition doll, c. 1840, with closed mouth, in original glazed case, 16in. (Lawrence Fine Arts) £165

A poured-wax child doll with blue wired sleeping eyes, the stuffed body with bisque limbs in original nightgown, 21in. high. £320

A wax over composition shoulder headed doll with short, blonde, curly wool wig, 1810-15, 14in. high. (Christie's) £240

Wood has been used as a doll making medium since earliest times, as the Paddle dolls of ancient Egypt testify. Nowadays, however, most collectors will be looking for jointed wooden dolls dating from the 18th century at the earliest, which are often referred to as Queen Anne dolls. Good examples have ball joints and well-carved hands, while cheaper ones might have only the body carved of wood. An eighteenth century development was the application of a moulded mask or brotteig to the plain turned head core.

These continued to be made throughout the 19th century alongside the new Grödnertals. These cheap little wooden figures, characterised by frequent use of combs in their hair, came from the area of that name in Bavaria. The classical Grödner type, slim waisted and high busted, reached its production peak in 1820, after which time the style became much more stolid.

Folk type dolls, some of which were known as penny woodens, were also made throughout this period, but these were seldom of high quality.

Towards the end of the century it was American manufacturers who were producing the finest wooden dolls. Joel Ellis of Springfield, Vt., is generally accredited with having produced the first peg-jointed wooden doll on a commercial basis at his Vermont Novelty Works. His products were very much lady dolls from only one mould, which was adapted by painting in different styles. The tradition was carried on by Mason & Taylor and later by the Schoenhut Company, who produced different models almost every year.

An early 19th century painted wooden Grodnertal doll with yellow comb, dressed in contemporary rose silk dress, 5½in. high. (Christie's)   £462

A painted wooden Grodenthal type doll with grey curls, circa 1835, 12½in. high. (Christie's)   £550

An early 19th century group of painted wooden headed dolls, 'There was an old woman who lived in a shoe', 5in. long. (Dacre, Son & Hartley)   £120

German early Grodenthal peg-wooden doll, circa 1820, 9¼in. high.   £200

A pair of carved and painted wooden nodding figures, with moving lower jaws, 8in. high, probably South German, circa 1850. (Christie's)   £176

American carved wooden swivel headed doll by Joel Ellis, circa 1878, 13in. high.   £694

A George III wooden
doll with painted face,
circa 1780, 20in. high.
£3,250

An early English wooden
doll, circa 1770, 16½in.
high.   £3,500

An early 19th century crudely
carved wood doll with blue enamel
and nail eyes and painted limbs,
15½in. high.   £150

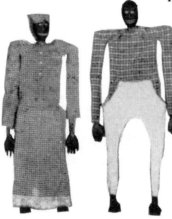

A carved and painted wooden
doll, with rouged cheeks, dark
enamel eyes, stitched brows
and lashes, carved ears and
adolescent figure, circa 1740
(arm missing, two fingers broken,
legs detached), 18in. high.
(Christie's S. Ken)   £10,450

A George I wooden doll,
the gesso-covered head with
finely painted blushed cheeks,
English, circa 1725, 16in. high.
£12,100

Two large carved and painted
articulated dancing dolls,
American, early 20th century,
43½in., 41in. high respectively.
(Christie's)   £1,038

A George III wooden doll,
circa 1800, the carved ovoid
head with the remains of a
styled ginger wig, jointed pine
legs and primitively carved
feet, 67cm. high. (Henry
Spencer)   £1,600

Carved wooden shoulder-
head doll with original odd-
shaped straw stuffed muslin
body, probably Austrian,
circa 1910.   £355

A George II wooden doll
with blonde real hair nailed-
on wig, English, circa 1750,
16in. high.   £11,000

Mid 18th century wooden doll in contemporary costume.   £3,500

A William and Mary wooden doll with a wisp of real auburn hair and nailed-on stitched linen wig, English, circa 1690, 16¾in. high.   £17,600

Late 18th century East European wooden doll with pinned ball joints, height to knee 21¼in.   £2,090

A late 18th century wooden doll with natural brown plaited wig, the straight legs peg jointed at the hip, 12in. high. (Phillips)   £460

Two wooden rod puppets with painted faces. £100

A painted wooden doll, with inset enamel eyes, rouged cheeks, "stitched" eyebrows and eyelashes, 19in. high, English early 19th century. (Christie's S. Ken)   £770

A turned and carved painted wooden doll, the wooden body with kid arms, dressed in original organza skirt, 13in. high, circa 1840. (Christie's)   £990

A George III wooden doll, circa 1780, the carved ovoid head with high forehead, black and white enamelled eyes and pink mouth, 59cm. high. (Henry Spencer)   £650

A painted wooden child doll the jointed wooden body (one foot missing) 17in. high, probably by Schilling.   £198

A turned and painted wooden doll with inset enamel eyes, circa 1810, 14in. high, in a wooden glazed case.   £1,500

American wooden character doll of Felix, by Schoenhut, 9in. high.   £350

French wooden manne-quin doll with articula-ted body, 20th century, 21in. high.   £300

A carved and painted wooden doll, with rouged cheeks, dark enamel eyes, stitched brows and lashes, circa 1740, 18in. high.
(Christie's)   £10,450

A rare William and Mary wood-en doll in original clothes, circa 1690. (Phillips)   £24,000

A very rare carved and painted Charles II wood doll, with bright pink rouged cheeks, 13in. high, circa 1680.
(Christie's)   £71,500

A Grodnertal wooden doll, the domed painted head with black hair, finely painted features and rings for earrings, 29cm.
(Phillips)   £420

An English William and Mary wood doll, circa 1690, 14½in. high.
(Sotheby's)   £67,100

An early Grodenthal type painted wooden doll with brown eyes, circa 1820, 18in. high. (Christie's)   £1,400

DOLL'S HOUSES

The earliest English dolls houses date from the early 18th century, though in Germany they appeared some two centuries earlier. They were not children's toys, but were usually commissioned by rich noblemen either for themselves or as gifts, beautifully made and lavishly appointed, with miniature furniture which was exquisite in its detail.

By the 19th century the average dolls' house had become less grand, and represented rather a middle class suburban villa. Genuine antique dolls' houses are quite rare and many collectors have turned to buying good reproductions, and then filling them with genuine old furniture.

In the 1920s and 30s such companies as Lines Bros. began making modern versions specially for children, and these can often be of very high quality.

A painted wooden doll's house, of five bays and four storey's, opening to reveal ten rooms with hall, staircase and landings, 50in. wide. (Christie's) £11,000

A painted wooden dolls' house of four bays and three storeys, 50in. high x 46in. wide on stand, circa 1840. (Christie's) £4,950

A painted wooden dolls' house of two separated storeys, with original wall and some floor coverings. (Christie's) £308

A fine late 19th century dolls' house, the front removable to reveal a six roomed interior with original papers, 41½in. wide. (Phillips) £750

A painted wooden dolls' house, simulating stone with red roof and bay windows flanking the marbelised porch, 43in. high. (Christie's) £715

Victorian House Diorama, America, late 19th century, mixed media including wood, printed paper cutouts and straw flowers, case 16 x 20in. (Skinner) £593

A mahogany dolls' house of two bays and two storeys with castellated bow window, 47in. high, late 19th century. (Christie's) £1,430

223

DOLLS & TOYS

An English Gothic-styled Victorian doll's house with steeply gabled roof, circa 1870. £500

English late 19th century interior of an open room in Georgian style, 23in. wide. £600

A doll's house, the gabled roof with pocket watch movement mounted within the pediment, 34in. wide. £350

19th century wooden Mansard roof doll's house with painted brick front, 23¾in. high. £300

A model doll's house of Harethorpe Hall, a two-storey mansion, with painted brick front, 23 x 47 x 13in. deep. £1,000

Belgian doll's house, model-led as a detached town villa with three bays, 1870's. £2,750

A 19th century wooden kitchen, maker unknown, several pieces marked Germany, 26 x 15 x 15in. £1,500

Late 19th century yellow Victorian doll's house and furniture, 26¾in. wide. £300

A wooden doll's house painted to simulate stonework of two bays and two storeys, circa 1850, 57in. approx.   £400

English late 19th century painted wooden doll's house of Victorian design, 42in. wide.   £750

A large Victorian doll's house with two hinged front sections, mounted on wheels, circa 1890, 40in. wide.   £750

Large doll's house in the form of a two-storey suburban house with arched roof, English, circa 1930, 45in. high by 73in. long. £1,000

A wooden doll's house painted to simulate stonework of five bays and three storeys, 46in. wide.   £4,000

A printed paper on wood doll's house, by Lines Bros., 43in. wide.   £1,200

A painted wooden doll's box-type town house of three bays and three storeys, 25in. high.   £450

American wooden doll's house by the Bliss Toy Co., Rhode Island, circa 1900, 18 x 12 x 9in.   £500

DOLL'S HOUSES

A wooden doll's house, opening at the front to reveal six rooms, hall and staircase, the kitchen with dresser and fire surround, with Christian Hacker stamp on the base, 33in. high. (Christie's S. Ken) £583

A model of a Georgian house with portico entrance and large bay, two storeys with basement, the case 19in. wide. (Christie's) £605

A painted wooden doll's house modelled as a Swiss chalet, opening to reveal three rooms with original lace curtains, floor and wall papers, furnished, German, circa 1920, 21in. wide. (Christie's S. Ken) £605

A wooden doll's house, of three bays and two storeys, opening at the front to reveal four rooms with staircase and landing, interior doors and fire surrounds, by G. and J. Lines, circa 1910, 37in. high. (Christie's S. Ken) £1,320

A painted wooden doll's house, of five bays and four storeys, opening to reveal ten rooms with hall, staircase and landings, interior doors, bathroom fittings, four side windows and contemporary wall and floor papers, 50in. wide. (Christie's S. Ken) £11,000

A painted wood and printed brick paper on wood doll's house, opening at the front to reveal four rooms with original kitchen paper, dresser and fire surrounds, 28in. high, (Christie's S. Ken) £220

A painted wooden dolls' house, simulating stone with brick quoining and window and door surrounds, 37in. wide, late 19th century. (Christie's) £495

A late Georgian wooden carpenter made doll's house, painted to simulate brickwork, circa 1830, 4ft. long, 45in. high. (Christie's S. Ken) £2,200

A wooden doll's house, painted to simulate brickwork with grey roof with scalloped eaves, opening to reveal four fully furnished rooms, circa 1900, 50in. high. (Christie's S. Ken) £2,420

226

DOLL'S HOUSES

A 19th century English wooden dolls' house, the deep red brick painted exterior having four gables, 64in. high, circa 1880. (Phillips) **£1,800**

A model house and garden in a boxed scene, with balconies and balustrading to the first floor and simulated slate roof, circa 1850, 19in. wide. (Christie's S. Ken.) **£418**

A painted wooden dolls' house, simulating brickwork with slate roof, the base with shaped apron, furnished, 41in. high. (Christie's S. Ken) **£638**

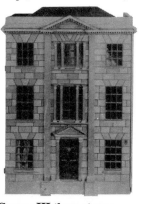

A George III three storey painted wooden baby house, of three bays, with pedimented dentil cornice, 37½ in. wide. (Christie's S. Ken) **£2,640**

A painted wooden doll's house of late Georgian style, opening in three hinged sections to reveal seven rooms, the staircase rising from the front hall to the first floor with separate treads, early Victorian, 46in. wide. (Christie's S. Ken) £1,540

A carpenter made wooden dolls' house with white painted gothic details and brass pediment, 23in. high. (Christie's) **£935**

An early 20th century English dolls' house, the wooden superstructure with nine windows to the façade, 30in. high, probably G. & J. Lines, circa 1900–1910. (Phillips) **£480**

A wooden box-type dolls' house, of four bays and two storeys painted on upper storey to simulate brickwork, 28in. wide, third quarter of the 19th century, English. (Christie's S. Ken) **£660**

An English wooden doll's house, the cream painted and simulated brick papered facade with eight windows, 51in. high, 1910, probably G. and J. Lines Bros. (Phillips) **£660**

227

DOLLS & TOYS

A lithographic paper on wood doll's house with decorative front porch and balcony, 12½in., German, circa 1915. £450

Victorian painted doll's house with porticoed doorway flanked by columns, English, circa 1890, 32½in. high by 37½in. wide £1,750

A late Victorian wooden doll's house in the shape of a two-storey villa, with pitched slate roof, front divided and hinged, 71 x 33cm. £1,000

Doll's house copied from original family house, with Gothic shaped door, gabled roof and two chimneys, English, circa 1910, 33in. high by 39½in. wide. £1,750

A lithographic paper on wood doll's house, with steps leading to front door, 13in. high, American, circa 1910. £400

Early 20th century American wooden gabled roof doll's house with glass windows, 24¾in. high. £350

Victorian wooden doll's house, cottage style, with working door with brass knob at front, circa 1890.   £1,250

A custom crafted Colonial-style doll's house, circa 1890, with ten rooms of furniture, rugs, textiles and accessories, 28in. high, 53¾in. long.   £1,500

An early 20th century doll's house, paper covered to simulate brickwork, 88cm. high.   £400

An early 20th century two-storeyed doll's house, facade 20 x 18in., depth 12in.   £400

A Jacobean style wood and composition doll's house of four bays and two storeys, 27in. wide.   £500

American diorama of an early 19th century hallway, circa 1950, fitted with dolls and furniture, 19½in. wide.   £250

German tinplate clockwork figure of Jumbo the Elephant. £40

A printed and painted tinplate elephant and Indian native boy rider, 7in. high, probably German, circa 1925. (Christie's) £275

19th century papier-mache elephant with glass eyes, 18in. long. £350

Toy tin elephant, riding a scooter and balancing an object on it's trunk, marked 'U.S. Zone, Germany', circa 1950's. £35

A grey leather covered clockwork walking elephant, with bone tusks, glass eyes and serrated wheels on the feet, 10in. long, probably by Roullet et Decamps. (Christie's S. Ken) £242

A Britains lead and tinplate flywheel-drive Rajah on Walking Elephant, flywheel modelled as Rajah's parasol, circa 1890. (Christie's) £495

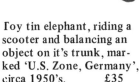

A lithographed Penny Toy of an Indian Elephant on green wheeled undercarriage, 10cm. (Phillips) £90

Nurnberger Blechspielwarenfabrik, clockwork novelty toy in the form of a circus elephant with roller ball shute, 1950, 24cm. high. £100

A toy tin 'balancing ball' elephant, marked 'U.S. Zone Germany', 1950's. £45

A 2in. scale model of a Shand Mason horse-drawn twin cylinder fire appliance built by F. Lynn, Sunderland, 15 x 22in. (Christie's S. Ken)   £2,750

A model of a horse-drawn fire engine of the Birmingham Fire Brigade built in 1914.   £2,750

Unusual Bing tinplate horse-drawn fire engine, hand-enamelled, circa 1903, 12in. long.   £6,000

Jep tinplate fire engine, French, circa 1935-40, 9¼in. long, with six crew members.   £150

A Tipp Co clockwork fire engine complete with two crew, circa 1930, 1ft. 7in. long.   £250

A fine Ernst Plank painted tinplate and brass steam horse-drawn fire engine, having vertical copper boiler with sight glass, circa 1903, 13½in. long without shafts. (Christie's S. Ken)   £16,500

A Schuco 6080 Elektro-Construction tin-plate fire engine, in original box, circa 1955. (Osmond Tricks)   £250

Early 20th century child's metal toy fire truck painted red.   £250

Dinky No 955/555 fire engine with extending ladder. (James of Norwich)　　£38

Karl Bub printed tinplate clockwork Fire Brigade turntable ladder truck, with electric headlamps and four crew, circa 1931, 18in. long. (Christie's S. Ken)　　£528

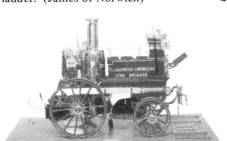

A 2in. scale model of a horse-drawn 1875 Shand Mason fire engine, 21in. long overall.　　£3,500

A Distler tinplate and clockwork fire engine, 37.5cm. long overall.　　£400

A 1½in. scale model of a spirit-fired Shand-Mason horsedrawn fire engine of 1894.
£1,000

'Fire Brigade', a printed and painted tinplate fire engine, 15½in. long, by Distler, circa 1936.　　£350

Keystone sheet metal fire truck, circa 1930, 28in. long.　　£350

A Bing hand-enamelled model of an early fire engine, circa 1902, 10½in. long.　　£850

GAMES

Anyone who was a child before the age of television still remembers evenings spent playing board games. The nostalgia element plays a large part in the collecting of games, of which many survive. Typical old favourites were Ludo, Snakes and Ladders and card games like Happy Families, while others, such as word games and general knowledge games, had a more educational bent. In the 1930s came Monopoly, the most famous of all board games, which was launched, ironically, at the height of the Depression.

It is interesting to note that the leading game and card manufacturers, Chad Valley, Waddington and Spear's, a company with strong German connections, are all still going strong today, and still producing many old favourites alongside constantly changing new ranges. When collecting vintage games, these should obviously be complete, and come with dice and shakers where applicable.

A set of six pottery carpet bowls, with a red, green or blue cross-hatched design, some glaze chipping.
(Bearne's)   £210

Early 20th century tartan-ware whist marker.

Oscar, the Film Stars Rise to Fame.   £12

Russian Novelty Clockwork Bus Track, circa 1960's.
                    £15

Bystander 'Fragments' Playing Cards by Chas. Goodall & Son Ltd.   £30

American 'General Grant's marble game', circa 1870, diam. of marbles 1.1/8in.
                    £400

An Edwardian table racing game with folding mahogany board painted in green with a race track with baize centre, and a mahogany box containing ten lead horses and riders, dice, tumblers and ivory markers, 60in. long. (Christie's London)   £825

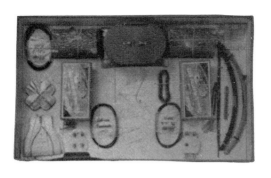

A Schuco-Varianto 3010 Motorway, in original box, US Zone W. Germany, circa 1955. £175

'Find the Car', by C. W. Faulkner, 1920. £5

A Schoenhut indoor golf game: 'set No. G/10, in original box with instructions, comprising: a 'Tommy Green' figure, a water hazard, and a putting green, etc. (Christie's) £462

Late 19th century parquetry folding cribbage board. £10

'James Bond, Secret Service Game', Spear's. £15

'The Popular Game of Halma', Squadron Edition. £8

'Wireless Whist, Score Cards', The Dainty Series, 1920's. £5

'The Game of Motoring', by Chad Valley, circa 1908, with original box. £150

Victorian wooden building game in a fine pictorial box. £45

'Steeplechase & Race Game'. £75

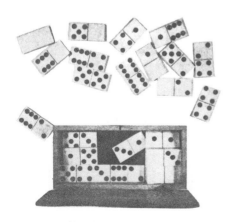

Victorian set of bone dominos in an oak box. £50

'The Portland Chess & Draughts Board', Robinson & Sons. £4

The Rose Chess Set with metal
pieces.   £25

1950's game of Lotto,
complete with cards and
counters.   £6

1950's Zoo-m-Roo space
pinball game.   £10

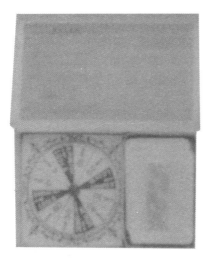

Tut-Tut or A Run In A Motor Card, A New
and Exciting Game, with forty-eight cards
depicting an Edwardian open tourer, contained in original box.   £85

'A Figuren Alphabetspiel', a set of twenty
fine printed paper on wood alphabet blocks
German, circa 1910.   £350

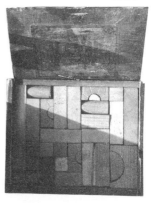

A deck of fifty two playing
cards manufactured by Goodall
& Son, London, circa 1882.
(Christie's S. Ken)   £330

Victorian pictorial play
block, 4in. square.   £5

Victorian box of wooden
building bricks, 9in. square.
     £10

Happy Families by Chad Valley, circa 1910.
£9

Drunken Coachman card game. £6

Sport-a-Crest, Dennis's 'Dainty' Series
N. G829. £3

Tops and Tails Around the World, made in
Austria. £1

Lindy card game. £7

The Cavalry Game. £6

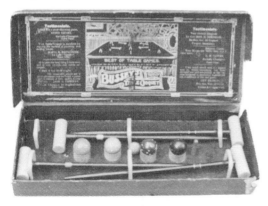

Bussey's Table Croquet game, complete with
balls. £50

History of England card game. £6

A model of a Dorset Wagon, complete with hay racks, carved light draught horse, dog, carter and a small pack mule, carved by George Gill of Branscombe. £1,000

A German tinplate horse-drawn open carriage finished in cream and green, the felt covered tinplate horse supported on a flywheel setting the horse in motion. £1,250

Dent cast iron three horse hook and ladder, early 1900's, 29in. long. £350

A zebra cart toy, probably French, circa 1900, 10½in. long. £250

Late 19th century painted 'Dandy Dan' riding horse toy, America, 3ft.9in. long. £500

Britain's Farm, horse-drawn milk float with milkman and two churns, No. 131F, in original box. (Milkman has broken neck.) £75

Late 19th century Wilkins cast iron trolley, 'Broadway Car Line 712', 12in. long. £1,500

Cast-iron circus van, red enclosed wagon, red driver and two black horses, circa 1920's. £150

Cast-iron Police Patrol wagon, black trotting horse pulls open yellow wagon, with driver and three policemen, 11in. long, circa 1910.
£125

A painted wooden toy carter's dray with carved and painted dapple grey horses, 36in. long, possibly English, circa 1900. (Christie's S. Ken) £330

Late 19th century painted tin horsedrawn coach, overall length 29in. £2,000

An F. Martin tinplate Hansom Cab, French, circa 1905, 9in. long. £300

A late 19th century wooden model Hay-wain, 26in. long overall. £250

A rare painted and lithographed tinplate hansom cab, with brown galloping horse on a metal wheel, driver and passenger, in original paintwork, probably by Gunthermann, circa 1908, 8½in. long. (Christie's) £1,045

A model of a horse-drawn cart by Benefink & Co. £500

A Britains' farmer's gig, No. F28 with horse, unboxed. £50

JIGSAW PUZZLES

The jigsaw puzzle was invented by a map-maker and engraver, John Spilsbury, around 1760. At first called a dissected puzzle, its original form was of a map to teach children geography in an entertaining way. The educational aspect continued paramount in the early days, and jigsaws were made in the form of historical or scientific tables and then portraits of English Kings and Queens from the Conqueror onwards, which also incorporated lists of famous events and people of the time. Religious themes were also popular.

The earliest jigsaws consisted of hand coloured lithographs mounted on mahogany, and cased in a mahogany box with sliding lid. Soon, however, whitewood came to replace mahogany, both for puzzle and box, as being much cheaper.

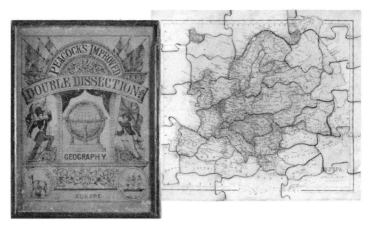

Peacocks Improved 'Double Dissection', Europe on one side, Nursery rhymes on the other. Puzzles cut in sympathy with the map (ie round borders) with large interlocking edge pieces to hold it all together, circa 1895, fine hand-coloured label to whitewood box lid, 11x12in. £140

'Ireland' — for teaching youth geography, circa 1820. Unknown, probably William Darton, some replacement pieces and missing necks, 11 x 10in. £125

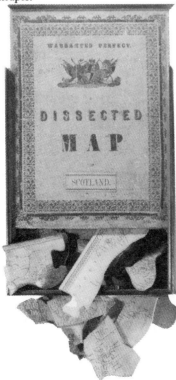

Dissected Map of Scotland, by Peacock, 19th century. £50

'Venice', Vera Picture Puzzle, made in France, 1930's, and box, finely cut, with contour cutting and shapes, difficult. Made specially for Truslove & Hansen of London SW1, 9 x 12in. £20

Dan Dare Jigsaw Puzzle,
Waddington's, 1950's.
£10

'The Romans at Caerleon', one of the series of 43
puzzles made by Chad Valley for the G.W.R. Co.
during the 1920's and 1930's. Box of slip-case
type from the 1930's, 14 x 14in.   £30

'The Eton Coach', popular or fashionable artists' works were often the
subjects of jigsaw puzzles between the wars. This one, of a Cecil Aldin
painting, has been cut in the style of the Huvanco firm, 6 x 19in. £20

DOLLS & TOYS

'A Labour of Love', 'Society Dissected Picture Puzzle — The Latest Craze' made for Hamley Bros. to sell in their store in London during the 1920's. The box label is typical of those made also for other stores, who had their names printed in the space provided, 8 x 6in. £15

'Journey into Egypt', probably amateur cut, all pushfit pieces, typical of its type and style for the period, 1920's, 9 x 7in. £15

'Captain Cuttle', one of a series of twelve Dickens characters made into puzzles and issued by A. V. N. Jones in the 1930's, 10 x 8in. £25

'Good Companions', 1930's example of a Douglas Jigsaw Library Puzzle, with its unusual and unrepetitive shapes that make it more challenging to assemble, 14 x 18in.   £25

'A Welcome Intrusion', a 1930's Chad Valley puzzle with its characteristic patented— 'book-box' design of container with guide picture, 10 x 14in.   £20

'Aladdin meets the Sultan's daughter',
Huvarco puzzle, 1920's/30's, no box
(often Huvarco puzzles were sold
ready-made-up and without a box).
£25

'De Dame Te Amsterdam', Dutch made puzzle,
1930's. Amateur, but intricately cut (not a
manufactured puzzle), difficult, 10 x 13in.   £20

'Cunard Liner Berengaria', Chad Valley for
Cunard Steam Ship Co., 12 x 16in., with box.
£35

'Changing the Guard at Buckingham Palace',
Raphael Tuck military puzzle, 1930's
distinctive style of cut different to their two
styles of zag zaw puzzle (one of which is
interlocking, the other push-fit, but both of
which include intricate shapes), 15 x 10in.,
with box.   £20

'Washington returning from Fox Hunt',
Parker Brothers pastime puzzle and box (USA),
1920-1930's. Finely cut with shapes and
colour contoured, a difficult puzzle, 10 x 13in.
£30

'The History of Joseph and his Brethren', circa 1835. Unknown maker, possibly Edward Wallis. Hand coloured wood blocks, plain mahogany box, lacking original label, 9 x 10in.
£200

'The Edge of the Common', Chandos puzzle (F. Hanse), 1920's/30's, 11 x 17in., and box.
£40

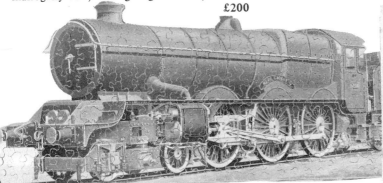

'King George V loco', Chad Valley for the Great Western Railway Co. 1930's, 8 x 22in. overall, contoured edge, hand coloured photographic print, and box.
£45

'Daffodils', Chad Valley 1920's (early Chad Valley cutting style), 14 x 10in. with box.
£25

'At Pharaoh's Court', Victory artistic puzzle, 1950's, 14 x 18in. with box. No guide picture is supplied with these puzzles, which include strips of traditional victory shapes amongst the interlocking pieces.
£20

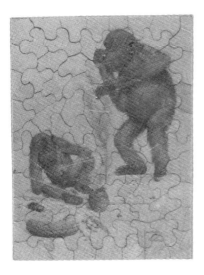

'First Whiff', a Lawson Wood cartoon made into a puzzle, probably by an amateur, 1930's. Humour was always a popular subject for amateurs (who often cut to professional standards, and usually with an interpretive flair) and Lawson Wood has become highly collectible now, 10 x 8in.   **£20**

Double sided puzzles became very popular during the inter-war jigsaw 'craze' years; they were mass produced on a large scale, since they offered 'two for the price of one'. This one has typically sentimental subject for each side, 7 x 10in.   **£15**

A rare Barfoot puzzle, a double sided map dissection, showing the Eastern and Western hemispheres (normally Barfoot had a non-map picture — eg historical or mathematical tables — on the reverse side of a map), 12 x 8in., circa 1855.   **£300**

'The Victory', one of The Delta Fine Cut
'National' Series of puzzles from the 1930's.
The box lid bears a traditional design that
has a family resemblance to the Victory box,
13 x 18in.   £25

'The Milkmaid', 1930's 'Chandos' puzzle by Frederick Warne, it has a
distinctive and easily-recognisable style of cut which can make it
awkward to assemble, 7 x 9in.   £15

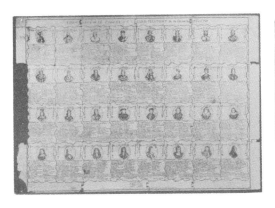

Snow White, Walt Disney, 1938. £15

Jigsaw Puzzle, John Wallis's chronological Tables of English History for the Instruction of Youth, 1788, one piece missing. £175

'Coronation 1953', a characteristic commemorative puzzle of the 1950's by Victory, the box is large enough to take the fully assembled puzzle, 8 x 10in. £25

Sunny Jim's Jigsaw Puzzle, No.9, 1930's. £15

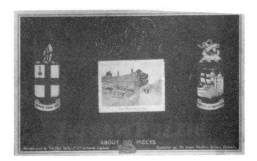

Anne Hathaways Cottage, Great Western Railway Jigsaw 1930. £20

'Sporting Days', a 1920's Raphael Tuck 'Oilette' picture puzzle by H. Drummond, 6 x 9in. £25

Coronation Jigsaw Puzzle, 1953. £5

BBC TV 'Dr Who and the Daleks', 1973. £10

The Duke of Edinburgh, Victory Jigsaw. £5

Famous Footballers, No. 1, Tommy Lawton. £5

Giselle, Victory Plywood Jigsaw, 1950's. £5

The Piglets, Beatles Take-Off, Waddington's, 1964.   £8

'The Horse', one of a series of 'Graphic illustrations of animals showing their utility to man', by Roake & Varty, circa 1840, 12 x 15in.   £100

'Primrose and Violet', with traditional shapes, an early Victory (Hayter & Co.), with interesting box design showing common pictorial theme of the period, 1920's, 11 x 13in.   £25

LEAD SOLDIERS

In 1893 W Britains developed a technique to replace the semi-flat figures which had hitherto been popular, whereby the figure became hollow and realistically proportioned. These were lighter and cheaper than their foreign competitors, and it was Britains who were to lead the field in lead soldier production for the next 60 years. They are particularly sought after in the USA, where as many as 100 million were exported in the 20s and 30s. The figures are characterised by attention to detail especially with regard to the uniforms.

Lineol made 5/32, Wehrmacht standard bearer, tin colour one shoulder, 1938. (Phillips) £60

A German made tinplate sentry box with 60mm. mounted sentry of The Royal Horse Guards, in original box, 1890. £400

Britains full band of the Cold-stream Guards, 22 pieces in all, in 'Armies of the World' box, no. 37. (Lawrence Fine Arts) £242

Britains rare individual United States cavalry figures in steel helmets, probably exported to USA without set boxes, circa 1940. (Phillips) £650

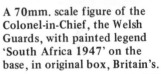

A 70mm. scale figure of the Colonel-in-Chief, the Welsh Guards, with painted legend 'South Africa 1947' on the base, in original box, Britain's. £1,500

German made, a tinplate sentry box with 120mm. Sentry of the Foot Guards, in original box, 1890. £300

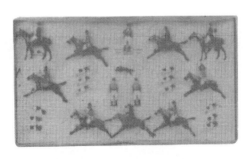

Britains Hunting Display Set No. 235, "Full Cry", in original green illustrated box, circa 1939. (Christie's) £264

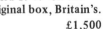

Lineol made model of Goering standing, Luftwaffe uniform, holding Marshal's baton, 1939. (Phillips) £90

Britains set of South African Mounted Infantry in its original box.   £100

Two Whistock boxes of Britains King's Royal Rifle Corps, No. 98, each box containing eight figures, circa 1905. £225

Britains set No 1470, The Coronation State Coach, including eight Windsor grays, four outriders, H.M. Queen Elizabeth II and Prince Philip, in gold painted state coach, in original box.   £250

Britains Royal Air Force, set 2011, twenty-two pieces.   £200

Heyde 30mm. hand-painted Indian elephant, with howdah, containing Maharajah and bower, an Indian lancer, 5 palm trees, six 54mm. scale figures and six other figures.   £175

Eight British Boer War soldiers wearing tropical helmets, in their original box.   £80

A collection of Britains and other makers World War I soldiers and some trees, circa 1920.   £70

Royal Horse Artillery at the halt, Service Dress with peak caps, khaki uniform, Set 318, in original box, Britain's. £6,500

Britains set No. 37, Band of the Coldstream Guards. £250

Britains set No. 315, 10th Royal Hussars, Prince of Wales' Own, at the halt with swords and bugler, in original box. £300

Set 2052, Anti-Aircraft Unit with AA gun, searchlight and instruments and operating crew of eight men, in original box, 1959 Britain's. £750

A collection of 38 French soldiers and Zouaves, including ski troops and one mule, made in France, circa 1940. £100

A mixed collection of 15 lead models, including soldiers, cowboys and red indians, Spanish warship blowing up, two men-of-war, etc., circa early 1920's. £35

Elastolin 100mm. scale hand-painted composition soldiers, Coldstream Guards, marching at slope arms in full equipment. £600

Royal Horse Artillery at the gallop in steel helmets, Set 1339, in original box, 1940 Britain's £7,000

Three officers mounted on galloping chargers and two armed Africans riding on a camel, circa early 1920's. £30

Britains very rare set 1904, Officers and Men of the U.S. Army Air Corps, four positions, in original green box, 1940. (Phillips)   £1,600

German made attractive first grade 52mm. hollowcast British Fusiliers at the slope with mounted officer, 1900. (Phillips)   £150

Britains special paint originally from the Poitier-Smith Collection, Royal Horse Guards, 1937. (Phillips)   £820

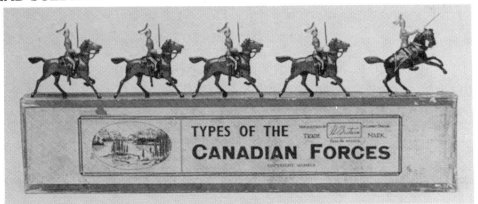

Rare set 1629, Lord Strathcona's Horse in original 'Types of the Canadian Forces' box, 1938. (Phillips) £1,800

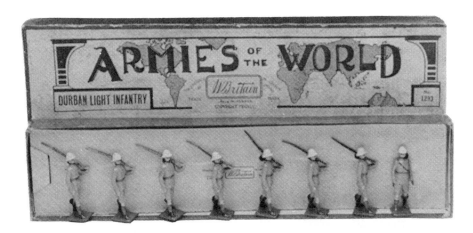

Britains rare set 1293, Durban Light Infantry at the slope, short trousers, unusual paint variation, 1934. (Phillips) £1,300

Britains, unusual set of British Infantry in steel helmets based on the U.S. Marine marching figure, one slight dent, 1940. (Phillips) £1,500

Britain's Set No. 2, The Royal Horse Guards, one officer and four troopers, at the trot, bearing swords (one sword missing), box torn but with label intact. **£100**

A Britains set No. 434, R.A.F. Monoplane, with two pilots and four R.A.F. personnel, in original box. **£1,200**

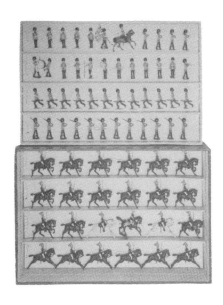

Britains extremely rare display set 131, including cavalrymen, infantrymen, bandsmen, sailors and Camel Corps soldiers, the largest set ever made by Britains. (Phillips) **£10,000**

Large display box Set 93, containing Coldstream Guards with mounted officer, four pioneers, thirteen-piece band, two officers, twelve marching, twelve running, two trumpeters, six troopers and fifteen normal troopers, 1938. Britain's. (Phillips) **£7,000**

Britains extremely rare Territorials in full dress standing at attention in red uniforms. (Phillips) **£2,700**

Britains set No. 1634, The Governor-General's Foot Guards, marching at the slope arms, with officer, in original box. (Christie's) £125

Britains early set No. 211, 18in. Howitzer No. 2, with ten horse team, in review order with No. 2 Howitzer and limber, in original box. £1,250

A Britains boxed set of The Royal Horse Artillery gun team. £6,200

Two Whistock boxes of Britains Bluejackets, No. 78, each box containing eight figures, circa 1905. £250

A Britains R.A.M.C. 4-horse covered ambulance waggon, in original linen cover, with 2 A.S.C. drivers and 2 seated R.A.M.C. orderlies, all full dress, and R.A.M.C. officer, nurse and stretcher. (Wallis & Wallis) £225

Twelve German made solid pewter model Boer soldiers, 45mm. high, circa 1900, in their original red box. £85

Part of an eighteen piece set of Britains model hunt, unboxed. £70

LEHMANN TOYS

The firm of Ernst Paul Lehmann was founded in 1881 in Brandenburg, away from the traditional centres of German toymaking, and they produced tinplate novelty toys which were very different from those turned out by Bing and Märklin, where quality was paramount. In contrast, Lehmann's toys were flimsily built and had a studied frivolity. Even the names were humorous – 'Toot toot' for example being the name of a car driven erratically by a driver blowing a hunting horn. Lehmann's products were cheap and cheerful, decorated with coloured lithography, which was often, notwithstanding, of a very high standard, and parts were joined by tabs, rather than by soldering. Motors had pressed tinplate gears and spiral, rather than coil springs. Nevertheless, they were extremely attractive, and Lehmann is one of the most famous tinplate toymakers of the 1920s.

After the Second World War, Brandenburg found itself in East Germany, and Ernst Lehmann's cousin, Johann Richter, set up a new enterprise, the Lehmann Company, near Nuremberg.

Lehmann 'Zig-Zag' tin wind-up toy, 1910-45, 5in. long. £450

'Baker and Sweep', E.P.L. No. 450, by Lehmann, circa 1905, in original box. £2,000

Lehmann, Japanese coolie in conical hat pulling rickshaw, with spring-motor action operating woman's fan and spoked wheels, 1930's. (Christie's S. Ken) £1,320

Lehmann clockwork sailor dressed in white summer uniform discoloured, 18.5cm. high, circa 1912. (Phillips) £207

A Lehmann tinplate 'Oh My', No. 690, the articulated figure holding the clockwork mechanism, circa 1920, 10½in. high. £500

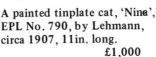

A painted tinplate cat, 'Nina', EPL No. 790, by Lehmann, circa 1907, 11in. long. £1,000

An early Lehmann, EPL marque, 'Paddy riding his pig to market', with clockwork mechanism, circa 1910, 5½in. long. £375

Lehmann Performing Sea Lion, No. 445, in original cardboard box, German, circa 1900, 7½in. long. £200

A Lehmann tinplate Anxious Bride, No. 470, German, circa 1910. £750

A Lehmann Mikado Family, No. 350, German, circa 1898, 6½in. long. £700

'Dancing Sailor', a printed and painted tinplate sailor, in blue cloth uniform, 7½in. high, by Lehmann, circa 1912. (Christie's) £200

'Bulky Mule, The Stubborn Donkey', EPL No. 425, by Lehmann, circa 1910, 7½in. long. £250

Early 20th century Lehmann waltzing doll, head with EPL trademark, 9in. high. £625

Lehmann, early flywheel driven 'Africa', EPL No. 170. £400

'New Century Cycle', EPL 345, with clockwork mechanism, by Lehmann, circa 1910, 5in. long. £1,000

Kadi, a printed and painted teabox with two Chinese coolies, clockwork mechanism concealed in box, by Lehmann, circa 1910, 7in. long. (Christie's S. Ken) £600

Lehmann 'Naughty Boy' tin wind-up toy, 1904-35, 4.5/8in. long.   £250

'Echo', EPL 725, an early printed and painted tinplate motorcyclist with clockwork mechanism operating a metal painted spoked wheel, by Lehmann, circa 1910, 8¾in. long.   £2,000

A rare tin plate beetle by Lehmann, Germany, which walks and flaps its wings.   £150

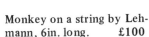

A Lehmann 'Lo and Li' tinplate toy.   £1,250

"Zulu", EPL 721, a painted and lithographed tinplate ostrich pulling a two wheel mail cart, by Lehmann, circa 1920, 7½in. long. (Christie's)   £605

Monkey on a string by Lehmann, 6in. long.   £100

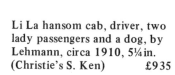

An early printed and painted tinplate automobile, 'Tut Tut' EPL No. 490, by Lehmann, circa 1910, 6¾in. long. £1,000

Oh My, a lithographed tinplate dancing negro, with hand-cranked clockwork mechanism, by Lehmann, circa 1912, 9¾in. high. (Christie's S. Ken)   £385

Li La hansom cab, driver, two lady passengers and a dog, by Lehmann, circa 1910, 5¼in. (Christie's S. Ken)   £935

MARTIN TOYS

Fernand Martin set up his toymaking business in Paris in 1878, and his tinplate clockwork toys came to rival their German counterparts in quality. Martin specialized in comical figures, often satirizing Paris society, and his toys were often dressed in fabrics, making them more realistic. He believed in having figures where the movement was amusing in its own right, such as a drunkard struggling to maintain his balance.

The firm was taken over by Victor Bonnet & Co. in the early 1920s. Martin's work was *FM* within a circle.

French 'Le Faucheur' scythe man by F. Martin, circa 1900, 7½in. high.
£500

A painted tinplate toy of a cooper, by F. Martin, Paris, circa 1902, 7½in. long.
£700

A German painted tinplate clockwork nursemaid, with rocking upper torso, umbrella, apron, cap and eccentric walking action, circa 1910, 6½in. high.
(Christie's S. Ken)
£528

F. Martin, clockwork L'Eminent Avocat, 22cm. high, boxed in excellent to mint condition, with Code Civil.
(Phillips)
£1,300

Fernand Martin, 'La Madelon casseuse d'assiettes', clockwork painted tinplate maid, dressed in blue with white apron and cap, circa 1913.
(Christie's S. Ken)
£550

A painted toy of a skater, with clockwork mechanism, by A. F. Martin, French, circa 1890, 8½in. high.
£1,000

A painted tinplate parlour maid chasing a mouse with a broom, dressed in pale blue dress with white collar, 19cm., probably by Martin.
(Phillips)
£820

'Our New Clergyman', a stained and carved wood, metal and tinplate preacher, probably by F. Martin, circa 1890, 10½in. high.
£1,750

MECCANO

The Meccano company was founded by the great Frank Hornby of train fame, in an attempt to wean the Sons of Empire away from the French and German model trains, cars etc., which were flooding the market. So successful was he that Meccano has become almost a generic name for assembly kits for planes, cars, engines, even ferris wheels, and all early examples fetch good prices today. They must however be in their original boxes, and be complete and in good condition.

Meccano expanded and diversified through the first half of the century, and its heyday was probably between 1958 and 1964. Then, through bad management and financial control it went into decline, sold out to Triang-Lines Bros., who in turn went bankrupt in 1971.

Meccano Aeroplane Constructor Outfit No. 1, silver, disassembled, in original box with instructions, circa 1931. (Christie's S. Ken) £1,045

Meccano Aeroplane Constructor Outfit No. 1 (2nd series), blue and cream, assembled as a Monoplane Racer, with pilot, circa 1936, 18½in. wingspan. (Christie's S. Ken) £462

Meccano No. 2 Motor Car Constructor Outfit, green and cream, assembled as a Grand Prix Special, circa 1937, 11¾in. long. (Christie's S. Ken) £440

Dealer's Meccano Display Model, red and green opening and closing No. 2 Outfit, electric motor, on wood base, circa 1960, 15in. wide. (Christie's S. Ken) £330

Rare Meccano Mechanised Army Outfit No. MA, in original box, with instructions, circa 1939. (Christie's S. Ken) £935

Meccano Elektron Electrical Experiments Outfits, comprising Sets No. 1 and 2, including electric motors, circa 1936. (Christie's S. Ken) £385

Meccano Steam Engine, a live steam spirit fired vertical steam engine, with japanned boiler, original fittings, circa 1929, 7½in. high. (Christie's) £715

Rare Italian Meccano Outfit No. 3, red and green, with removable tray, in original box, circa 1928. (Christie's S. Ken) £143

Meccano Aeroplane Constructor Outfit No. 2 (2nd series), silver and red, assembled as a single seater fighter, with pilot, circa 1932, 18½in. wingspan. (Christie's S. Ken) £396

Meccano Kemex Chemical Experiments No. 3L, with assorted glass bottles, in original box, circa 1933. (Christie's) £352

Meccano No. 2 Special Aeroplane Outfit, red and cream, assembled as a three engine airliner, with No. 2 Aero motor, circa 1937, 20½in. wingspan. (Christie's S. Ken) £495

Meccano Dealers Parts Display, blue and gold, on original card, circa 1936. (Christie's S. Ken) £440

Dealer's Meccano Display Model, yellow and blue Double Ferris Wheel fairground ride, electric motor, on wood base with Meccano signs, late 1970s, 19½in. wide. (Christie's S. Ken) £275

Rare Meccano Dealers Display Cabinet, red and green, six drawers, original velvet card, circa 1928. (Christie's S. Ken) £1,760

Assembled blue and gold Showman's Engine, electric motor, steerable front wheels, circa 1934, 29½ x 20in. (Christie's S. Ken) £704

Meccano Radio Crystal Receiving Set No. 1, on wood board, with phones, circa 1921. (Christie's S. Ken) £396

Assembled early nickel plated 'B' type Omnibus, with clockwork motor, 1916 parts, 21¾in long. (Christie's S. Ken) £308

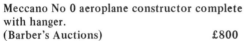

Meccano No 0 aeroplane constructor complete with hanger.
(Barber's Auctions)   £800

A Meccano No. 1 dealer's display cabinet, circa 1929, with six drawers, made up to 1938 specifications.
(Christie's S. Ken)   £770

A Meccano motor car constructor No. 2, assembled as a grand prix racing car, with clockwork mechanism, circa 1934.
(Lawrence Fine Art)   £715

A good Marklin tinplate fairground carousel toy, circa 1910, beautifully hand-painted, original paint and transfers, original hand-cranked musical movement, six sided centre column finished in white lined gold, and with painted floral decoration to alternate faces, plaster figures riding contemporary hide covered pigs, and white and gold painted shell-form chairs, diameter of base 41cm.
(Sotheby's)   £47,300

A Marklin tinplate 'Aeropal' hand or steam operated lighthouse roundabout, circa 1909, hand painted in red, white, green and blue including simulated stone on the centre lighthouse, six handsome sailboats with passengers which spin about, with stairways and many flags aloft, 19in. high.
(Christie's)   £12,100

Gunthermann wind-up painted tin merry-go-round, Germany, 1920's and 1930's, 10in. high, 10.3/8in. diameter.   £1,500

A merry-go-round with a wheel driven mechanism.
£300

A Bing painted tinplate clockwork Maypole with rotating suspended figures, a girl in a red dress and apron, and two boys in blue, and grey suits, circa 1910, 11in. high. (Christie's S. Ken)   £1,760

An airship musical go-round, possibly French, circa 1915, featuring three bisque-headed doll aviators suspended from dirigibles, when mechanism is wound, the airships circle the base as music plays. (Christie's)   £1,694

A Doll & Co. printed and painted carousel with a handcranked clockwork mechanism, 11½in. long, circa 1914.   £400

A tinplate model of a fair-ground traction engine, with a four-wheeled car containing a carousel, by Bing, circa 1906.   £700

A painted miniature pine blanket chest, attributed to Joseph Long Lehn, Pennsylvania, circa 1890, decorated with floral decals and landscapes, 8½in. wide. (Christie's)

£552

Bird's-eye maple cannon ball doll's bed, America, circa 1830, the turned base on ball posts, 8¾in. high. (Robt. W. Skinner Inc.) £228

A William and Mary miniature walnut veneered and marquetry chest, 16in. wide. (Henry Spencer) £1,000

A brocade covered display case in the form of a miniature sedan chair, 16in. high. (Christie's) £242

A fine early 19th century miniature dressing chest, 14in. wide, and a similar chest of drawers. (Henry Spencer) £780

A miniature Dutch gilt metal mounted mahogany armoire, the top with a pierced gallery, late 18th century, 18½in. wide. (Christie's) £2,860

A Dutch marquetry miniature bureau with hinged slope enclosing drawers and pigeon holes, 16in. wide. (Christie's) £2,640

A 19th century Continental miniature bone piano, fitted with shelves above the keyboard, carved with the name Badenweler, 6½in. high. (Christie's) £297

A Danish parcel gilt and stained elm miniature commode with moulded waved top, 14in. wide. (Christie's) £2,530

Miniature Biedermeier nightstand with marble top and tiny oval mirror, 1in. scale.   £100

A George III miniature mahogany chest of drawers, 14¾in. wide.   £150

Contemporary miniature hanging cradle, by Carol Anderson, painted by Natasha, 1981, 1in. scale.   £125

A miniature upright piano in burr walnut with central inlay, brass candlestick holders and ivory keyboard, 15½in. high. (Christie's) £1,045

19th century miniature maple dining-room set with carved legs and leather seats. £100

Contemporary wooden child's chair made by Eugene Beshenkovsky and painted by Natasha, 1982, 1in. scale.   £40

A burr-yew wood miniature chest inlaid with lines, on bracket feet, 11in. wide.   £3,250

An American late Federal mahogany miniature chest of drawers, 10in. wide.   £850

A 19th century painted miniature ladder-back armchair, American.   £200

Miniature 19th century
Biedermeier type dressing
table, 5in. long, trimmed
in marble-like stripes.
£175

Late 19th century Japan-
ese miniature steel and
gold overlay cabinet on
stand, 5.7/8in. high.
£1,250

Miniature natural wood
finish armoire with
three working cupboard
doors, 5 x 4in.   £275

Miniature contemporary
canopy bed in walnut
with quilted cover, 7½in.
high.   £125

Set of 19th century miniature
maple wood furniture including a writing desk and two
chairs, desk 5½in. wide. £125

A 19th century miniature
tilt-top tea table, 13in. high.
£200

Charles I miniature oak
cupboard with diamond-
inlaid panels, circa 1640,
2ft.7in. wide. £3,000

A miniature apprentice made
marquetry top table.   £200

19th century miniature
maple wood piano with
functioning keyboard,
5in. wide.   £40

An American, 19th century, miniature painted bannister-back armchair, 9½in. high. (Christie's) £400

A 19th century miniature grain painted bowfront chest-of-drawers, American or English, 12in. high. (Christie's) £1,000

A 19th century, American, miniature classical maple fiddleback chair, 10¾in. high, 8¼in. wide. (Christie's) £450

Mid 18th century miniature Chippendale cherrywood chest-of-drawers, 7¾in. high. (Christie's) £1,250

An American, 18th century, miniature Queen Anne maple and pine slant-front desk, with a cherrywood mirror, the desk 11in. high. (Christie's) £2,750

Late 19th century miniature Chippendale walnut slant-front desk, American, 7¼in. high. (Christie's) £1,250

Late 18th century miniature George III mahogany side table, English, 6in. high. (Christie's) £300

Late 18th century miniature Chippendale mahogany chest-on-chest, English, 16¾in. high. (Christie's) £1,500

An American, 19th century, miniature Federal mahogany four-post bedstead with canopy, 15½in. high. (Christie's) £250

A 19th century miniature green painted pine blanket chest, American, 9½in. high. (Christie's)   £300

Miniature paint decorated Windsor armchair, America, last half of 19th century, the black ground painted with floral decoration, 8¼in. high. (Skinner Inc.)   £429

Early 19th century miniature Federal mahogany tilt-top tea table, American, 9in. high. (Christie's)   £750

A 19th century miniature Federal mahogany picture mirror, American, 9½in. high. (Christie's)   £1,000

A 17th century miniature oak coffer of panelled construction, probably French, 35 x 21 x 23cm. (Phillips)   £850

Late 18th/early 19th century miniature Continental painted tall clock case, 17in. high. (Christie's)   £450

A miniature Chippendale mahogany desk and bookcase, Rhode Island, 1760-80, 16in. high. (Christie's)   £1,600

Two 19th century miniature painted side chairs, American, 9¾in. and 8¼in. high. (Christie's)   £450

A Dutch mahogany and oak miniature clothes press, 21in. wide, 33in. high. (Christie's)   £2,250

A Federal mahogany
miniature chest of
drawers, 1790-1810,
14½in. wide.   £750

19th century tin piano, 3½
x 4in., in excellent condition.
£75

Miniature raised panelled
settle by David S. White,
£50

Part of a set of 20th century miniature wooden furniture
in Colonial Windsor style.   £175

A doll's Jacobean style chair
upholstered in dark red velvet, 21in. high.   £800

A mid Georgian walnut miniature chest, the base with one
long drawer on bracket feet,
13½in. wide.   £1,300

A William and Mary walnut
oyster veneer and cross-
banded chest of small size.
£2,250

A miniature Federal secretary, America, circa 1830,
13½in. wide.   £2,000

Biedermeier miniature writing desk with marble writing surface, 3½ x 4½in.   £125

Part of a set of 19th century miniature maple wood furniture of a Gothic style settee and a set of shelves.   £100

A mid 19th century mahogany miniature tripod table, circa 1840, 9½in. diam.   £300

Miniature Napoleonic-style bed and chairs, 4½ x 4in.   £200

Group of 19th century miniature furniture of a cupboard and three chairs, cupboard 7½in. high.   £85

A Victorian mahogany and marquetry banded miniature chest of five drawers, 14in. wide.   £300

An Anglo-Indian miniature ivory bureau cabinet.   £7,500

A 19th century miniature, Empire mahogany and painted chest-of-drawers, American, 19½in. wide.   £600

Miniature Victorian wash boiler and dolly in brass. £20

Miniature gilt parlour lamp with a white milk glass shade, 1in. scale.   £300

A metal framed child's mangle with wooden rollers.   £15

Japanese porcelain child's teaset, each piece illustrates a scene from Little Orphan Annie, circa 1920.   £375

A plated and tinplate child's live steam kitchen stove, with five burners, three ovens, adjustable rings, Bing, circa 1920, 19in. wide. (Christie's S. Ken)   £462

A miniature tin dresser, 3½in. wide.   £8

A miniature cast metal mangle, 5in. high. £10

Set of tableware in wooden case with red suede lined interior, 1 x 2in.   £75

Pearson's miniature dictionary including magnifying glass, 1¼ x ¾in.   £8

Contemporary silver cash register in 19th century style, 1¼ in. high. £20

German miniature tin penny toy with handle which turns and produces a music-like sound. £50

A 19th century miniature wallpapered bandbox, American, 4½ in. high. £250

19th century hanging wall clock, 3½ x 1½ in., with brass clock frame. £60

Miniature Austrian set of porcelain and silver cutlery of nineteen pieces, in excellent condition. £175

Miniature 19th century banquet lamp with brown glass shade, 3in. high. £75

A miniature violin in original case with mother-of-pearl inlay, the case 5in. long. £300

A miniature set of die cast 'pots and pans' by Crescent. £10

A presentation child's set of French 19th century Victorian miniature dishes in case, 17 x 19in. £300

MODEL AIRCRAFT

The first toy planes made by the Dinky Toy Company were launched on the market in 1934 and given the identification Number 60. The scale used was roughly 1/200. Planes were issued in boxes of six to be sold boxed or singly. Production continued until 1939 when it slowed down and by 1941 came to a standstill because of the lack of raw materials which were needed for the war effort. The original models were made of lead alloy but before 1939 this was replaced by a substitute called Mazak which was an alloy containing aluminium, copper, zinc and some magnesium. Sometimes trace elements that were present made the alloy brittle and cracks appeared. Examine any Dinky toys well because cracks will only get worse. Always store in a cool, dry place out of direct sunlight. The most common model plane produced was the Percival Gull which was produced in many colours but after 1940 the planes were always camouflaged and Spitfires, Hurricanes, Blenheims, Fairey Battles, Armstrong Whitworth Whitleys, Ensigns, Leopard Moths and Vickers Jockys joined the range. Because they were only produced for a short time they are rare and valuable. Boxed sets which are available are The R.A.F. Presentation Set, The Camouflaged Set and The Presentation Set. After the war, Dinky planes were back in production and new ranges were produced in 1946 and in the 50s. Probably the most sought after model to any Dinky collector is number 992 Avro Vulcan. This model of the most famous of the R.A.F. V-Bombers, was produced between 1955 and 1956. The model is quite large and finished in silver.

JU89 Heavy Bomber, 67A, 1940-41, German markings, boxed. £200

Nimrod Dinky Comet (Conversion). £120

Dinky F-4 U.S.A.F. Phantom, U.S. Market only. £100

Shetland Flying Boat No. 701, 1947-49, boxed. £600

Camouflaged Whitworth Ensign Liner No. 68A, 1940-41. £200

Dinky Hurricane, ME109. £40

Dinky Diamond Jubilee Spitfire, boxed. £100

Pre-war Frog Penguin, unmade in kits. £20

Bristol Britannia No. 998, 1959-65, boxed.
£180

A large scale model of the British airship
R100-G-FAAV, 10ft. long, with tower, 4ft.
£1,750

Meccano No. 2 special model aeroplane constructor outfit complete and good order,
play damage to paintwork, pilot missing,
circa 1939.
(James of Norwich)   £210

Atlantic Flying Boat, boxed.   £300

Lockheed Constellation No. 60C, produced
by Meccano France, 1957-63, boxed.   £140

Camouflaged Frobisher Air Liner.   £220

A rare printed and painted tri-engine cabin
biplane, with red and blue lining and RAF
roundels, by Wells, circa 1936, 21¼in.
(Christie's)   £440

Hindenburg, a rare printed and painted tinplate airship, with clockwork mechanism,
in original paintwork with swastikas, German,
10in. long. (Christie's S. Ken)   £462

Post-war Spitfire No. 62A, 1945-49. £15

60u Armstrong Whitworth Whitley No. 62T, Silver 1937-41. £85

Shooting Star No. 70F, 1947-62. £10

719 Dinky Spitfire, 1969-78. £10

British 40-seat Air Liner No. 62X, 1939-41. £60

726 Modern Dinky ME109, 1972-76. £10

Four-engined Liner No. 62R, 1945-49. £30

Dinky Viking No. 70c, 1947-62. £10

Monospar No. 60E, 1934-41. £85

DM Comet Racer No. 60G, 1945-49. £30

Hawker Hurricane No. 62H, 1939-41. £45

Ensign Air Liner No. 62P, 1938-41. £50

Flying Boat Clipper III, No. 60W, 1938-41. £55

Seaplane No. 700, 1945-49. £15

Auro York No. 70A & 704, 1946-59. £30

Fairey Battle No. 60N, 1937-41. £50

Twin-engined Fighter No. 70D, 1946-55. £15

Spitfire No. 62E, 1940-41. £50

Armstrong Whitworth Whitley No. 62T, Silver, 1937-41, boxed.   £150

Frog Hawker Hart Mark II Day Bomber, with accessories and instruction book, in original box, with Hamley's retail label, circa 1935.
(Christie's S. Ken)   £990

A pre-war Frog de Havilland 80A 'Puss Moth' in original box with winding key, accessories.
(Christie's)   £275

Flying Fortress No. 62G, 1939-41, boxed.   £150

Dinky pre-war Set No. 60 Aeroplanes (2nd Issue), including Imperial Airway Liner, D. H. Leopard Moth, Percival Gull, Low Wing Monoplane, General 'Monospar' and Cierva Autogiro, in original box, circa 1934. (Christie's)   £4,180

Douglas Air Liner No. 60T, (supposed to be a DC3 by many, but is probably a DC2) boxed.   £160

A Meccano No. 1 Aeroplane Constructor Outfit, assembled as a light biplane, silver plates, R.A.F. roundels, circa 1931.
(Chrsitie's)   £180

Armstrong Whitworth Ensign Air Liner No. 62P, 1938-41, boxed.   £100

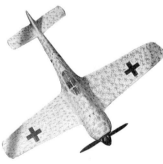

A detailed model of the Focke-Wulf FW 190-A6 single-seater fighter, serial No. 1-5 with considerable external detailing, finished in camouflage, 6 x 15$\frac{1}{2}$in.
(Christie's)   £220

A well detailed ⅛th scale flying model of the Hawker Typhoon 1B Serial letters RB222, built by D. Banham, 65in. (Christie's) £770

Mayo Composite Aircraft No. 63, 1939-41, boxed. £300

A modern painted tinplate Fairey Swordfish torpedo bomber, by Tin Pot Toy Co., 14in. long. (Christie's) £198

Dinky pre-war set No. 60 Aeroplanes (2nd Issue), with markings and instructions, in original box. (Christie's S. Ken) £462

The first Dinky boxed set, No. 60, issued in 1934 to 1940. £1,000

Kings Aeroplane (Envoy) No. 62K, 1938-41, boxed. £180

A pre-war Empire Flying Boat No. 60R, 1937, boxed. £170

Britains rare set 1431 Army Co-operation Autogiro with pilot, in original box, 1937. (Phillips) £2,100

Frobisher Class Air Liner No. 62, 1939-41, boxed. £180

Douglas Air Liner No. 60T, (supposed to be a DC3 by many, but is probably a DC2). £70

DM Comet Racer No. 60G, 1935-41. £45

A post-war Giant High Speed Monoplane No. 62Y, R/H Gree. £35

French Meccano Farman 360, No. 61C, 1935-40. £75

Japanese Aeromini 747, 1973 -77. £65

Gladiator Fighter No. 60P, 1937-41. £50

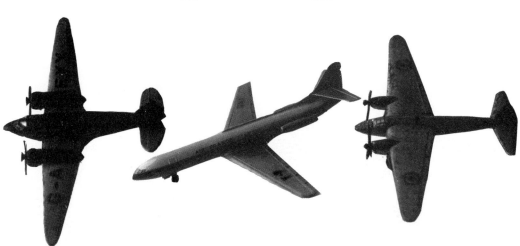

Kings Aeroplane (Envoy) No. 62K, 1938-41. £55

Air France Caravelle No. 997 — £40 for an English one or £55 for one of French manufacture.

Amiot 370 No. 64AZ, French sold in U.K., 1939-40. £35

JU89 Heavy Bomber, 67A, 1940-41, German markings. £125

Comet 4 Airliner No. 702, 1954-65. £20

British 40-seat Air Liner No. 62X, 1939-41, boxed. £150

Avro Vulcan No. 992, issued 1955, (not issued in U.K., unknown number released in Canada). £1,400

BEA Viscount No. 708, 1957-65. £35

A pair of Fairey Battles, known as the Mirror Image Pair, 1939-40. £125

A pre-war Empire Flying Boat No. 60R, 1937. £55

French Meccano Mystere IUA, No. 60A, 1957-63. £20

Mayo Composite Aircraft No. 63, 1939-41. £120

Shetland Flying Boat No. 701, 1947-49. £200

Imperial Airways Liner No. 60A, 1934-40. £100

French Meccano Sikorsky S.58 Helicopter No. 60D, 1957-61. £25

Frobisher Class Air Liner No. 62R, 1939-41. £55

Air France Viscount No. 706, 1956-57. £45

Tempest II Fighter No. 70B, 1946-55. £12

Bristol Britannia No. 998, 1959-65. £55

·JU90 Air Liner No. 62N, 1938-41. £85

Iomica (Japanese) F-14A Tomcat, 1978-80.
£20

Lockheed Constellation No. 60C, produced
by Meccano France, 1957-63.   £125

A pre-war Giant High Speed Monoplane No.
62Y, R/H Gree.   £55

Hawker Hunter No. 736, 1955-63. £10

Japanese Aeromini F-4 Phantom, 1973-77.
£40

Large monoplane model, made by Charles R. Witteman, Staten Island, New York, circa 1912, 62in. long, wingspan 78in.   £1,250

A model of a Bleriot-type (Morane) monoplane, with engine, wingspan 40½in.   £125

A Lehmann Ikarus tinplate aeroplane, No. 653, German, 10½in. long.   £1,250

Tipp Co., clockwork lithographed bomber bi-plane TC-1029, wing span 36.5cm., 25.5cm. long, key, lacking pilot, three bombs. £400

A Marklin monoplane in cream and green, fitted to a double bogie, plane 20cm. long.   £300

A Britain's set No. 434, R.A.F. Monoplane, with two pilots and four R.A.F. personnel, in original box.   £1,500

A 1:24th scale wood and metal model of the Royal Aircraft Factory SE5a, built by R. Walden, 1976.   £275

Biplane No. 24, with clockwork mechansim, Deutsche Lufthansa markings, wingspan 20¼in. long, by Tipp, circa 1939.   £500

French tinplate Paris-Tokio bi-plane, clockwork mechanism driving the wheels, circa 1935, 9in. long.   £300

A J.D.N. clockwork tinplate model bi-plane, made circa 1928.   £500

A Mettoy jet airliner, No. 2016/1, in original box with four mechanical sparking replacements, the box 20½in., English, circa 1935.   £250

'Strato Clipper', a printed and painted tinplate four-engine airliner with battery mechanism, by Gama, circa 1956, wingspan 20in.   £175

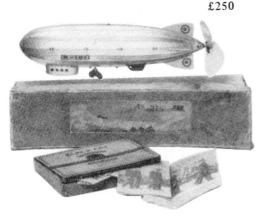

A pre-war Japanese R101 airship by GK, the aluminium body with tinplate gondolas and fins, 13in. long, together with newspaper cuttings, circa 1930.   £600

A flying scale model of the Gloster Gladiator single seater fighter Serial No. K.8032 with external details, finished in silver with R.A.F. markings, wingspan 56in.   £500

American Flyer Manufacturing Co., Model No. 560 spring-driven monoplane, 54cm. long, span 60cm., boxed.   £300

An Exhibition Standard 1:30 scale model of the prototype Panavia Tornado F-2 Multi Role Combat Aircraft, wingspan 17½in.   £2,750

P1B Lightning Fighter No. 737, 1959-68.
£15

Bristol 713 Helicopter No. 715, 1956-62.
£15

Flying Fortress No. 62G, 1939-41. £60

A post-war Empire Flying Boat, 1949. £30

Camouflaged Whitworth Ensign Liner No.
68A, 1940-41. £65

Sea Vixen No. 738 Naval Fighter, 1960-65.
£20

Modern Dinky Phantom 730, 1972-76. £15

Vickers Viking No. 70C, 1947-62. £15

DOLLS & TOYS

Four-engined Flying Boat, No. 60W, 1945-49.
£20

French Meccano Air France Viscount No. 60E, 1957-60.
£40

Westland Sikorsky S.51 Helicopter, 1957-62.
£15

Gloster Javelin No. 735, 1956-66.   £10

Ensign No. 62P, 1938-41.   £50

Nord Noratlas No 804, 1960-64.   £125

Vautoor No. 60B, French Issue, 1957-63.
£30

Bloch 220, No. 64BZ, French made Dinky, sold in U.K., 1939-40.
£55

A 19th century wooden and papier-mache butcher's shop, several pieces marked Germany, 12 x 6in. £300

A Peek Freans biscuit tin 'Castle' made of four different sections, manufactured by Huntley Bourne & Stevens, 1923. £300

A large 20th century model bird house. £35

A late 19th century glazed and cased model of M. Osborn's — The Butcher's Shop, 46.5 x 43.5cm. £1,500

A Crown illuminated Panorama optical toy theatre, illuminated by a candle mounted behind, 9½in. wide. £225

Britain's Army Building No. 1739, circa 1940, a model of gunners' quarters. £1,250

Early 20th century Bing lithographed tin garage, Germany, with key-wind open car and closed sedan type car, 5½in. and 6½in. £300

A Victorian Christmas cracker house. £30

Wooden and paper toy theatre, manufactured for F. A. O. Schwartz Toys, circa 1885, 25 x 25in. £100

A splendid Marklin tinplate hand-painted castle with revolving moat, finished in tones of tan and green, with red and blue accents, 13in. high.
(Christie's) £1,936

A wooden and paper lithograph stable, circa 1875, 24 x 15 x 12in. £275

A model of a hall with marquetry floor dividing at the landing into stairs on either side going up to a galleried landing, 26in. wide.
£350

"Auto Garage", a fine painted and lithographed tinplate garage, with printed windows and two opening doors, to reveal two cars, by Bing, circa 1925. (Christie's)
£308

A card model of a three bay stuccoed villa, laid out with a garden containing seven Grodnerthal dolls, 24in. wide, in glazed case, circa 1860.
(Christie's S. Ken) £385

A painted wooden toy stable, with two stalls, coach house and furnished living quarters above and with blue cart and composition horses, 28½in. wide.
(Christie's S. Ken) £330

English butcher's shop, mid 19th century, 26½in. high.
(Christie's) £4,840

A Marklin hand-painted kitchen, circa 1900, featuring a sideboard, sink, shelves, pots, pans and elaborate cookstove, 37in. wide.
(Christie's) £5,445

Water mill, one of three Marklin working models, in original paintwork, German, circa 1936.
(Christie's) £165

A wooden toy grocer's shop, stencilled and lined in brown, with printed paper labelled drawers, 21¼in. wide, German, circa 1930s. (Christie's S. Ken)   £495

Peepshow — hand coloured peepshow of the Palais Royal, extending to 492mm. in 5 sections, 128 x 189mm., Paris (?), circa 1820.
(Phillips London)   £420

A good hand cranked cardboard JWB Patent. Excursion to London, moving panorama.
(Christie's S. Ken)   £352

A painted wooden toy Butcher's Shop, with transfer decoration, marbelised slabs, two original tables, plaster joints, carcases, butcher and customers, 20in. wide, stamped C. H. Schutzmarke on base for Christian Hacker, circa 1895.
(Christie's)   £5,720

A painted tinplate kitchen, the corner stove with hood, a painted glass window at the back and with utensils including a copper hot water bottle, 11½in. wide, late 19th century, possibly Marklin.
(Christie's)   £605

A hand cranked cardboard 'The Royal Illuminated Panorama', with rear mounted candle holder and internal paper strip of views.
(Christie's S. Ken)   £330

MODEL SHIPS

Model ships can really be divided into two distinct types. The first consists of the craftsmen built or builder's model type, faithful scale models of the original and exact in every detail, designed to be set in glass cases and wondered at. Some of the earliest examples of these were manufactured by French prisoners of war during the Napoleonic period and sold by them to obtain money to eke out their rations. They were made from left over bones, string and straw, and embellished with scraps of wood, ivory or metal. These now fetch many thousands of pounds, as do the more conventionally built builders' models, the price reflecting the care and precision which has gone into the making. Beloved by collectors too are the ship in a bottle types, many of which have been lovingly made by old sailors.

Strictly speaking, however, these are not really toys, and it is to the tinplate manufacturers of the turn of the century that we must look for the earliest examples of the second type. While the first were accurate in every scale detail, the charm of the second type lies often in their bright colours and disproportionate sizes. The earliest were not even meant for the water, but had detachable wheels so that they could be 'sailed' on the carpet! Early examples, even in poor condition, are all likely to be of value, particularly the large (up to 36") German models with steam or clockwork mechanisms. Tinplate boats from the 1930s are also worth looking out for, and even those from the 1950s by German makers such as Arnold can fetch hundreds. The record is £125,000 paid in 1989 for an 1885 Märklin boat, the Imperator.

Ernst Plank, a large hand painted battleship with guns, handrails, finished in grey with red lining, 60cm. (Phillips West Two) £2,000

An early wood/composition base toy of a Dreadnought with three funnels, 12.5cm., circa 1905. (Phillips West Two) £50

A German painted tinplate steam riverboat, finished in red and white, blue and red lined, and yellow funnel with red star, circa 1905, 30cm. long. (Christie's S. Ken) £385

Ingap, clockwork lithographed twin funnelled river boat, the main body finished in cream, on four silver spoked wheels, 15.5cm. (Phillips) £184

A Third Series painted tin-plate clockwork ocean liner, by Bing, circa 1925, complete with masts and rigging, the hull fitted with clockwork mechanism, 16in. long. (Christie's) £1,760

Carette, a lithographed tinplate flywheel driven carpet toy sailing vessel, with eccentric rocking action and lithographed card sail (lacks flywheel), circa 1905, 24cm. long. (Christie's S. Ken) £242

An Arnold four funnel ocean liner, with clockwork mech-anism powering two three blade propellers, German, circa 1920 (some parts missing, flags missing, patches of rust, worn), 15½in. long. (Christie's) £286

Hornby Speed Boat No. 2 'Hawk', green and white, in original box, circa 1936, 9¼in. long. (Christie's S. Ken) £88

A shipbuilder's model of the schooner yacht 'America', American, circa 1850, 28in. long.   £3,500

Mid 19th century English contemporary model of a sailing ship hull, 9in. long. £200

A 20th century carved and painted model of the paddle steamer 'City of Key West', American, in wooden and glass case, 38in. long.   £1,000

Mid 19th century English model of the brig 'Vanda', probably sailor-made, 15in. long.   £1,250

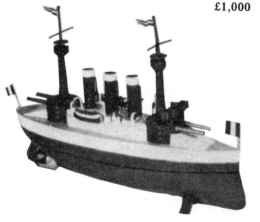

A restored and repainted early Marklin three-funnel tinplate battleship, German, circa 1910, 17in. long.   £700

A 1:100 scale model of the three masted auxiliary schooner 'Cruz del Sur' built by W. M. Wilson, Silloth, 12 x 17½in.   £400

A carved and painted model of ocean liner 'Liberte', executed for the Companie Generale Transatlantique, circa 1950, in wooden and plexi-glass case, 54in. long.   £4,000

A builder's mirror back half model of a single screw cabin motor cruiser built by John I. Thorneycroft & Co. Ltd., London, 6 x 26in. (Christie's)   £1,500

Late 19th century model of a fore-and-aft schooner 'Swallow', 55in. long, on stand.　　　　　　　　　　　　£600

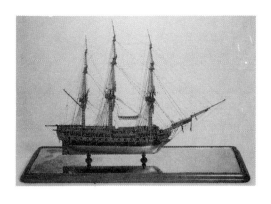

Early 19th century prisoner-of-war boxwood model of the 48-gun Ship-of-the-Line 'Glory', 20 x 28in.　　£15,000

A 19th century model of a Gloucester fishing schooner, 'Columbia', fully rigged with wooden sails, 20.3/8in. long.　　£650

A fully planked and rigged model of a 72-gun man-o'-war, built by P. Rumsey, Bosham, 26 x 37in.　　　　　　　　　£1,750

A carved and painted model of the 'Royal Ark', by J. R. Whittemore, on a moulded wooden base, 43in. long.　　　　　£1,500

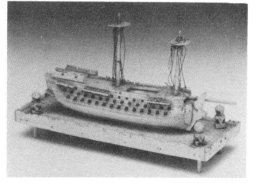

Early 19th century prisoner-of-war bone model of a frigate, 7in. long, under glass dome.　　　　　　　　　　£1,200

A fully planked and rigged bone and wood model of a topsail schooner built by P. Rumsey, Bosham, 10 x 14in.   £550

An exhibition standard 1:75 scale fully planked and rigged model of the French 60 gun man-of-war 'Le Protecteur' of circa 1760, built by P. M. di Gragnano, Naples, 31 x 38in.   £6,000

A 1:60 scale model of the late 18th century French Ceremonial Galley 'Reale de France', built by J. Cherrill, Weybridge, 25 x 42in.
                                    £1,000

An exhibition standard 1:384 scale model of H.M.S. Rattlesnake, circa 1781, built by J. Evans, Whyteleaf.   £2,000

A finely carved and detailed contemporary early 19th century boxwood model of the 28-gun man-o'-war H.M.S. Nelson, 13½ x 10½in.   £10,000

A contemporary model of a Bristol slaver, English, circa 1810, 45in. long.   £1,750

A finely engineered and detailed live steam, spirit fired model of the Passenger Tramp Steamer Belle Morss of London, 22½in. x 51½in. (Christie's) £1,650

A finely detailed electric powered radio controlled model of the paddle steamer Albion, 16in. x 52in. (Christie's) £1,650

A well detailed and presented fibreglass wood and metal electric powered, radio controlled model of the Lowestoft Herring Drifter Gull, Licence No. H241, built by W.A. Williams, London. 68in. x 35in. (Christie's) £2,200

Sutcliffe live steam spirit fired battleship, with burner, in original paintwork, circa 1928, 16½ in. long, in original box. (Christie's S. Ken.) £187

Cased, carved and painted ship model, America, late 19th/early 20th century, polychrome model of the steam ship City of New York, 35½in. wide. (Skinner Inc.) £903

An ⅛th scale wooden display model of the German cruiser S.M.S. Viktoria Louise, the hull carved from the solid, masts and rigging and deck details including anchors, deck rails, bridge, stayed funnels, guns in turrets and other details, 29in. x 67½in. (Christie's) £462

Kron Prinzessin Cecilie, a rare hand painted tinplate display model of the Norddeutscher Line Trans-Atlantic liner, by Fleischmann, Germany, circa 1907, 154cm. long. (Christie's S. Ken) £7,700

A finely planked and pinned unrigged model of the ship rigged sloop Myridon of circa 1881, built by P. Danks, Leighton Buzzard, from plans supplied by the National Maritime Museum, 8in. x 32in. (Christie's) £1,430

A well presented fully planked and framed
model of a 30ft. Royal Navy armed pinnace of
circa 1877, built by P. Smith, Ealing, 15in. x
23.5in.
(Christie's) £484

An extremely fine and detailed exhibition
standard fibreglass wood and metal, electric
powered radio controlled model of H.M.S.
Warspite built by G. Edwards, Cheddington,
17¹/₂in. x 61in. (Christie's) £4,180

A well detailed and presented 1:150 scale
static display model of the Spanish paddle/sail
corvette San Isldefonso of circa 1840, built by
W.M. Wilson, Carlisle, 10¹/₂in. x 19in.
(Christie's) £242

A well presented radio controlled, electric
powered model of the Mississippi Stern Wheel
Steamer Creole Queen, built by R. Burgess,
Mayfield, 15¹/₂in. x 48in.
(Christie's) £330

Shadow box with model of the 'Cumberland',
America, late 19th century, of polychrome
wood, paper and thread, 15¹/₂in. x 26in.
(Skinner Inc.) £488

A finely detailed and well researched fully
planked and framed electric powered radio
controlled model of a Thornycroft 55ft. coastal
motor torpedo boat, built by R.R. Bullivant,
Leighton Buzzard, 14¹/₂in. x 38in.
(Christie's) £990

A fine and detailed exhibition standard ¹/₇₅th
scale model of the French 64-gun ship of-the-
line Le Protecteur, built to drawings supplied
by Le Musee de la Marine, Paris, 32¹/₂in. x
39in.
(Christie's) £2,200

An extremely fine and detailed builder's model
of the steel schooner rigged single screw steam
yacht Wakiva, built by Ramage & Ferguson
Ltd. of Leith for W.E. Cox, Boston,
Massachusetts, 19in. x 52in.
(Christie's) £33,000

A fully planked and rigged model of the
'Wasa' of circa 1628, built by J. M. R. Brown,
Darwen, 31 x 40in. (Christie's) £1,210

A finely detailed and well presented
3/32 in.:1ft. scale fully rigged model of the
clipper ship 'Timaru', of circa 1874, built
to drawings of H. A. Underhill by E. V. Fry,
Cowes, 16 x 27½ in. (Christie's) £3,520

A well detailed and presented waterline
display model of the Thames Sprit's'l
sailing barge 'Emma' of London, No. 221,
built by W. H. Crook, York, 13½ x 16in.
(Christie's) £490

A finely detailed and well presented fully
planked and framed, fully rigged ¼in.:1ft.
scale model of the frigate H.M.S. 'Endymion',
of circa 1792, built by M. Salville-Smithin,
Bristol, 43 x 67in. (Christie's) £2,420

A fully planked and rigged model of the
clipper 'Cutty Sark', of circa 1869, built by
J. M. R. Brown, Darwen, complete with masts,
spars, standing and running rigging and full
suit of stitched linen sails, 25½ x 44in.
(Christie's) £1,210

A well detailed fibreglass, wood and metal
¼in.:1ft. scale model of the armed trawler
H.M.S. 'Sir Agravaine' Pennant No. T230,
built by N. Howard-Pritchard, Blackpool,
18½ x 35in. (Christie's) £990

A wood and metal unrigged model of the Royal Naval 90-gun ship of the line H.M.S. 'Albion', built by A. Brown, St Austell, 18 x 44in. (Christie's)   £660

A fine and detailed planked and framed, fully rigged model of the screw/sail man of war H.M.S. 'Rattler', complete with masts, yards, standing and running rigging with scale blocks and deck details, 35 x 60in. (Christie's)   £2,860

A well detailed and presented 3/8th in.:1ft. scale model of a Royal Naval gaff-rigged schooner of circa 1760, built by I. H. Wilkie, Beardisely, 29 x 36in. (Christie's)   £440

A well detailed 3.32 scale wooden model of the three masted barquentine 'William Ashburner', built in Barrow, 1876, and modelled by J. Kearon, Southport, 10 x 15in. (Christie's)   £660

A well detailed and presented fully planked and rigged model of the bomb ketch H.M.S. 'Firedrake', of circa 1741, built by P. N. Smith, London, 20½ x 34in. (Christie's)   £1,980

A well detailed free rigged and planked model of H.M.S. 'Victory', built by J. M. R. Brown, Darwen, complete with masts, yards with stun's'l booms, standing and running rigging and deck details, 27 x 40in. (Christie's)   £1,430

An early 20th century American steamship model, diorama scene in mahogany case, 48in. wide. £600

Mid 19th century English sailor-made half-block ship model of a paddle steamer, 30in. wide. £575

Mid 19th century shipping diorama, depicting the three-masted clipper 'Solway', together with a fishing smack, English, 39in. wide. £650

Mid 19th century English sailor-made half-block model of a clipper, 34in. wide. £400

A 1/24 scale fully planked electric powered model of the Herring Drifter 'Supernal', built by G. Wrigley, 1979/80 from drawings by R. Neville, 24 x 24in. £1,750

A 1:48 scale fibreglass, wood and metal, electric-powered model of the coastal cargo ship S.S. Talacre of Liverpool, built by R. H. Phillips, 13 x 33in. £600

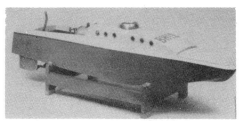

An exhibition standard 'One Metre' class steam boat 'Papua', BH 19, built by A. Broad, Bromley, 8 x 40in. £450

A well detailed wood and metal static display model of the Leander class frigate H.M.S. Aurora, Pennant No. F10, stand 14 x 16in. £725

A wooden framed working model of a single screwing boat 'The Swift', circa 1904, Greenock, 32½in. long.   £300

A shipbuilder's model of Lord Ashburton's steam yacht 'Venetia', Scottish, 1893, 67½in. long.   £7,500

An English mid 19th century sailor-made shipping diorama, 30½in. wide.   £400

A mid 19th century sailor-made model of the coaster 'Susan Vittery', English, 29½in. long.   £600

A live steam spirit-fired wooden model of the paddle tug 'Alert' of Yarmouth, 21 x 39in.   £1,750

Late 19th century carved and painted model of the 'William Tapscot', in a glass and mahogany case, 38in. long.   £1,250

A builder's mirror backed half model of the schooner rigged steam yacht 'Rona', built for A. H. E. Wood Esq., by David and William Henderson & Co., 1893/4 to the order of Thomas and Campbell, designed by G. L. Watson & Co., 10 x 71in.   £4,000

A builder's model of the single screw cargo ship M.V. 'Deerwood' of London, built 1955 by Wm. Pickersgill & Sons Ltd., for Wm. France, Fenwick & Co. Ltd., 12½ x 53in.   £1,250

303

DOLLS & TOYS

A tinplate model liner, entitled 'The Queen Mary', probably German, circa 1930, 29in. long. £800

A Marklin tinplate and clockwork warship, H.M.S. Albion, 21in. long. £700

JEP: No. 3, clockwork streamline speedboat painted in pale blue and cream with driver, 36cm. long. £75

Early 20th century Walbert lithographed tin wind-up ferry boat, 13¾in. long. £200

Fleischmann tinplate clockwork model of a two-funnelled ocean liner, 10½in. long. £200

A Bing repainted three-funnel liner with clockwork mechanism, 14¾in. long, circa 1925. £500

An early Carette carpet toy tinplate sailboat, with fly-wheel mechanism, German, circa 1905, 11¾in. long. £250

Dinky pre-war set No. 50, 'Ships of the British Navy', together with five other warships and 'Famous Liners'. £225

A late 19th/early 20th century ships model of a harbour dredger, 78in. long. £1,000

'Unterseeboot', a painted metal submarine, by Bing, circa 1902, 17¾in. long. £700

A Falk tinplate painted clockwork battleship, HMS Invincible, 37cm. long. £525

Fleischmann, tinplate clockwork liner No. 67, 51cm. long.   £1,000

An early painted metal gun-boat with clockwork mechanism, by Bing, circa 1904, 10½in. long.   £275

Tin clockwork steamboat, probably Gebruder Bing, Germany, 1920's, 32in. long.   £1,500

A hand enamelled 'New Orleans Paddle Wheeler', probably by Dent, U.S.A., circa 1903, 10½in. long.   £450

A Hess printed and painted tinplate toy of Dreadnought, with clockwork mechanism, circa 1911, 8½in. long.   £100

A painted wood waterline dreadnought, probably by Carette, circa 1904, 5in. long, in original instruction box. £400

A painted tinplate river paddle steamer with clockwork mechanism, 11in. long, by Uebelacker, Nuremberg, circa 1902. £650

A painted tin wind-up tanker, by J. Fleischmann, Germany, 1950's, 19in. long. £200

A tinplate model of a three-funnel ocean liner, with clockwork mechanism operating two propellers, by Bing, circa 1920, 15½in. long.   £1,000

Early 20th century shipbuilder's model of the cargo vessel 'Nailsea Manor' built by Bartram & Sons Ltd. of Sunderland, 54in. long. £2,500

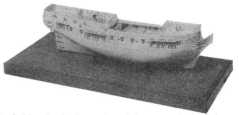

A fully planked un-rigged boxwood model of H.M.S. Circe, circa 1875, built by T. Wake, Stockwood, 5 x 17in. £1,000

A builder's mirror back half model of the single screw cargo ship 'Persistence', 15 x 49¼in. overall. £3,500

Late 19th century shipbuilder's half-block model of a Barquentine 'Sound of Jura', English, 67in. long. £1,500

A 1:100 scale model of the Le Havre Pilot Boat 'Henriette', pennant No. H2, of 1866, built by M. Deveral, Folkestone, 8 x 8in. £300

An exhibition standard 1:72 scale planked and fully rigged model of the French frigate 'La Venus' of circa 1782, built by P. M. di Gragnano, Naples, 31 x 44in. £5,000

A builder's 3/16in.:1ft. scale model of H.M.S. 'Transport Ferry No. 3016', built for the Royal Navy by R. & W. Hawthorn, Leslie & Co. Ltd., Hebburn-on-Tyne, 1945, 16 x 63½in. £3,500

A boxwood, lime and walnut model of 'H.M.S. Endeavour', made by Brian Hinchcliffe, English, modern, 30in. long. £6,000

A contemporary model of Sir Henry Segrave's record breaking power boat Miss England, length of vessel 12in., in glazed case. £400

Early 20th century shipbuilder's model of the turret deck steamer 'Duffryn Manor', English, 44in. long, in glazed mahogany case. £2,500

Late 19th century English shipbuilder's half-block model of a yacht, 24in. long. £450

A painted tinplate model of an early 4-funnel torpedo boat, by Bing, circa 1912, 16in. long. £400

A 1:100 scale model of a Trouville trawler of circa 1866, built by M. Deveral, Folkestone, 6 x 6½in. £300

Late 19th century possibly builder's model of the fully rigged model of a yawl believed to be the 'Constance' of 1885, built for C. W. Prescott-Westcar by A. Payne & Sons, Southampton and designed by Dixon Kemp, 28 x 35¾in. £4,500

A half-block model of the Coaster 'S.S. Ardnagrena', Scottish, built by G. Brown & Co., Greenock, 1908, 42in. wide. £1,200

Early 20th century model of the Clyde steamer 'Duchess of Fife' made by N. S. Forbes, 54in. long. £3,500

A 20th century model of a fully rigged
4 masted barque with planked wooden hull.
(R.K. Lucas)   £310

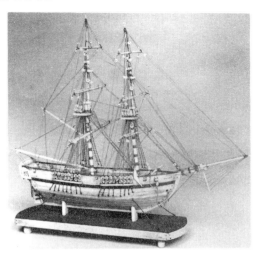

An early 19th century Prisoner of War bone
model ship, 13in. overall.
(Dreweatt Neate)   £1,150

A Carette painted tinplate steam ocean-going
steamship, the horizontal boiler with usual
fittings, single oscillating cylinder to propellor
shaft and flywheel, circa 1905, on a wooden
base, 21in. long.
(Christie's S. Ken)   £4,400

A detailed ¼in.: 1ft. scale builder's model of
the Train Ferry Steamer 'Drottning Victoria',
Trelleborg, built by Swan Hunter & Wigham
Richardson Ltd., 30 x 91in.
(Christie's)   £8,800

Chinese Export bone model of an English
frigate, 19th century, with mother-of-pearl
inlaid rosewood base, glass case, 23in. long.
(Skinner Inc.)   £5,000

Wooden ship model of the New Bedford
whaler 'Alice Mandell', well detailed, height
24in.
(Eldred's)   £1,014

A painted wood model of the topsail schooner 'Anne Marie' in 52in. glazed wood case.
(Anderson & Garland)   £420

A Bing painted tinplate clockwork twin-funnel 'American-outline' ocean liner 'Columbia', with single screw, deck fittings and detail, circa 1906, 26in. long.
(Christie's S. Ken)   £4,400

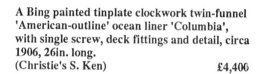

A large tinplate model of a toy torpedo battle ship, 'The Olympia', the hull made in four parts, 156cm. long, 26cm. wide, fitted with spirit fired boiler and commercially produced German engine finished in black, 20cm.
(Phillips)   £5,060

Two builders $1/4$in.: 1ft. scale models of the torpedo boat destroyers H.M.S. 'Cheerful' and H.M.S. 'Viper' built by R. & W. Hawthorn, Leslie & Co. Ltd. Engineers and Shipbuilders, Newcastle-Upon-Tyne, mounted side by side in the original mahogany table mounted bronze framed glazed case, $86 1/4$in. long.
(Christie's)   £14,300

An early 20th century model of the brig 'Marie Sophie' by L.D. Taylor, the two masted ship painted in blue and white, with standing rigging, planked deck and hatches with lift off covers, 41in. long overall.
(Spencer's)   £800

A carved and stained wood model of a 16th century three masted galleon, circa 1920, with metal sails, fully rigged and with various deck details, 46in. long overall.
(Spencer's)   £180

Mid 19th century half-block model of a clipper with carved wooden sails, 24in. long, in glazed wall case.   £450

Model of a steam-driven day yacht 'Lady Eleanor', 59½in. long, with stand below.
£700

A well detailed live steam, spirit fired, radio controlled, fully planked and framed model of the Barry Pilot Cutter 'Chimaera' of circa 1918, built by Marvon Models, Doncaster, 24½ x 47in.
£1,250

A contemporary mid 19th century model of the Paddle Steamer 'Atlanta', 18½ x 41in.
£6,000

A Bing battleship 'H.M.S. Powerful', German, circa 1912, 29in. long.   £1,200

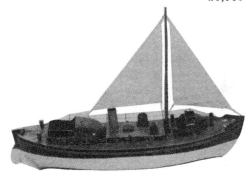

A wood and metal electric powered model of a Watson Type self-righting lifeboat, circa 1925. 24in. long, by Bassett-Lowke.   £450

A 1/8in.:1ft. scale builder's model of the single screw steam newsprint carrier 'Sarah Bowater' of London, built 1955 by Denny Bros., Dumbarton for the Bowater Paper Corporation Ltd., 12 x 52in.   £2,250

A display model of the motor tanker 'London Glory', built by Messrs. Sir James Laing & Sons Ltd., Sunderland for London & Overseas Freighters Ltd. Yard No. 793, 1952 and modelled for the builders by I. R. Amis Ltd. London, 7 x 31in.   £850

A wood waterline model of the R.M.S. Edinburgh Castle built by Bassett-Lowke, the ship 30in. long, in glazed case.   £500

Bassett Lowke three-funnel torpedo boat, circa 1920, 54in. long on stand.   £500

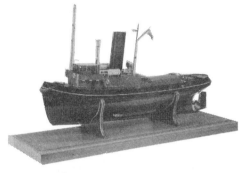

A model of the single screw tug 'Devonmoor', built by J. Gregory, Plymouth, 18 x 34in.   £1,200

Modern scale model of the barque 'Harriet McGregor', with copper-sheathed wooden hull, 26in. long.   £300

Early 20th century model gun-boat Chinese, 9½in. long, on carved wood simulated sea.   £500

Early 20th century English model of a barge with detailed fittings, 25in. long.   £650

A model of a paddle steamer 'Caledonian', English, circa 1900, 56in. long.   £650

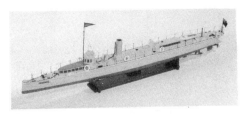

An exhibition standard ¾in.:1ft. scale model of the steam yacht 'Turbinia', as developed to 1895 and modelled by A. Broad, Bromley, 18½ x 77in.   £1,500

A 20th century American model of the clippership 'Cutty Sark', on a walnut base, fitted in a glass case.   £1,250

A contemporary early 19th century French prisoner of war bone and horn model man of war reputed to be the French ship of the line 'Redoubtable' of 74 guns, 20½ x 26¾in.   £10,000

Late 18th century prisoner-of-war carved ivory ship, with rigging and thirty-four gun ports, Europe, 13½in. long.   £1,000

A planked and rigged model of a Royal Naval Cutter built by I. H. Wilkie, Sleaford, 36 x 42in.   £450

A planked and framed fully rigged model of the Royal Naval armed brig H.M.S. 'Grasshopper' of circa 1806, built by R. Cartwright, Plymouth, 32 x 41in.   £750

Early 19th century prisoner-of-war bone model of a ship-of-the-line, 7¾in. long.   £2,750

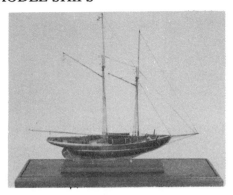

A 20th century American model of a fishing schooner, 'Kearsar', fitted in a glass case, 33½in. long.   £850

A 19th century three-masted ship model, sails furled, approx. 36in. long.   £500

A detailed ¼in.:1ft. model of a twelve gun brig of circa 1840 built to the plans of H. A. Underhill by M. J. Gebhard, Tottenham, 36 x 47in.   £3,250

A 19th century carved bone model of a frigate, probably French, 16½in. long. £2,750

An early 19th century French prisoner-of-war bone model of a ship-of-the-line, 8½in. long.   £2,500

Early 19th century prisoner-of-war bone model of a First Class ship-of-the-line, 21in. long.   £7,500

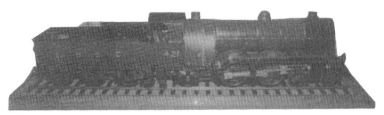

Model steam locomotive, London Brighton & South Coast, 'Atlantic' class, 4-4-2, 3½in. gauge. (H.P.S.) £2,500

Toy trains were being manufactured in France, Germany and England shortly after the introduction of the real thing, but it was to be another 50 years before they had any track to run on. Made of wood or tinplate, early examples were carpet toys designed to be pushed or pulled along.

The earliest train sets in the form we know them today were produced by Märklin in the early 1890s, when they produced impressive figure-8 layouts for clockwork trains. Their beautifully painted accessories, in the form of railway stations etc. are all highly sought after today.

Standardising scale in some way was a pressing necessity, and by the early 1900s two major gauges, 0 and 1, had been established. The larger no. 1 ran on a track 45mm wide, while the smaller 0 gauge was used for indoor displays.

In England, Wenham Bassett-Lowke, son of a Northamptonshire engineer, was determined to make near perfect scale models, and produced his famous gauge 1 Lady of the Lake in 1904. This and his first clockwork models formed a serious challenge to the German manufacturers.

The First World War brought building to a halt and had the further effect of inhibiting the hitherto fruitful cooperation between British and German firms. This proved to the advantage of Hornby, who began making model railways in the 1920s, and by the end of the decade could boast a full and comprehensive range of train sets and accessories. The value of Hornby sets often varies with their livery, Southern Railway engines, for example being quite rare. By and large this is true of all makes.

A (3-rail) electric model of the LNER 4-4-0 No. E220 special locomotive and tender No. 201 'Bramham Moor'. (Christie's S. Ken) £935

A Marklin tinplate 'Rocket' gauge 1 train set, German, circa 1909. £30,000

Hornby, 3.R.E. Princess Elizabeth and tender, boxed. £1,250

MODEL TRAINS

Model steam locomotive, London Brighton & South Coast, Brighton terrier class, 0-6-0, 5in. gauge. (H.P.S) £2,000

Rare Hornby-Dublo pre-war (3-rail) EDL7 S.R. 0-6-2 tank locomotive No. 2594, in original box, circa 1938. (Christie's S. Ken) £605

Painted and stencilled tin train, Stevens and Brown, Cromwell, Connecticut, 1868-1872, black, green and red engine inscribed *Thunderer,* engine 6in. long. (Skinner Inc.) £2,454

A rare clockwork model of the SAR 0-4-0 No. 1 tank locomotive No. 7206, in original box, circa 1926. (Christie's S. Ken) £308

A finely detailed exhibition standard 7¼in. gauge model of the GWR Class 1101 0-4-0 Dock tank Sisyphus, originally built by the Avonside Engine Company, Bristol, 19 x 38½in. (Christie's S. Ken) £6,050

Model steam locomotive, London Midland & Scottish, shunting tank engine, 0-6-0, 5in. gauge. (H.P.S) £2100

A rare (3-rail) electric model of the 0-4-0 No. LE220 locomotive No. 10655, finished in green livery with grey roof, circa 1934. (Christie's S. Ken) £1,430

315

Marklin, gauge 1, clockwork 4-4-0 locomotive and tender No. 1031. £500

Marklin for Gamages, gauge 1, clockwork 0-4-0 G.N.R. locomotive and tender No. 294. £400

Hornby pre-war gauge 0 No. 0 vans, including two milk, ventilated refrigerator, perishable, meat; two No. 2 high capacity wagons and a Bing LNWR open wagon. £300

Marklin gauge 1 (e-rail) electric model of a Continental 4-4-0 'Compound' locomotive and six-wheeled tender No. 65/13041. £300

A Stevens's model dockyard, 3¼in. gauge live-steam spirit fired brass model of an early 2-2-0 locomotive, in original box, circa 1900. £275

A Hornby pre-war gauge 0 No. 2 tank Passenger train set, in original box. £525

Hornby No. 00 train, early 1920's clockwork tin printed MR locomotive and tender No. 483, with key. £125

Bing, gauge 1, clockwork 0-4-0 locomotive and tender No. 48, (unnamed). £375

A Bing for Bassett-Lowke gauge O clockwork model of the LMS 4-4-0 'Compound' locomotive and tender No. 1053 'George the Fifth'. £150

A Bassett-Lowke gauge 0, 3-rail, electric model of the GWR 2-6-0 'Mogul' locomotive and tender No. 4331, in original paintwork. £700

A gauge 0 clockwork model of the LNER 4-4-0 No. 2 special locomotive and tender No. 201, 'The Bramham Moor', by Hornby. £700

A 4in. gauge LMS model tank engine, heavy goods type, steam driven, on oak stand. £1,300

A Hornby pre-war gauge 0 clockwork No. 2 tank goods set, in original box, and an M1 locomotive. £400

A 7¼in. gauge model of the Great Eastern Railway 0-4-0 locomotive No. 710, steel boiler with 7in. barrel and superheater, cylinders 2.1/8in. x 3¾in., driving wheels 8in. diam. £2,500

A Bing gauge 0 clockwork model of the LNER 4-6-0 locomotive and tender No. 4472, 'Flying Fox', in original paintwork. £450

An early gauge 1 (3-rail) electric (4v) model of the LNWR 4-4-0 'Compound' locomotive and tender No. 2663, 'George The Fifth', by Marklin, circa 1912. £600

DOLLS & TOYS

A Leeds Model Company clockwork model of the S.R. 0-6-0 goods locomotive and tender, in original box, circa 1933. (Christie's) £352

A Bing clockwork model of the L.S.W.R. 0-4-4 'M7' tank locomotive No. 109, circa 1909. (Christie's) £990

A very rare Hornby gauge 0 clockwork model of the Great Indian Peninsula 4-4-2 No. 2 special tank locomotive No. 2711, circa 1937. (Christie's) £462

A rare Bassett-Lowke gauge 0 (3-rail) electric model of the GWR 2-6-2 'Prairie' tank locomotive No. 6105, in original green and black livery, circa 1937. (Christie's) £935

A rake of three Darsted gauge 0 CIWL Bogie coaches (39cm), including a sleeping car, a dining car and a baggage, all in fine original paintwork, circa 1965. (Christie's) £770

A rare Marklin gauge 0 clockwork model of the 0-4-0 electric locomotive No. RS1020, in original dark green paintwork, with red and black chassis, circa 1927. (Christie's) £330

A rake of three very rare gauge 1 Central London Railway four wheel passenger coaches, inscribed 'Smoking', by Marklin circa 1903 (one coupling broken). (Christie's) £6,050

A well restored gauge 0 (3-rail) electric model of the SR 2-6-0 'Mogul' locomotive and six wheel tender No. 897, in original green livery, by Marklin for Bassett-Lowke, circa 1927. (Christie's) £770

An Exhibition Standard two-rail electric model of the L.N.W.R. Webb 0-6-2 coal tank locomotive No. 588 built by J. S. Beeson, Ringwood, 3½ x 9in. (Christie's) £2,420

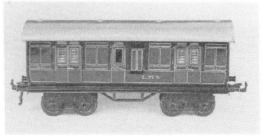

One of two Bing lithographed bogie coaches No. 62/190/0 G.W.R. passenger coach No. 3295, with tables and chairs, circa 1924, in original box. (Christie's) Two £220

A Lionel No. 700E gauge 0 (3-rail) electric model of the New York Central Railway 4-6-4 'Hudson' locomotive and tender No. 5344, in original black livery. (Christie's) £935

A Hornby (3-rail) electric (20v) model of the LMS4-6-2 locomotive and tender No. 6201 "Princess Elizabeth", in original paintwork, circa 1938. (Christie's) £770

A rake of three Hornby S.R. No. 2 passenger coaches, in original boxes, circa 1936 (boxes lids torn, one lid missing).(Christie's) £935

A rake of three Bing gauge 1 MR four wheel coaches, including two 1st/3rd coaches and a brake van, circa 1912. (Christie's) £110

A Bassett-Lowke gauge 0 (3-rail) electric model of the SR 2-6-0 'Mogul' locomotive and tender No. 866, in fine original paintwork, circa 1927. (Christie's) £715

A Hornby gauge 0 (3-rail) electric model of the SR 4-4-0 No. E420 locomotive and tender No. 900 'Eton', in original green paintwork, circa 1937. (Christie's) £605

319

A rake of three fine gauge 1 Great Western Railway twin bogie passenger coaches, by G. £400

A gauge 1 clockwork model of the London and and North Western Railway 4-6-2 'Bowen-Cooke' tank locomotive No. 2663, in black livery, by Marklin for Bassett-Lowke, circa 1913. £1,000

An early Bing 2½in. gauge II live steam spirit fired Midland Railway 4-4-0 locomotive, with a six-wheel tender and a six-wheel carriage, the locomotive 14in. long, circa 1902-06. £700

A gauge 0 clockwork model of the North Border Railway 4-4-0 pannier tank locomotive, by Bing for Bassett-Lowke, and a Bassett-Lowke clockwork mechanism. £200

A fine gauge 1 clockwork model of the London and North Western Railway 4-4-2 'Precursor Tank' locomotive No. 44, in black livery, by Bing for Bassett-Lowke, circa 1910. £475

A rake of three gauge 1 Midland Railway twin bogie passenger cars, including two first class coaches and a 3rd class brake car, by Bing for Bassett-Lowke, circa 1927. £425

Two gauge 1 Great Northern Railway, teak, 1st/3rd class twin bogie passenger cars, Nos. 2875, by Marklin, circa 1925. £300

A gauge 3 live- steam spirit-fired model of the London and South Western Railway 4-4-0 locomotive and tender, by Bing for Bassett-Lowke, circa 1904. £3,000

A contemporary mid 19th century 4½in. gauge brass model of the 2-2-2 locomotive 'Apollo' of 1844 built by Franklin & Co., Manchester, 9¾ x 14¼in. £3,500

A Marklin 3RE 20 volts 4-4-0 LMS locomotive and four wheeler tender, the first/third class carriages and brake van, Bing controller. £525

Two gauge 0 C.I.W.L. twin bogie passenger coaches, restaurant car, Ref. No. 1746/GJ1, and sleeping car, Ref. No. 1747/GJ1, by Marklin.   £150

A 3½in. gauge model of the London and North Eastern Railway Class V2 2-6-2 locomotive and tender 'Green Arrow' built by A. Ficker, Radlett, 10½ x 53in.   £1,750

A 5in. gauge model of the London and North Eastern Railway Class J39 0-6-0 locomotive and tender No. 2934, built by K. Edge, Peterborough, 13¾ x 59in.   £2,750

A Bing spirit fired 0-4-0 LNWR locomotive and tender No. 1942 with separated lamps and a Bing gauge 1 signal.   £350

A gauge 1 (3-rail) electric model of a Continental 4-4-0 locomotive and tender, by Bing, circa 1910.   £400

A gauge 0 (3-rail) electric model of the 0-4-0 locomotive, Ref. No. RF66/12920, by Marklin.   £300

A 7¼in. gauge model of the Hunslet 0-4-0 contractor's locomotive designed by M. R. Harrison and modelled by J. Maxted, Ramsgate, measurements overall 33½ x 98in.   £3,000

'Juliet', a 3½in. gauge live steam coal fired 0-4-0 tank locomotive, together with a trailer, 20in. long overall.   £300

A gauge 1 London and North Western Railway twin bogie 3rd class brake car, by Bing for Bassett-Lowke, circa 1922.   £175

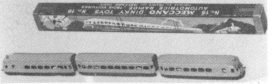

Pre-war French Factory 16Z diesel streamlined train by Dinky.   £400

A 7¼in. gauge model of the Great Western Railway Armstrong Class 4-4-0 locomotive and tender No. 8 'Gooch', built by T. Childs, Churchill, 20¼ x 88in. £7,500

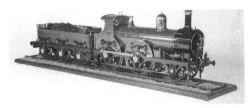

An exhibition standard 5in. gauge model of the Great Western Railway River Class 2-4-0 locomotive and tender No. 69 'Avon' as running in 1906, built from builder's drawings and photographs by R. W. Gale, Newport, 14¼ x 53¼in. £8,000

A well engineered 3½in. gauge model of the Great Western Railway County class 4-6-0 locomotive and tender No. 1022 'County of Northampton', 10 x 47in. £2,000

A 3½in. gauge model of the British Railways Class 7 4-6-2 locomotive and tender No. 70013 'Oliver Cromwell, built by H. C. Luckhurst, Oxley, 10¼ x 52½in. £2,500

A 5in. gauge model of the London Midland and Scottish Railway Class 2F 0-6-0 side tank locomotive No. 11270, 13 x 27½in. £2,250

A 7¼in. gauge model of the London Midland and Scottish Railway Class 2F 0-6-0 side tank locomotive No. 11270, built by C. Ottaway, Chippenham, 18½ x 41in. £5,000

A 3½in. gauge model of the Southern Railway 0-4-2 side tank locomotive No. 2036, built to the designs of Juliet by M. Darlow, 1972 — 10 x 21in. £500

A Hornby gauge 0 (3-rail) electric model of the No. 1 LNER 0-4-0 special locomotive and tender, original paintwork, (loco in original box). £350

322

A well engineered 2½in. gauge model of the London Midland and Scottish Railway 4-4-0 locomotive and tender No. 1000, built to the designs of Eagle by G. Ward, 8 x 31in.

£500

An exhibition standard 5in. gauge model of the Great Northern Railway Stirling Single 4-2-2 locomotive and tender No. 53, built from works drawings and photographs by J. S. Richardson, Halifax, 14 x 56in.

£6,000

A finely detailed 7mm. finescale two rail electric model of the Deutche Bundesbahn 144 Bo Bo class electric outline locomotive No. E44070 built by Hego Modellbahn for the Nuremburg Toy Fair, 1976, 4 x 13½in.

£600

A mid 19th century live steam spirit fired 4¾in. gauge brass model of the 2-2-2 locomotive and tender 'Express', built by Steven's Model Dock-yard, 11¾ x 30in.

£2,250

A fine Marklin gauge 1 clockwork model of the LB & SCR 4-4-2 'Atlantic' tank locomotive No. 22, in original paintwork, with lamps, circa 1920 (1 loose bogie).

£2,250

A gauge 1 (3-rail) electric model of the G.N.R. 0-4-0 side tank locomotive No. 112, in original paintwork by Bing for Bassett-Lowke (lacks 3 buffers).

£350

An exhibition standard 5in. gauge model of the Great Western Railway Armstrong Class 4-4-0 locomotive and tender No. 14, 'Charles Saunders', built by P. J. Rich, Rhiwderin, 14 x 62in.

£12,000

A fine contemporary late 19th century 3¼in. gauge brass and steel spirit fired model 4-2-0 locomotive and tender, built by H. J. Wood, London, 8½ x 21½in.

£750

DOLLS & TOYS

A spirit fired 4-4-0 locomotive and 8 wheeled bogie tender, finished in black with red and gold detailing, circa 1909, slight chipping.
(Phillips)   £3,400

A Märklin hand-painted bogie Midland Railway family saloon, with opening roof, detailed interior, opening doors and seated figures, circa 1907.
(Christie's S. Ken)   £1,265

A clockwork 4-4-0 Paris-Lyon Mediterranee painted tinplate 'windcutter' locomotive and 6 wheeled tender CV 1022, finished in dark green with gold and red banding and lining, circa 1905.
(Phillips)   £4,200

A 3-rail electric 20v 4-8-2 ME locomotive and 8 wheeler tender finished in pale green, dark green and red.
(Phillips)   £3,600

Hornby control system: lever frame and 'Windsor' signal cabin, in original boxes, with adjustable No. 2 20in. control rail, two control points and nine rod guide brackets, circa 1925.
(Christie's S. Ken)   £385

A Hornby Series 'Palethorpes' sausage van, in original box, circa 1939.
(Christie's S. Ken)   £418

A 3-rail electric 4-4-2 NBR locomotive and tender No. CE 6513021, finished in brown with red, yellow and black lining, excellent condition, tender sticky.
(Phillips)   £1,600

A 3-rail electric, 20v, 4-6-2 HS pantograph locomotive, finished in brown with orange lining and black roof, slight retouching.
(Phillips)   £3,400

A spirit fired NBR 4-4-2 locomotive and 6 wheeled tender No. 4021, finished in brown with red, yellow and black lining.
(Phillips)   £1,500

DOLLS & TOYS

A rare Hornby Series E120 Special Electric FCS Argentinian tank locomotive, in lake, red and gold livery, circa 1938.
(Christie's S. Ken) £660

A well detailed 7in. gauge static display model of Stephenson's 'Rocket' of 1829, 22 x 31³/₄in.
(Christie's S. Ken) £1,980

A rare Märklin-bodied Bassett-Lowke clockwork Great Western 'King George V' and matching six wheel tender, circa 1936.
(Christie's S. Ken) £1,870

A rare Hornby Series FCS Argentinian refrigerator van, with open axle-guards, early hinged doors and handles, in original box with Argentinian label, circa 1927.
(Christie's S. Ken) £528

A Märklin hand painted and stamped station newspaper kiosk, with four-gable roof, pay windows, clocks and relief work, circa 1910, 5in. high.
(Christie's S. Ken) £2,860

A Hornby Series 'Crawford's' biscuit van with opening doors and white roof, in original box, circa 1927.
(Christie's S. Ken) £440

A 3-rail electric 0-4-4-0 steeple cab PO-E1 locomotive, with forward and reverse lever, finished in green with pale green and black detail, gold window frames, black roof.
(Phillips) £1,000

An extremely fine mid-19th century 5¹/₂in. gauge spirit-fired model of the Sheffield to Rotherham Railway Stephenson 2-4-0 locomotive and tender No. 45 'Albert', signed *Alfred Chadburn Maker 1855*, 14³/₄ x 36in.
(Christie's S. Ken) £13,200

A 3-rail electric, 20v, 4-0-4 Gotthard type locomotive No. S 64/13021, with forward and reverse action, finished in brown with orange lining.
(Phillips) £2,400

DOLLS & TOYS

Early Hornby gauge 0 rolling stock, including a 'Carr's Biscuits' van and an LNER Gunpowder van, circa 1924. (Christie's) £264

A well engineered and presented 3½in. gauge model of the Heisler 0-4-0 plus 0-4-0 geared logging locomotive No. 5, built by P. Higgins, Renhold, 10 x 28½in. (Christie's S. Ken) £1,870

An exhibition standard 5in. gauge model of the LMS (ex L & Y) 2-4-2 side tank locomotive No. 10637, built to the designs of Don Young by Major F. R. Pearce, West Byfleet, 14 x 39¼in. (Christie's S. Ken) £3,520

A well engineered and presented 3½in. gauge model of the Japanese Climax 0-4-0 plus 0-4-0 geared logging locomotive No. 3, built by P. Higgins, Renhold, 10½ x 28in. (Christie's S. Ken) £2,090

Hornby book of trains 1927-1939 (three incomplete. (Christie's S. Ken.) £825

A live steam spirit fired model of the L.N.E.R. Class A4 4-6-2 locomotive and tender No. 4468 'Mallard', by Aster for Fulgurex, 5 x 28in. (Christie's) £3,300

A rare early Hornby gauge 0 clockwork model of the LNWR 0-4-0 No. 00 locomotive and tender No. 2663 'George the Fifth', circa 1924. (Christie's) £990

A well detailed and finished model of an unusual L.M.S. (ex L.N.E.R.) twin bogie 3rd driving/trailer coach of circa 1901, 3½ x 15in. (Christie's) £220

The L.M.S. Class 5XP 4-6-0 locomotive and tender No. 5500 'Patriot' built by P. Hammond and painted by L. Richards, 3¾ x 17½in. (Christie's)   £1,210

A rare Marklin electric model of the G.W.R. 4-6-2 'Pacific' locomotive and bogie tender, circa 1909. (Christie's)   £3,850

5in. gauge live steam 0-6-0 tank locomotive in British Rail black livery No. 1505. (Hobbs & Chambers)   £850

A Hornby (3-rail) electric model of the LMS 4-6-2 locomotive and tender No. 6201 "Princess Elizabeth", in original paintwork, circa 1937. (Christie's)   £990

A Hornby clockwork L.M.S. 'No. 1 Tank Good Set', comprising an 0-4-0 tank locomotive, a 'Shell Motor Spirit', an open wagon, a brake van and a circle of track, in original box, circa 1926. (Christie's)   £209

Wells clockwork 'Mickey Mouse Circus Train', comprising an 0-4 0 A4 locomotive No. 2509 'Silver Link', a tender with Mickey Mouse and a lithographed 'Circus Dining Car', circa 1948, (Christie's)   £880

A well detailed two-rail electric model of the G.W.R. 48XX Class 0 4-2 side tank locomotive No. 4837 and auto coach No. 187 built by B. Miller, 3¾ x 25¾in. (Christie's)   £5,500

A rare Marklin Jubilee Set No. AR12930/35/3, comprising a 'Planet' locomotive and tender, a stage type coach and an open carriage, all in original paintwork, circa 1935. (Christie's)   £3,850

Set No. 1771RW, gauge 0 No. 1681 Hudson type locomotive 2-6-4, 8-wheel 1936 version tender and three pullmans, American Flyer Lines.   £550

A gauge 1 Bing locomotive 4-4-0 with 6-wheel tender, circa 1915.   £1,250

A Hornby O gauge 'Bramham Moor' 4-4-0 clockwork locomotive and tender, finished in LNER apple green, with brass nameplate to each side, circa 1925.   £425

A Voltamp gauge 2 trolley No. 2123, 0-4-4-0, circa 1913.   £2,500

Carette green locomotive, 2-2-0, 4-wheel tender, alcohol burner, together with an olive 4-wheel baggage car, circa 1905.   £750

A Hornby O gauge 4-4-2 electric locomotive 'Lord Nelson', finished in Southern region, together with an SR tender, circa 1900.
£300

A 7¼in. gauge model of the North Eastern Railway Class G5 0-4-4 side tank locomotive No. 505, built by D. W. Horsfall, Northowram, 20½ x 52½in.   £2,250

A 5in. gauge model of the Great Western Railway 57XX Class 0-6-0 pannier tank locomotive No. 5702, built by C. G. Balding, Bideford, 13½ x 34in.   £1,850

A 3½in. gauge live-steam 2-4-0 locomotive, 27½in. long, circa 1880's.   £1,450

Hornby gauge O clockwork 4-4-0 locomotive 'Bramham Moor', No. 20, with six-wheeled tender.   £300

A 'Washington Special', No. 385E locomotive with tender and cars, circa 1934.   £1,750

A 2½in. gauge live-steam coal-fired engineered model of a 2-6-2 Pannier Tank locomotive, 24in. long, modern.   £1,800

A gauge 1 (3-rail) electric model of the Great Northern Railway 4-4-2 'Atlantic' locomotive and tender No. 1442, by Bing for Bassett-Lowke.   £750

A Bassett-Lowke gauge O electric 'Flying Scotsman', English, circa 1935, finished in British Railways Caledonian blue and black lined cream.   £600

An exhibition standard 5in. gauge model of the British Railways Duke-dog Class 4-4-0 locomotive and tender No. 9014, built by I. P. Watson, 14 x 60in.   £6,000

A late 19th century 3¾in. gauge spirit fired brass model of the Great Northern Railway Stirling 2-4-0 locomotive and tender No. 152, built by H. J. Wood, London, 10¼ x 35in.   £1,500

A rake of four gauge 1 Great Northern Railway teak passenger carriages, all by Marklin, circa 1925.   £400

A Marklin gauge 1 tinplate bogie Kaiserwagen, German, circa 1901, 11in. long.   £700

A Stevens & Brown painted tin train, 'Thunderer' black and red engine, green tender and two yellow passenger cars, America, 1870's, engine 7in. long.   £2,500

Hornby gauge O clockwork 4-4-2 tank locomotive, No. 2221, finished in G.W.R. green and black lined gold.   £100

The L.M.S. Streamlined Pacific 4-6-2 locomotive and tender No. 6220 'Coronation' built by Duchess Models, 3¾ x 20¾in. (Christie's) £1,100

A rare Hornby gauge 0 clockwork model of the DSB 4-4-2 No. 2 special tank locomotive No. 3596, in original maroon livery, circa 1934. (Christie's) £385

A well engineered and presented 3½in. gauge model of the Shay 0-4-0 plus 0-4-0 geared logging locomotive No. 2 built by P. Higgins, Renhold, 11 x 27½in. (Christie's S. Ken) £2,310

A Bing 'Miniature Table Railway', a lithographed tinplate railway set, comprising a L.M.S. 2-4-0 locomotive and tender, circa 1925. (Christie's) £385

The L.M.S. 'Jinty' 0-6-0 side tank locomotive No. 7469 built by Duchess Models and painted in L.M.S. black livery by L. Richards, 3½ x 8½in. (Christie's) £605

A Bassett-Lowke remodelled gauge 0 (3-rail) electric model of the LNER 4-6-2 'Pacific' class locomotive and tender No. 4472 'Flying Scotsman', circa 1937. (Christie's) £264

A rare Marklin electric model of the Paris-Orleans Railway E.1. electric locomotive, with glass windows, circa 1919. (Christie's) £660

A gauge '0' three rail electric model of the B.R. Class 7P 4-6-2 locomotive and tender No. 70004 'William Shakespeare', by Bassett-Lowke, 3¾ x 19½in. (Christie's)

£2,200

A rare gauge 0 (3-rail) electric model of the SBB CFF 'Re 4/4' No. 427 diesel electric locomotive, by H. and A. Gahler, Switzerland, circa 1947. (Christie's)

£605

A (3-rail) electric 'Coronation Scot' train set, comprising the L.M.S. 4-6-2 class HP streamlined 'Pacific' locomotive and tender, by Trix Twin Railways, circa 1937. (Christie's)

£1,210

A rare Bing gauge 1 live steam, spirit fired model of a German 4-6-2 Pacific Class locomotive and twin-bogie, finished in original black livery, circa 1927. (Christie's) £1,870

A Bassett-Lowke gauge 0 clockwork BR Goods Set, including a 4-4-0 'Compound' locomotive and tender No. 62453 'Prince Charles', in original display box, with instructions, circa 1960. (Christie's)

£286

An early and rare Marklin M.R. 1st class bogie coach, with opening roof and side doors, circa 1904. (Christie's) £605

'Hamburg Flyer' a Marklin (3-rail) electric model of the two-car diesel unit Ref. No. T.W.12970, with operating front and rear lights, circa 1937. (Christie's) £605

A 7¼in. gauge model of the Great Western Railway 15XX Class 0-6-0 Pannier tank locomotive No. 1500, rebuilt by F. West, Lee Green, 21 x 55in. **£6,000**

A gauge 0 (3-rail) electric model of a Continental 4-6-2 'Pacific' locomotive and twin bogie tender, Ref. No. HR64/13020, by Marklin, circa 1930. **£1,750**

A gauge 0 live steam spirit-fired model of the S.E.C.R. steam railcar, by Carette, circa 1908. **£1,250**

A 3½in. gauge model of the 4-4-0 locomotive and tender No. 573 built to the designs of 'Virginia', 11½ x 45in. **£1,100**

A collection of the Great Western Railway coaching stock including the twin bogie full brake No. 188, the six wheel full brake No. 95 and the four wheel horsebox No. 88, painted by L. Goddard. **£350**

A 7mm. finescale two rail electric model of the London Midland and Scottish Railway Class 7P 4-6-2 locomotive and tender No. 6231 'Duchess of Athol' as built in 1938, the model by D. Jenkinson and painted by L. Goddard, 3¾ x 20½in. **£850**

A 7¼in. gauge model of the Great Western Railway 4-6-0 locomotive and tender No. 1011 'County of Chester' rebuilt and reboiled by F. West, 21¾ x 10in. **£12,500**

A gauge 0 (3-rail) electric model of a Continental Doll BLS electric engine, with overhead pantograph, by Bing, circa 1930. **£300**

A 5in. model of the London and North Eastern Railway Class A3 4-6-2 locomotive and tender No. 2568 'Sceptre' built by K. Edge, 1975, 15 x 75in. **£3,500**

An exhibition standard 5in. gauge model of the William Dean diagram 21 Brake Composite twin bogie passenger coach No. 3391 of 1897, 13 x 57in. **£2,250**

DOLLS & TOYS

A detailed exhibition standard 5in. gauge model of the British Railways Class 7 4-6-2 locomotive and tender No. 70000 'Britannia', 14 x 76in. **£7,000**

A 7mm. finescale two rail electric model of the London Brighton and South Coast Railway Stroudley Class D1 0-4-2 side tank locomotive No. 351, built by B. Miller, 3¾ x 8¾in. **£525**

A 5in. gauge model of the Great Western Railway 4-6-0 locomotive and tender No. 6011 'King James I' built by K. Edge, 15 x 73in. **£6,000**

A 5in. gauge model of the Great Northern Railway Stirling Single 4-2-2 locomotive and tender No. 9 built by H. Bannister, Burton-on-Trent, 15 x 58in. **£3,500**

A 3½in. gauge model of the London and North Eastern Railway Class B1 4-6-0 locomotive and tender No. 8301 'Springbok' built by T. Dyche, York, 10¼ x 47in. **£2,500**

A 5in. gauge model of the London Midland and Scottish Railway re-built Scot Class 4-6-0 locomotive and tender No. 6154 'The Hussar' built by K. Edge, Peterborough, 15½ x 70in. **£3,500**

A 5in. gauge model of the Great Western Railway 0-6-0 Pannier tank locomotive No. 9716 built to the designs of Pansy, 13½ x 34in. **£1,750**

A 7mm. finescale two rail electric model of the British Railways (ex L.M.S.) 0-6-0 'Jinty' side tank locomotive No. 47469, built by M. H. C. Models, Bolton, 3½ x 8½in. **£550**

A gauge 0 clockwork model of the London Midland and Scottish Railway 4-4-0 locomotive and six-wheel tender No. 5320 'George V', by Bing for Bassett-Lowke. **£200**

An exhibition standard 5in. gauge model of the Great Western Railway Dean Single 4-2-2 locomotive and tender No. 3012 'Great Western', 14 x 61in. **£7,500**

No. 5 thin rim locomotive lettered 'B & O R.R.', circa 1907.   £1,700

Marklin 4-4-0 live steam spirit-fired gauge 'one' locomotive, German, circa 1915.   £425

Exhibition standard 4mm. scale electric model of the Metropolitan Railway tank locomotive No. 106, 6½in. long.   £500

A gauge 1 clockwork model of the Great Northern Railway 2-4-0 side tank locomotive, by Marklin. £525

A gauge 1 clockwork model of an 0-4-0 Peckett saddle tank locomotive No. 204, by Carette for Bassett-Lowke.   £400

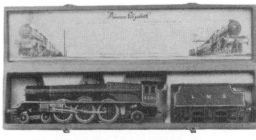

A (3-rail) electric model of the LMS 4-6-2 locomotive and tender No. 6201 'Princess Elizabeth', in the original maroon paintwork, circa 1937. (Christie's S. Ken)   £1,760

A 3½in. gauge copper and brass spirit fired 2-4-0 locomotive, No. 715, English, circa 1880's, 17¼in. long. £1,250

A gauge 1 clockwork model of the London Tilbury and Southend Railway 4-4-2 side tank locomtovie No. 10 'Grays'.   £750

A Bassett-Lowke gauge O clockwork
0-4-4 tank locomotive, 'Shallow Horse',
No. 109.   £600

A 3½in. gauge model of the old
Canterbury & Whitstable Railway
'Invicta',   £550

A 6½in. gauge 1¼in. scale electrified display
model of the Glasgow and Garnkirk Railway
Robert Stephenson 'Four Coupled Planet'
0-4-0 locomotive and tender of 1831, 15 x
36in.   £2,250

Late 19th century boxed Marklin wind-up
train set, sold by F.A.O. Schwartz, New
                          £1,500

One of two Marklin gauge '1' tinplate passenger coaches, hand-painted, German, circa
1902.   £1,400

A 7mm. finescale two-rail electric
model of the London and North
Eastern Railway 'Coffee Pot' 0-4-0
saddle tank locomotive No. 7230.
                          £500

A gauge 1 clockwork model of an
0-4-0 Peckett saddle tank locomotive
No. 810, by Carette for Bassett-Lowke.
                          £400

A 5in. gauge model of the Great Western
Railway 'Metro' 2-4-0 side tank locomotive.
                          £1,750

An exhibition standard 2in. scale model of the Clayton Undertype Articulated wagon, built by E. W. D. Sheppard.   £1,750

Early 20th century miniature Eskimo model of dogsled and team, wooden sled, and four rabbit skin covered papier mache dogs, sled 12.3/8in. long.   £400

An early 20th century wood model of the 1860 horse-drawn goods wagon owned by Carter Paterson & Co, London and Suburban Express Carriers, 17in. long. £400

Marklin for Gamages, a spirit fired portable horizontal overtype steam engine, with single cylinder driving governer, circa 1910 (worn), 27cm. long.
(Christie's S. Ken)   £638

An unusual Marklin pond, circa 1900, the circular base moulded and painted to resemble a grassy slope with footpath to enclosed "stone" pond with boat and cupola at centre, 16in. wide.
(Christie's)   £968

'Caravan Novelty', a lithographed tinplate gypsy caravan, by Chad Valley for Jacobs, circa 1937, 6¼in. long.
(Christie's)   £165

Marx, Armoured Floating Tank Transporter, boxed.   £60

A Bing clockwork threshing machine, circa 1905.   £800

A gauge 1 signals gantry, with four signals, oil fired lamps and ladders on both sides, by Bing, circa 1910, 21in. high.   £600

An exhibition standard $\frac{1}{8}$ in. scale model of an Oxfordshire wagon, circa 1830, built from plans drawn from the original wagon by John Thompson, 8½ x 32½in.
(Christie's S. Ken)   £264

A finely engineered model twin cylinder compound undertype stationary steam engine built to the designs of A. H. Greenly, by P. C. Kidner, London, 14½ x 24½in.
(Christie's)   £1,500

An approx. 4in. scale Foden type twin cylinder overtype two speed steam lorry, built by A. Groves, Watford, 1937 and restored by M. Williams at the British Engineerium, Hove, 1983, 36½ x 88in.   £6,000

A 3in. scale model Foden 'C' type twin cylinder steam lorry entitled 'Patricia', measuring 6ft long and 2ft 5in. wide.
(Hobbs & Chambers)   £3,100

A Louis Marx tinplate 'Main St.' Tramway, the loop track with overhead power pylons with trams and trucks moving between station and terminal, 24in. long.   £125

A Punch and Judy toy theatre booth, the interior with painted landscape back drop, and four composition head puppets, theatre 16in. high.
(Phillips)   £420

A fine early doll and cie ferris wheel ride, entirely hand-painted, consisting of six swinging gondolas, each with two passengers, 13½in. high.
(Christie's)   £2,299

An exhibition standard 3in. scale model of the Savage horse-drawn Electric Light Engine No. 357, built by C. J. Goulding, Newport, 27 x 47in. (Christie's)   £2,800

A rare set of lithographed tinplate petrol pumps, with oil cupboard opening to insert battery, advertising "Pratt's", "BP" and "Shell", by Tipp & Co., circa 1935, 9½in. wide. (Christie's)   £825

MONEY BANKS

Modern type money boxes began to appear in Europe in the 17th century and in the 18th, Staffordshire pottery money banks in the form of cottages were popular. 19th century Prattware examples also fetch good sums.

It was the 19th century that saw the manufacture of money boxes designed especially for children. Understandably, these had to be of a tougher material than pottery, and the first were of cast iron. Often, these were in the shape of animal or human heads, open mouthed to receive the coins, or of figures and buildings with slits in the top.

In comparison with the United States or even Europe, British versions were fairly unimaginative. Few mechanical versions were produced (though find one by John Harper & Co. and it could be worth a considerable amount).

It is however American money boxes which fetch the highest prices today. During the last 30 years of the 19th century such firms as Shephard Hardware and J & E Stevens of Cromwell, CT produced cast iron banks in such forms as acrobats, bucking broncos, and Punch & Judy. Most were mechanical, some operated simply by the weight of the coin, while others had a lever or catch action. The Jolly Nigger was a favourite example, and when a coin was placed on the tongue the eyes would roll. This 'Sambo' type was copied in the UK, though usually as a 'still bank' with no mechanical action.

There have been many more modern replicas of Sambo and his female counterpart Dinah, some of which have been aged to increase their value.

'I always did 'spise a mule' mechanical bank, by J. & E. Stevens, patented 1879, 8in. high. £350

American cast iron money bank, 'Hall's Lilliput Bank'. (Phillips) £280

A William Tell cast iron money bank, 1896, the figure firing coins placed on his crossbow into a slot above a boy's head, 10½in. £600

A 'Jolly Nigger' mechanical money bank, in the form of a negro wearing a top hat, 21.5cm. high. (Phillips) £75

'World's Fair' cast iron mechanical bank, J. & E. Stevens, Co., pat. 1893, 8¼in. long. £750

'Tammany Bank', a cast iron mechanical bank, the seated gentleman with articulated right arm, 5¾in. high, by J. and E. Stevens Co., circa 1875. £150

American late 19th century Paddy and the Pig cast iron mechanical bank, 8in. high. £750

Late 19th century American cast-iron leap frog mechanical bank, by Shephard Hardware Co., 7½in. wide. £500

Late 19th century American cast-iron 'Santa Claus' mechanical bank, 6in. high. £750

Pussycat chromium cast money bank, with key, circa 1935. (Auction Team Koeln) £21

Stevens cast-iron Indian and Bear mechanical bank, Conn., circa 1875, 10.9/16in. long. £1,000

'Stollwerck Bros. Post Savings-Bank', modelled as a chocolate dispenser, circa 1911, 6½in. high. £250

A tinplate monkey mechanical bank, German, circa 1930, 6½in. high. £400

Late 19th century cast iron 'Speaking Dog' mechanical bank, by J. & E. Stevens Co., 7¼in. long. £1,000

Stump Speaker, a cast iron mechanical moneybox, with movable right arm and unusual counterbalanced talking mouth, pat. June 8 1886, 25cm. high. (Christie's S. Ken) £880

DOLLS & TOYS

A cast iron 'Eagle and Eaglets' mechanical bank, by J. & E. Stevens, patented 1883, 6¾in. long. £400

'Chief Big Moon' cast iron mechanical bank, J. & E. Stevens, Co., pat. 1899, 10in. long. £1,000

Organ and Monkey mechanical bank, patented 1882, 7¼in. high. £350

Jolly Nigger bank, with movable right arm, in original paintwork, by Shepard Hardware Co., Buffalo, N.Y., circa 1883, 7in. high. (Christie's S. Ken) £187

Late 19th century cast iron owl money bank. £150

'Trick Dog', a mechanical cast-iron moneybox, by J. & E. Stevens, circa 1888, 8¾ x 3in. £500

Plated clockwork Bulldog Savings Bank by Ives Blakes-lee & Co. 18cm. high. (Auktionsverket, Stockholm) £613

Wooden Jug savings bank, with key, circa 1920. (Auction Team Koeln) £12

A mechanical cast iron money box, as a football player with articulated right leg, causing the player to shoot a coin into a goal and ring a bell, circa 1890, 10½in. long. £850

DOLLS & TOYS

German 7.11/16in. Symphonion musical savings bank, 17½in. high, circa 1905.
£2,750

A J & E Stevens painted cast iron 'Creedmoor Bank', designed by James Bowen, marksman firing at target, 6½in. high.
(Christie's S. Ken) £220

Late 19th century English cast-iron 'Giant in the Tower' mechanical bank, 9¼in. high. £2,750

Black and gold Jep tin money bank, in the form of an old safe with combination lock, French, circa 1920. (Auction Team Koeln) £43

A cast iron novelty bank, by J. & E. Stevens Co., the building with front door opening to reveal a cashier, American, late 19th century.
£350

Late 19th century American cast-iron 'Punch & Judy' mechanical bank, by Shepard Hardware Co., 7½in. high. £750

A cast iron money bank of a golly, 15.5cm. high.
£125

'Bull Dog Bank' cast iron mechanical bank, J. & E. Stevens, Co., pat. 1880, 7½in. high. £600

A German lithographed tinplate money box, with lever action eyes and extending tongue, 1920's, 7½in. high.
(Christie's S. Ken.) £330

'Transvaal Moneybox', a mechanical cast-iron money box of Paul Kruger.   £200

Late 19th century American cast-iron 'Trick Pony' mechanical bank, by Shepard Hardware Co., 7in. wide.   £600

Late 19th century cast-iron Hall's Excelsior bank, American, 5¼in. high.   £400

A 20th century Kenton cast iron flatiron building bank, America, 8¼in. high.   £250

A cast iron 'Always Did 'Spise a Mule' money bank, American, circa 1897, by J. Stevens & Co., 10in. long.   £1,000

Late 19th century American 'Uncle Sam' mechanical bank, by Shepard Hardware Co., 11½in. high.   £350

Late 19th century cast iron clown mechanical bank, 9½in. high.   £600

Lion and Monkeys cast iron mechanical bank, Kyser & Rex Co., Pat. 1883, 10in. long.   £450

A 20th century English cast-iron 'Dinah' mechanical bank, by John Harper & Co. Ltd., 6½in. high.   £150

DOLLS & TOYS

'Bad Accident' cast iron mechanical bank, J. & E. Stevens, Co., 1891-1911, 10.3/8in. long. £850

American late 19th century 'Artillery Bank' cast-iron mechanical bank, 8in. long. £350

Late 19th century American reclining 'Chinaman' cast-iron mechanical bank, 8in. long. £1,500

A cast iron two frogs mechanical bank, American, late 19th century, 8½in. long. £650

An amusing savings bank in the form of a typewriter. (Auction Team Koeln) £15

Early 20th century English 'Hoopla' cast-iron money bank, 8½in. long, by John Harper & Co. £450

A mechanical bank, girl skipping rope by J. & E. Stevens, designed by James H. Bowen, 8in. high. (Christie's) £13,602

A mechanical bank, a horse race, with flanged base, by J. & E. Stevens, designed by John D. Hall, 8in. high. (Christie's) £6,505

Late 19th century American cast-iron 'Negro and Shack' money bank, 4¼in. long. £400

DOLLS & TOYS

A Pratt money box modelled as a chapel, inscribed Samuel Townsend 1848, 17cm. £500

An unusual tin 'Combination Safe' money box. £30

A Prattware cottage money box in the form of a two-storeyed house with blue tiled roof, 12.5cm. high. £450

An unusual wind-up drummer boy money box, 6in. high. £60

Oliver Hardy money box, late 1950's. £20

One of a pair of German electroplated Britannia metal 'porker' money boxes, 13.7cm. long. £350

A money box modelled as a chapel, inscribed Salley Harper Hougate March 16th 1845, 6¾in. high. £500

Red and black painted tin money box in the shape of a 'pillar box', circa 1930, 6½in. high. £50

Jgeha money box clock by Buerer Spar, in enamelled case. £125

A tinplate toy gramophone, printed 'Made in Germany', 1930's, 8¼in. long.   £75

Thorens Excelda cameraphone, ultra portable gramophone in the form of a folding camera with Excelda No. 17 sound pick up, crank and arm, circa 1932.
(Auction Team Koln)   £268

Luxus Necessaire-Etui with music box and dancing couple, melody 'Tales from the Vienna Woods', couple retract on closure, circa 1920.
(Auction Team Koln)   £107

A Monopol 7½in. disc musical box formed as a child's pull along car with original red paintwork, 20in. long, with six discs.   £600

An Amourette organette in the form of a chalet, with seventeen discs, 14in. wide, the discs 9in.
(Christie's)   £495

An early Kammer & Reinhardt 5in. Berliner Gramophone, with three Berliner records.
(Phillips)   £1,300

A small Victorian musical box, the top decorated with children playing, 6 x 4in. £60

20th century 'Jiving Jigger' musical drum, 4in. diam. £50

A Tanzbaer automatic accordion with trigger-operated twenty-eight key mechanism, in grained wood casing, with fourteen rolls. (Christie's) £1,870

Portable gramophone by Peter Pan now much sought after by collectors, circa 1920. £200

A Triola mechanical zither with 25-note roll mechanism and twenty-four hand-played strings, on ebonized base. (Christie's S. Ken) £2,200

A German printed tinplate musical cathedral, printed marks DRGM, Made in Germany, 17.5cm. high. £100

NOAH'S ARKS

Noah's Arks were particularly popular in the 19th century, when, in pious households, because of their Biblical associations they were the only toy when children were allowed to play with on Sundays. They had the further advantage that they could be made by anyone reasonably handy with wood, and in fact very few appear to have been made commercially by actual companies. The vast majority came from Bavaria, an area with a particularly strong wood-carving tradition. They were also made in Sweden and the USA.

Arks can vary hugely in size and content, from 12" long and containing 15 pairs of animals, to double that length with 100 pairs of animals. They usually took the form of a house, often painted to represented two storeys, resting on a boat. The roof or walls could slide off to hold the animals.

Among the arks that appear now for sale, many animals and birds are, inevitably, missing or damaged. The paintwork on the ark itself is often faded or worn, but should on no account be restored. Those decorated with inlaid wood or straw work are particularly sought after.

A large carved wood Noah's Ark, with twenty-two pairs of carved wood animals and two members of the Noah family, German, probably Erzegebirge, circa 1880. (Christie's S. Ken)   £660

A painted wood Noah's Ark, Erzegebirge, Germany, circa 1870, 23¾in. long, approximately 205 animals.
                                                                £1,000

A painted wood Noah's Ark, the flat bottom vessel with twenty-three pairs of animals, three others, six members of the Noah family, German, probably Erzegebirge, late 19th century, 12¾in. long. (Christie's S. Ken)   £385

An Edwardian painted wooden model of a Noah's Ark, containing approx. 120 painted carved wooden animals, 56cm. long. £800

A painted wood Noah's Ark on wheels, with opening roof, door and windows, German, circa 1890, 31in. long.   £300

A coloured straw-work Noah's Ark, with sliding panel and a quantity of painted wooden animals including Noah's family, insects, deer and a peacock, 13in. long, (some damages). (Christie's)   £935

A painted wooden Noah's Ark, decorated with columns and a printed paper frieze, with sliding side containing over two hundred animals and eight figures, including moles, grasshoppers, rabbits, flies, monkeys, camels, dogs, cats and anteaters, 27in. wide, Sonneberg, 19th century. (Christie's)   £6,600

'Joey the Clown and his dog Spot',
by P. A. Purton.   £8

'See-Saw Margery Daw', Jigsaw Picture Book.   £5

'Sewing Pictures' 1940's.   £5

'Dean's Home Stencil Book, No. 1', by Dean &
Son, 1930's.   £8

'If I could only get the door down, I should
see them all for nothing'.   £30

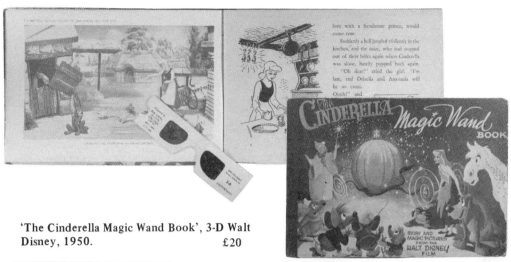

'The Cinderella Magic Wand Book', 3-D Walt
Disney, 1950.   £20

'My First Jig-Puz Book', Five Jigsaws.   'Dan Dare's 'Anastasia' Jet Plane', by Wallis Rigby.   £35
£40

'The Big Book Of Shops', fold-over book, 1930's.
£35

OPTICAL TOYS

The Victorians were fascinated by photography and viewing instruments, as the host of optical toys dating from the period bears witness. They have wonderful names, such as graphoscope, mutoscope, stereoscope, and enchanted adults and children alike. Perhaps most fun of all is the zoescope, or 'wheel of life' in which figures on the inside of a rotating cylinder are made visible through slots, providing an illusion of animated motion. The forerunner, in fact of modern cinematography.

A Magic Disc phenakisticope optical toy with 8 discs, each 7in. diam., a viewing disc, 9in. diam., and a Fantascope disc, 5in. diam. £600

A pressed and pierced metal magic lantern with fluted chimney and lens, 11¹/₂in. high. (Christie's S. Ken) £154

A 19th century box stereoscope, the case decorated with flowers on a black ground. (Michael Newman) £360

The 'Improved Phantasmagoria Lantern, by Carpenter & Westley, with patent argand solar lamp with a quantity of lantern slides. (Christie's) £220

Rosewood stereo viewer, table top, manufactured by Alex. Becker, N.Y., circa 1859. £350

A mohagany-body bi-unial magic lantern with a pair of two-draw brass bound lenses each with rack and pinion focusing, all in a fitted combined container. (Christie's S. Ken) £1,980

British projection lantern for max 19 x 19cm. slides, having wood and brass Petzval type optics with gear drive and red filter equipped for 21cm. diam. condensor, original gas burner. (Auction Team Köln) £227

A mahogany body table Achromatic Stereoscope by Smith, Beck and Beck, with a pair of focusing eyepieces and original mirror. (Christie's S. Ken) £495

A metal bodied Flickergraph optical toy with viewing lens, handle and one reel, printed paper labels *For use with the Animated Pictorial.*
(Christie's S. Ken)   £352

A burr walnut Brewster pattern stereoscope with rack and pinion focusing, shaped lens hood mounted on hinged lens section. (Christie's S. Ken)   £198

A moulded black-plastic body OTHEO Stereo Viewer x5 with red illuminant button and a pair of focusing eyepieces by Ernst Leitz Canada Ltd., in maker's fitted box.
(Christie's S. Ken)   £605

A Brewster-pattern hand-held stereoscope with Japanese lacquer-work decoration depicting flying storks and trees. (Christie's S. Ken.)   £440

A mahogany and brass-fitted biunial magic lantern with a wood-mounted snow effect mechanical slide with printed label *E.H. Wilkie*, in a fitted wooden box.
(Christie's S. Ken)   £990

A mahogany sliding box camera obscura front section with lens and turned wood lens cap, body stamped By His Majestys Special Appointment. Jones, (Artist.) London.
(Christie's S. Ken)   £418

Gaumont, Paris, a 45 x 107mm. mahogany bodied table stereoscope with internal mechanism and slide holders. (Christie's S. Ken)   £352

A 20 x 14cm. Polyrama Panoptique viewer with diced-green paper covered body, brass fittings, and black leather bellows with thirteen day and night views.
(Christie's S. Ken)   £660

A mahogany-body pedestal Scott's Patent Stereoscope with rack and pinion focusing eyepiece section, with plaque *Negretti & Zambra.*
(Christie's S. Ken)   £605

Rowsell's parlour grapho-scope, folding table model, base 23 x 12in., circa 1875.
£175

A London Stereoscopic Co. Brewster-pattern stereoscope with brass mounted eye pieces, in fitted rosewood box, 13in. wide. (Christie's) £380

A Fantascope optical toy comp-rising a fitted mahogany box with drawer containing fifteen picture discs. (Christie's) £4,950

A metal-body upright magic lantern type 720 by Ernst Planck, Germany, with gilt-metal decoration lens, chimney and illuminant.
(Christie's S. Ken) £220

A twelve inch diameter black painted Zoetrope and a quan-tity of picture strips each with a printed title and *'Entered at Stationer's Hall'*.
(Christie's S. Ken) £308

A 'The Designoscope' kaleido-scopic toy, contained in maker's original box bearing the legend *The Designoscope. An endless source of artistic pleasure.* (Christie's S. Ken)
£50

Negretti and Zambra, a mahogany stereoscope with focusing section, hinged top lid and hinged rear reflector.
(Christie's) £935

Ernst Planck, Germany, a hot-air powered Praxinoscope comprising a removable spirit burner, condens-ing pistons and 6in. diameter prax-inoscope drum with three picture strips.
(Christie's) £3,850

A 7in. diam. 'Spin-E-Ma' zoe-trope with three picture strips each labelled *Kay. Made in England. Copyright.* (Christie's S. Ken) £242

A wood and brass magic lantern with brass bound lens and chimney with a slide holder and a small quantity of slides in wood box. £200

A mahogany-body Kinora viewer with inlaid-wood decoration and a picture reel no. 273 showing a white polar bear. (Christie's S. Ken) £665

A Le Praxinoscope optical toy with shade and ten picture strips, by Emile Reynaud, drum with seller's label. £175

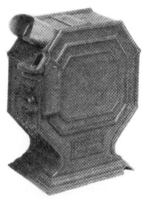

A burr walnut pedestal stereo-scope with focusing eye-pieces and internal mechanism. (Christie's) £352

An Ive's Kromskop colour stereoscopic viewer, in wood carrying case. £750

A mutoscope in cast iron octagonal shaped case, electrically lit, 22in. high. £750

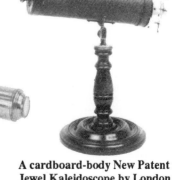

A 12-inch diameter black metal drum zoetrope mounted on a turned mahogany stand with 7½ inch diameter friction-drive wheel with handle. (Christie's S. Ken) £825

An upright cylinder lantern with red and gilt decoration on barrel with chimney by Ernst Planck, Nuremberg. (Christie's) £605

A cardboard-body New Patent Jewel Kaleidoscope by London Stereoscopic Co., with brown morocco-leather finish, and ball-socket mounting section. (Christie's S. Ken) £880

An Austin A40 pedal car complete with operative electric headlamps, circa 1950. £500

Post war tinplate pedal car 'Austin Devon' with battery operated headlamps, 60in. long.   £400

A Richardson and Allwin painted wood and metal model Bullnose Morris pedal car, with folding hood, measuring 3ft 9in. long. (Hobbs & Chambers)   £4,000

Rare child-sized model of the Austin Seven racing car.   £1,000

An early Lines Bros. pedal car, the wooden body painted suede grey with sprung chassis, 39in. long.   £750

A painted metal model of an Austin J40 Roadster pedal car, 64in. long, British, circa 1950.   £850

Volkswagon 'Beetle' cabriolet with fibre glass white body, 5 h.p. Briggs & Straton engine, 6ft.6in. long.   £1,250

A 1930's Lines Bros. pedal car with wooden body and chassis, mock honeycomb radiator grill, and pneumatic tyres 47in. long. (Andrew Hartley)   £775

'ABC in Living Models', Bookano, 1930's. £35

'The Story of Jesus', Bookano, 1938. £15

'Prince Albert Driving His Favourites'. £20

'Album Victorianum'. £25

'Bookano Stories', 1940's.   £35

'Hans Andersen's Fairy Stories', Bookano. £35   'Into Space with Ace Brave!', 1950's. £15

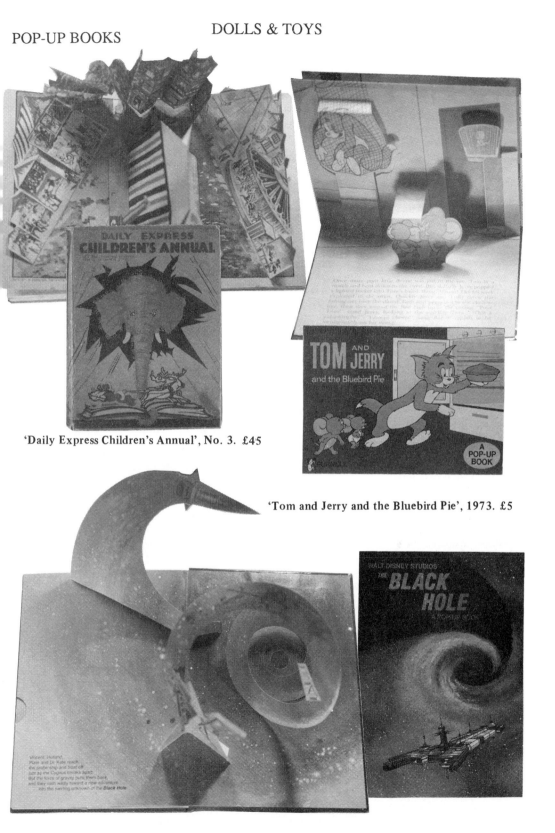

'Daily Express Children's Annual', No. 3. £45

'Tom and Jerry and the Bluebird Pie', 1973. £5

'The Black Hole', Walt Disney Studios, 1979. £8

PRAMS

The earliest known baby carriage in Britain was made in 1730 (for the children of the 3rd Duke of Devonshire), and designed to be pulled along by a small animal. The first of the baby carriages manufactured for public use was made in 1840. This was a three wheeled version with iron tyres and it still had to be pulled along. About the mid 19th century, a handle was fitted to the back so that the pram could be pushed and this version was called the perambulator. The three wheeled perambulator remained in popular use until about 1880 when it was displaced by the new four wheeled bassinette. The early four wheeled prams were, at first, categorised by the authorities as road vehicles but as they became more popular, this was rescinded.

The pram has always been something of a status symbol and the early prams were no exception. They were coachbuilt with bodies made of wood, sometimes of leather, and dressed with fittings of brass. They were lavishly trimmed and the interiors were often upholstered in soft skins or leatherette.

An early safety feature perhaps worth noting is the pram fitted with two handles, one at each end. This was not merely a fashionable 'extra' but a necessity for the safe-keeping of the infants who were trundled around the treacherous roads of the early perambulating days. Pavements were either very narrow or non existent and traffic regulations for coaches and carriages still a bit sketchy, which made turning a pram for the return journey, a hazardous business. With a handle fitted at both ends, the prampusher only had to pass alongside the pram to reverse direction in safety.

A beechwood child's perambulator, with gilt metal fittings, painted dark green, upholstered in American cloth, 52in. long, circa 1880. (Christie's S. Ken) £550

Painted and decorated baby carriage, America, 19th/20th century, painted light green and heightened with red and black pinstriping. (Skinner Inc.) £212

A baby carriage with maker's name plate attached, A. Mitchell, Margate, height to hood 31in. (Worsfolds) £320

An interesting Victorian child's horsedrawn carriage, the wicker seat lined with buttoned leatherette cushions, 150cm. long. (Henry Spencer) £1,700

A fine Landau baby carriage, circa 1870, by S. H. Kimball, Boston, Mass, featuring a turned push bar, 40in. long. (Christie's) £3,025

The 'London' baby coach with wooden body and fabric cover. £75

1950's doll's pram with tin body and fabric hood.   £45

A metal bodied Leeway pram with plastic interior.   £65

1950's Royal' pram with plywood body.   £60

Wooden bodied doll's pram with vinyl interior and fabric hood.   £55

Doll's pram with scroll and lattice wicker-work body, 30in. long.   £85

Tri-ang doll's pram with metal body and plastic and fabric hood, 1960's.   £35

Country style oak framed back to back twin pram with brass hubs.   £300

A rare Bassinett two-handled double pram with painted leather body, circa 1860. £350

A large 1960's Silver Cross pram with metal body and fabric and leatherette upholstery.   £50

Silver Cross 1930's twin hood doll's pram with metal and wood body and leatherette and fabric hood.   £75

1930's Pedigree pram by A. J. Dale & Son, Warminster.   £75

Tan-Sad wartime Cot-Kar pram, No. 3214, with wooden body and leatherette hood.   £100

1930's simulated leather doll's pram with folding hood and brake.   £50

1930's Stella doll's pram with plywood body, leatherette hood and umbrella holder.   £60

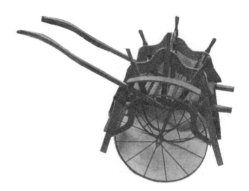

An early Star Manufacturing Co. round-head pram with leather trim and porcelain handle.   £300

Country style 'mail cart' push-chair with iron wheels.   £150

Victorian wicker and wooden doll's carriage with scrolled framework, circa 1880, 34in. long.   £300

A rare T. Trotmans patent 1854 folding pram with carpet back seating and wood and brass wheels.   £450

Wooden 'mail cart' pram with carved sides, leather hood and brass trim.   £350

Victorian wooden baby carriage, circa 1880, with slatted sides, 53in. long.
£300

1930's German wickerwork pram with alloy wheel arches and bumpers.   £100

A wicker and bentwood baby carriage, labelled Whitney, raised on wooden wheels, America, circa 1895, 55in. long.   £300

Victorian doll's wicker carriage, 29in. long, circa 1890, in good condition.   £275

1920's Acme pram with wooden body and 'C' springs, reg. no. 465485.   £125

Miniature cloth bear on wheels, circa 1900, 5 x 3in., with glass button eyes. £150

A 19th century circus wagon, 28in. overall, wagon 16 x 7½in. £150

Late 19th/early 20th century painted walking gait wooden horse toy, America, mounted on an iron frame, 28in. long. £600

A 19th century carved and painted wood horse pull toy, mounted on wooden base with wheels, 11in. high. £400

A skin covered horse on wheels with leather saddle and bridle, 16in. high, circa 1890. (Christie's) £300

Late 19th century hide covered horse pull toy, Germany, horse 24in. long, height on platform 27in. £500

Early 20th century goatskin goat pull toy, baa's when head is pressed down, Germany, 16½in. high. £600

An M. J. tinplate pull-along train, French, circa 1905, 11in. wide. £240

A wooden pull-along horse, the painted dapple body with carved features, metal stud eyes and leather cloth saddle, 18in. high. (Phillips) £220

A Bugatti Child's car, by Westwood, gas powered by single cylinder.
(Christie's)   £5,517

An Alfa Romeo P2, by CIJ of France, circa 1926.   £600

A printed tinplate clockwork model of Sir M. Campbell's land speed record car 'Bluebird', circa 1930, 10¾in. long.   £250

A Marklin tinplate clockwork constructor racing car, 1935, red, No. 7.   £375

Britains Bluebird, in original box.   £200

A Bing hand-enamelled early two-seater Benz racing car, with steerable front wheels, German, circa 1904, 11¼in. long.   £10,000

A Meccano racing constructor car with clockwork mechanism driving the rear axle, circa 1935, 11¾in. long.   £425

A J.E.P. tinplate P.2 Alfa Romeo racing car, French, circa 1930, 20½in. long.   £375

"Swift", a printed and painted tinplate single seater racing car, with clockwork mechanism, adjustable front tinplate wheels, by Seidel, circa 1928 (slightly rusted at front), 11in. long. (Christie's)   £165

A Meccano No. 2 Car Constructor Outfit, assembled as a racing car with clockwork mechanism driving rear axle, (slightly worn, rear wheels loose) circa 1935. (Christie's)   £528

A constructor Racing Car, probably French, with battery operated remote control, 29cm. long.   £175

Gunthermann, Gordon Bennett clockwork racing car, finished in yellow with gold detail, 28cm. long.   £4,500

Scamold clockwork die-cast Grand Prix racing car, in original box.   £200

A Meccano No. 1 Motor Car Constructor Outfit, assembled as a Grand Prix racing car, with clockwork mechanism, circa 1934, (Christie's)   £352

German clockwork racing car with original tyres.   £125

An early Mettoy wind-up racing car.   £125

DOLLS & TOYS

French Alfa-Romeo P2 clockwork tinplate racing car, circa 1935, 20½in. long.   £800

A Meccano motor car Constructor, no.2, assembled as a Grand Prix racing car, circa 1934. (Lawrence Fine Arts)   £715

A large cast aluminium desk top display model of 1000 HP Sunbeam Record Car of 1927 (World Speed Record of 203 m.p.h. at Daytona Beach 1927), 71cm. (Phillips)   £3,000

A finely detailed hallmarked sterling silver model of the Alfa Romeo Monza FYE 7 of 1933, by Theo Fennell, London, 1988, 42oz., 9½in. (Christie's Monaco)   £6,499

A 1/10th scale cast aluminium model of the Alfa Romeo Type 158 Racing Car, finished in red and silver, 40cm. long, with original box. (Onslow's)   £3,100

A Marklin Constructor Car, assembled as a Mercedes W125 Grand Prix racing car, with clockwork mechanism, German, circa 1934 (lacks mudguard, instrument panel and some nuts and bolts), 14½in. long. (Christie's)   £715

A Kingsbury Sunbeam racer, tinplate clockwork model complete with driver, steering wheel and original box. (David Lay)   £550

Sir Malcolm Campbell's Bluebird, a clock-work tinplate toy by Kingsbury, repainted, 18in. long. (Onslow's)   £220

A red aluminium 1/10 scale model Lancia
F1 D50 by Michele Conti with leather
upholstery, one of four made in 1955
specially for Gianni Lancia.
(Finarte)   £8,036

A Dinky DY-1 1968 E Type Jaguar, this is
the prototype of the first Dinky model
produced commercially by Matchbox Toys
Limited in November 1968, 10.3cm.
(Phillips)   £340

Carlo Brianza, an extremely fine and detailed
1:10 scale model of a 1976 Ferrari 512BB
constructed in brass and aluminium, presented
on a wooden plinth and enclosed in a case,
21in. long.
(Christie's New York)   £5,720

1936/7 Auto Union C Type Model, length
24in., the 1936 and 1937 V-16 6.1-litre,
520 b.h.p., C Type Auto Union was one
of the world's most powerful and spectac-
ular Grand Prix cars.
(Christie's New York)   £28,600

239 Vanwall Racing Car, No. 35, boxed.
(Phillips)   £110

C.I.J., clockwork P2 Alfa Romeo racing car,
early version, finished in green with shock
absorbers, drum brakes, and treaded tyres,
circa 1927, 52cm.
(Phillips)   £1,800

An early Structo constructional two seater racing
car, with hand cranked clockwork mechanism,
USA, circa 1910, marked 'Iwafame', 9½in. long.
(Christie's S. Ken)   £308

An American clockwork tinplate streamlined
record car finished in red with driver, 46cm.
(Phillips)   £862

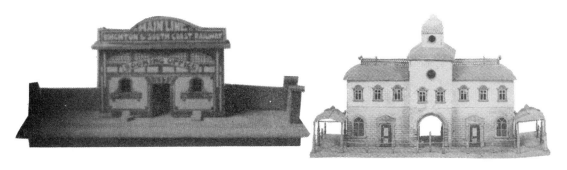

1930's wooden Booking Office for the Main Line station of the Brighton and South Coast Railway. £75

An early and rare gauge 1 hand enamelled tinplate mainline railway station, by Bing, circa 1908, 25½ x 9¼in. (Christie's)
£1,650

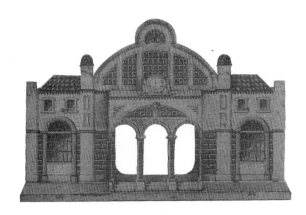

A lithographed tinplate station by Bing, circa 1910, 33.5cm. long. (Christie's) £330

An early Marklin gauge 1 mainline station, hand-enamelled, fitted for candle lighting, circa 1903. £750

A No. 2-E Engine Shed (lacks light fittings). (Christie's S. Ken) £308

An early Marklin station 'Harrogate', the painted tinplate building with opening doors and painted adverts, circa 1902, 40in. wide. (Christie's) £1,650

DOLLS & TOYS

'Bahnhof' country station with entrance foyer, ticket collectors foyer, waiting rooms under a removable simulated tiled roof, 48cm. long.
(Phillips)   £500

Two No. 116 Ives Union Stations, together with platform cover, circa 1928.   £1,500

A printed tinplate station, by **Carette**, circa 1912.   £250

A Marklin gauge 1 railway station, circa 1925, 53cm. long.
(Christie's)   £2,860

A Marklin hand painted tinplate Central Station, circa 1904.   £12,000

'Central-Bahnhof', an early Marklin railway station, with central arch and platform canopy, ticket office and waiting room, circa 1901. (Christie's)   £2,860

A fine Marklin tinplate Leipzig two storey station for gauge 1, circa 1930, with lithographed brickwork, roof tiles and cobbled courtyard, hand painted details including ticket hall, doors, water fountain and clock tower with paper clock face and metal hands, glazed windows with electric interior lighting.   (Sotheby's)   £9,900

A magnificent Marklin hand painted 'Gare Centrale' major railway station, gauge one, circa 1910, finished in varying shades of tan as simulated stone, with a green base and roof, the two storey building features an outside workable clock, twin arched passageways, ticket, baggage and waiting room areas inside, glass windows, telegraph transmitting roof wiring and two beige glass lamps hanging on the trackside, 18½in. x 34in. x 20½in. (Christie's)   £12,100

3in. scale model of Aveling & Porter steam road roller, by Bishop-Ellis, Birmingham, with boiler test certificate, 4ft. 6in. long. (Peter Wilson) £4,200

A 3in. scale model of a Wallis & Stevens 'Simplicity' Road Roller, built by D. G. Edwards, 1980, 24¾ x 35in. £1,250

A well engineered 2in. scale model of an Aveling and Porter twin crank compound two speed, four shaft Road Roller, 19½ x 35in. £3,500

3in. scale model of a Wallis & Stevens 'Simplicity' road roller, 35½in. long. (Peter Wilson) £1,250

An Exhibition Standard 2in. scale model of the Wallis & Stevens 'Advance' Road Roller, built by S. Jackson. (Christie's S. Ken) £4,000

A well engineered 3in. scale model of a Wallis and Stevens Simplicity road roller built by J.M. Gregory, Winchester, 25½ x 35in. (Christie's S. Ken) £3,190

ROBOTS

Robots are defined as machines capable of carrying out some human activities, and toy versions became immensely popular in the 1950s and 60s. Indeed, the toymakers of the time were producing examples which were in many cases more sophisticated than their scientific equivalents, and the whole concept was infused with a terrific mystique, further enhanced by such contemporary films as The War of the Worlds.

Battery operated, robots can be made of such various materials as plastic, tin, rubber or cloth. The most famous (and, to date, most valuable) is Robbie the Robot, based on the film The Forbidden Planet, who could walk, rotate his antennae and had pistons which moved up and down in his head.

Most early robots were made in Japan. They are now also produced in Macao and Hong Kong, and find their readiest market in the USA.

Value is often related to size – the larger the better, and to the number of movements they can carry out. Tin robots are more highly regarded than plastic versions. Association with a successful television series or film also adds cachet.

Early 1960's silver blue plastic robot with red flashing eyes and three different sonic sounds.
£75

Horikawa: Rotate-o-Matic Super Giant Robot, with automatic action, swing open door, blinking and shooting gun, in original box. (Christie's S. Ken)
£99

'Last in Space Robot', 1970 American, plastic battery operated robot.   £100

K9, scratchbuilt to a high standard, with battery operation causing his eyes to light up giving him an intelligent countenance. (Bonhams)   £220

Marx, electric robot and son, finished in grey, gold and maroon, 43.5cm. high. (Phillips West Two)   £200

A Yonezawa friction drive tinplate 'Talking Robot' with battery operated speech mechanism, retailed by Cragstan, in original box, circa 1960's (Christie's S. Ken)   £418

A Horikawa battery operated tinplate 'Fighting Robot', with transparent plastic chest cover, 1960's.
(Christie's S. Ken)   £200

'Space Explorer', Hong Kong plastic battery operated 1960's robot. £35

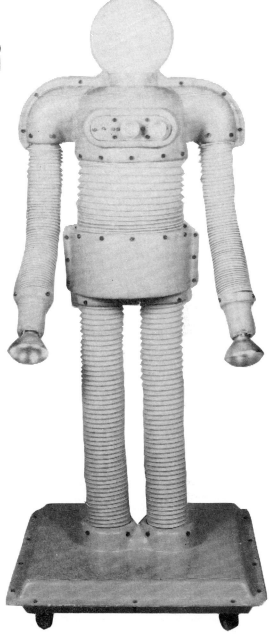

A coin operated Dalek kiddies ride, the six foot Dalek has a seat inside for the passenger, who enjoys a ride with backward, forward and sidewards movement, and can operate the Dalek controls. This model dates from around 1964 and is among forty believed to have been made by Edwin Hall & Co., London. The electric operation, and some of the exterior, is in need of attention.
(Bonhams) £550

'Rudolph', a robot light fitting designed by Frank Clewett, the orange fibreglass torso with rectangular central panel, the head formed by spherical glass shade, the adjustable arms with light bulbs forming the hands, the grey plastic concertina legs on square base with castors, 149cm. high.
(Christie's) £935

Television Spaceman, battery operated, moveable arms and legs, rotating eyes, screen in chest revealing a space scene, by Alps, Japanese, 1950's, 38.5cm. high.   £550

Planet Robot, battery operated with remote control, rotating antenna on top, with box, by Yoshiya, Japanese, 1950's, 23cm. high.   £550

High Wheel Robot, clockwork mechanism, moveable legs, with visible rotating wheels, sparks in chest, with box, by Yoshiya (mk. 4), Japanese, 1960's, 25cm. high.   £450

Gear Robot, battery operated, moveable legs with coloured wheel rotating chest and flashing head, possibly by Horikawa, Japanese, 1960's, 22.5cm. high.   £350

Busy Cart Robot, battery operated, pushing and lifting a wheelbarrow, with box, by Horikawa (mk. 6), Japanese, 1960's/1970's, 30cm. high.   £675

Ultraman, clockwork mechanism, moveable arms and legs, with box, by Bullmark (mk. 5), Japanese, 1960's, 23cm. high.   £200

Attacking Martian, battery operated, moveable legs, chest opens to reveal flashing guns, with box, by Horikawa (mk. 6), Japanese, 1960's, 23cm. high.   £575

Sparky Robot, clockwork mechanism, moveable legs and sparking eyes, with box, by Yoshiya, Japanese, 1950's, 19.5cm. high.   £325

Answer-Game, battery operated immobile, executes simple mathematics, flashing eyes, by Ichida (mk. 3), Japanese, 1960's, 35.5cm. high.   £1,350

Sparky Jim, battery operated with remote control, moveable legs and flashing eyes, Japanese, 1950's, 19.5cm. high. £700

Nando, the mechanism activated by air pressure through remote control, moveable legs and head, with box, by Opset, Italian, circa 1948, 13cm. high. £1,250

Astoman, clockwork mechanism, moveable arms and legs, by Nomura (mk. 1), Japanese, 1960's, 23.5cm. high. £600

Dyno Robot, battery operated, moveable legs, opening mask to reveal a flashing red dinosaur's head, with box, by Horikawa, Japanese, 1960's, 28.5cm. high. £450

Giant Robot, battery operated, moveable legs, chest opening to reveal flashing gun, possibly by Horikawa, Japanese, 1960's, 41cm. high. £650

Space Explorer, battery operated box transforms into Robot, revealing '3-D' television screen, with box, by Yonezawa (mk. 2), Japanese, 1960's, 29.5cm. high. £1,350

Talking Robot, battery powered, mobile, speaks four different messages, with box, by Yonezawa (mk. 2), Japanese, 1950's, 28cm. high. £850

Mr. Robot, clockwork mechanism and battery activated, with box, by Alps, Japanese, 1950's, 20cm. high. £900

Confectionery Dispenser, battery operated, with coinslot, transparent chest showing sweets, Italian, late 1960's, 139cm. high. £1,250

1960's Japanese flying saucer with robot operator.   £30

A Dalek, scratchbuilt to a high standard and realistically modelled and finished in grey and black, with battery operated eyes and internal controls for single person operation. (Bonhams)   £9,000

Japanese tinplate clockwork Sparking Robot finished in bright colours, with transparent chest and sparks, boxed, 15.5cm. (Phillips)   £45

A fine and rare 1960's Jupiter Robot the Space Explorer by Yonezawa of painted tinplate with battery operated mechanism, complete with box. (Christie's)   £3,000

Marx, electric robot and son, finished in black, red and silver, 43.5cm. high. (Phillips West Two) £160

'Dux-Astroman', No. 150, a plastic robot, with battery operated remote control, by Dux, W. Germany, 1950's, 12in. high. (Christie's) £176

Alps-Shoji, battery operated Robot Television Spaceman, 38cm. including aeriel, in working order. (Phillips) £170

'Planet Robot', 1960's Japanese plastic. £100

An unusual silver Horikawa Attacking Martian robot, in original box. (Christie's S. Ken) £385

'Astronaut', Japanese 1960, battery operated robot. £100

A Nomura painted tinplate 'Battery Operated Mechanised Robot' ("Robbie the Robot"), with black body, red arms and feet, circa 1956, 13in. high. (Christie's S. Ken) £1,375

Ko-Yoshiya, Japanese tinplate clockwork Planet Robot finished in black and red, with sparking face in colour picture box, 22cm. high. (Phillips) £220

A Yonezawa for Cragstan battery-operated tinplate 'Mr Robot', same body pressing as 'Talking Robot', 1960's. (Christie's S. Ken) £286

The earliest rocking horses had a boat shaped structure, consisting of two parallel semicircular panels held vertically by a small wooden seat between them.

By the late 17th century horses with free standing legs on a panel attached to bow-shaped rockers had become popular. These were now accoutred with saddles and bridles and had a prancing rather than galloping stance. Gallopers came in around a century later, beautifully and realistically carved. Dapple grey was the favoured shade. Earlier gallopers tended to be narrow, with irregular spots and steep bow rockers. Later, however, they became broader with more regular dapples and shallower rockers.

It was probably for safety reasons that the trestle base was developed in the 1880s. Legs were now attached to a pair of boards which swung on metal brackets mounted at the ends of a trestle base.

The first commercial makers of rocking horses were probably those who made fairground gallopers, wooden saddle trees etc. It was thus that G & J Lines began in the middle of the 19th century. Other notable manufacturers were the Liverpool Toy Industry, Woodrow & Co. of London, and Norton & Baker of Birmingham.

The points to look for when buying an old rocking horse are a well-carved, lively head, original paintwork and trappings, and a luxuriant mane and tail of real horsehair. Superficial damage indicative of a well loved, well used toy, is not necessarily prejudicial to the value. Look out in particular for three footed horses on trestles, which are very sought after.

Painted rocking horse, America, late 19th century, painted white with dapple grey spots having applied horse hair tail, 54½in. high. (Skinner Inc.)   £1,419

Hide covered rocking horse, attributed to Whitney Reed Corporation, Leominster, Massachusetts, 19th century, covered with dapple-brown hide, 43in. high. (Skinner Inc.)   £2,945

A carved and painted rocking horse with hair mane and tail, America, circa 1880, 52in. long.   £850

A large dappled rocking horse, on metal hinged rockers, 51½in. high.   £600

Small carousel stander, mounted as a rocking horse, circa 1900. 27in. high, 29in. long. (Robt. W. Skinner. Inc.)   £892

A 20th century wooden rocking horse, painted black, leather bridle and saddle and mounted on a boat-shaped rocker base, 6ft.7in. long.   £400

A Victorian carved wooden rocking horse. £600

A carved and painted wooden rocking horse, probably English, circa 1720, 24½in. long. £400

Painted wooden hobby horse, New England, early 19th century, painted dapple grey with green saddle and heart-shaped supports, 51in. wide. (Skinner Inc.) £650

A late nineteenth century painted wood and composition rocking horse, with jockey rider, 10½in. long, German. (Christie's) £715

A carved and painted rocking horse with horsehair mane and tail, glass eyes and leather bridle and saddle, America, circa 1880, 72in. long. £2,000

A 19th century carved wooden rocking horse, painted piebald with leather bridle, material covered saddle and grey horsehair tail, 7½ hands high. £1,500

A painted wood dapple grey 'pony size' rocking horse, with horse hair mane and tail, 56in. long, British. £450

A child's painted wooden rocking horse, probably Mass., with leather upholstered seat, 31in. high. £800

A painted wooden dapple grey rocking horse, on swing stand, 44in. long, by Lines Bros. (Christie's S. Ken) £715

SAMPLERS

Samplers, from the French exemplaire, were originally a record of embroidery patterns which could then be copied. The earliest dated one is English, made in 1586 and worked by Jane Bostock. Early examples are rare, for they were made only by the leisured upper classes. By the mid 1700s, however, sampler work was spreading to all classes. By this time too, the original function of the sampler changed to become more and more an apprentice piece for young girls, where they could practise and display the various stitches they could execute.

During the 18th and 19th centuries, most schools and orphanages set girls to stitch samplers as part of their general education. These could be of two types, plain sewing samplers, or embroidered examples, featuring the alphabet and numbers,.

Most embroidered samplers consist of one or two simple alphabets enclosed in a narrow border, and are usually done on coarse woollen tammy, or sometimes linen. 18th and 19th century samplers often included a moralising text or some pictorial content.

The great charm of the sampler is its intensely personal nature. It becomes to some extent a window through which we can glimpse these bygone times and the young sewer bent laboriously over her work. One is not buying just a piece of cloth, but hours, months, sometimes even years of a person's time and devotion. By and large, the earlier the sampler, the more money it will fetch, condition, intricacy and all else being equal. The USA is a particularly rich source of samplers, and it is generally early American examples which fetch the largest sums

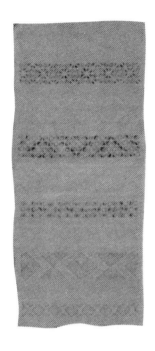

A 17th century whitework sampler, bearing the inscription *The fear of God is an Excellent Gift,* 44 x 20cm. (Phillips West Two)   £650

A 17th century needlework sampler, probably by Mary Tratt of Boston, 7½ x 22¾in.   £2,500

A sampler by ME, 1678, worked in coloured silks, with a central wreath surrounding the letters, 15 x 11in. probably Dutch, 17th century. (Christie's) £1,265

A fine spot motif sampler, the ivory linen ground with geometric samples, circa 1630.   £3,000

A long sampler worked in blue, purple, pink, yellow and green, by Mary Phippard 1685, 39 x 9½in., English 1685. (Christie's) £1,980

A mid 17th century unfinished linen sampler with six bands of reticella work, depicting strawberries and acorns, 90 x 13cm., English. (Phillips) £950

A 17th century needlwork sampler by Anna Stone, the linen ground worked in pink, green and blue silk threads, 41 x 19cm. £850

A 17th century whitework sampler, designed with bands of reticella of floral design, 45 x 23cm. (Phillips West Two) £800

A late 17th century needle-work sampler, embroidered in silks, 36 x 14cm. £400

Spot motif sampler with geometric panels in a variety of stitches, circa 1630. £2,000

Needlework sampler "Polley
Woodbery her sampler A 14
1787 Essex, Massachusetts',
10½ x 8in. (Robt. W. Skinner
Inc.) £397

A late 18th century
needlework sampler
by Jane Spurling,
1796, 16 x 12in.
£350

A sampler by Ann Ariss, 1756,
worked in coloured silks with
a central hexagonal border
framing the Lord's Prayer,
15 x 12in. (Christie's) £242

Needlework sampler, *Rachel
McClure, New York, 1760*,
worked with silk threads in
shades of blue, green, yellow and
brown, 16 x 14in.
(Skinner Inc.) £2,194

An early 18th century needlework sampler by Hephzibah
Tillsey finisht in the eleventh
year of my age in the year
1728, 51cm. x 37cm.
(Phillips) £600

A late 18th century Dutch
needlework sampler by
Maria Cornelia van der Bilde
Oude 10 Iaar 1784, 46cm.
x 44.5cm., lined. (Phillips)
£240

Needlework sampler, silk
yarns worked on ivory linen
ground fabric, by 'Harriatt
Shoveller, 1799', England,
12½ x 17in. £1,750

Needlework sampler, 'Betsey
Stevens, her sampler wrought
in 10th year of her age AD
1796', silk yarns on linen,
15 x 16in. £2,000

Needlework spot sampler,
Germany, 1759, vivid
polychrome silk yarns on
natural linen fabric, 12 x
21½in. £2,750

Late 18th century Spanish needlework sampler with silk embroidered stylised floral and geometric designs, 15½ x 18½in. £400

Needlework sampler, worked by *Elisabeth Lyon, aged 14 years 1791 New Haven,* Connecticut, 17¾ x 20¾in. (Skinner Inc.) £2,515

A needlework sampler worked in coloured silks with the alphabet by Mary Barne, February 26 1785, 16¾ x 11½in. (Christie's) £440

A late 18th century needlework sampler, designed with tulips, bluebells and animals around two verses of a poem, 34 x 32cm. (Phillips West Two) £320

A mid-18th century needlework sampler by Ann Clowes, the linen ground embroidered in autumnal coloured silks designed with a verse, 45 x 32cm. (Phillips) £700

A late 18th century darning sampler, by Maria Jesup 1799, the linen ground embroidered in mainly red, green and ochre silks, 45 x 42cm. (Phillips) £850

Late 18th century needlework sampler, worked in silk yarns of gold, light blue, red, brown, ivory and black on natural linen, 7 x 10½in. £3,500

Late 18th century English sampler, depicting a house, figure of a Major Domo, trees, flowers, and more, 11in. x 13in. (Eldred's) £232

Needlework sampler *Betsey Sergent's Sampler,* Stockbridge, Massachusetts, dated *September 28, 1788,* (faded) 12 x 7¾in. (Skinner Inc.) £839

Mid 18th century Boston School, Adam & Eve sampler, 6¾ x 11½in. £7,500

An 18th century silk embroidered sampler, Europe, 20 x 35in. £7,000

An embroidered band sampler by Elizabeth Woodworth, 1758. £1,000

A needlework sampler "Betsy Davis's sampler wrought at eight years of age, Providence October 22 1794", Balch School, Providence, Rhode Island, 11¾ x 8in. (Robt. W. Skinner Inc.) £965

Late 18th century framed needlework sampler, by Charlotte Richardson 13 years, Dec. 1786, American, 17 x 20in. £1,500

A Perpetual Almanack sampler, by Ellen Stackhouse, 1781, Walton School, with a naturalistic pot of flowers and scrolling motifs worked beneath in coloured silks, 16 x 11in. (Christie's S. Ken) £330

A sampler, 'Adam & Eve', by Mary Simpson Chamberlin, circa 1775, 10½ x 13¾in. £3,500

Mid 18th century Boston School needlework picture of a shepherdess and piper in a landscape, 19 x 14in. £50,000

Boston 'Adam & Eve' sampler by Lydia Hart, May the 28, 1744, 9 x 11½in. £25,000

Late 18th century needle-
work sampler family record,
10½ x 16in.   £3,500

A needlework picture, by
Mary Fentun, dated 1789,
21¼ x 16½in.   £3,000

An 18th century sampler,
by Kezi Ladell, July 11,
1799, 37 x 21cm.   £300

A late 18th century needlework sampler by Jane
Doughty, the linen ground
embroidered in coloured silks
designed with Adam and Eve
in the Garden of Eden,
62 x 53cm. (Phillips)   £2,000

A fine and rare needlework
sampler, by Alice Mather,
Norwich, Connecticut, 1774,
13¾ x 11½in. (Christie's
New York)   £31,132

A late 18th century needlework
sampler by Isabella
Cunningham, the linen ground
worked in blue, green, yellow,
ivory and crimson silk threads,
38cm. x 30cm.
(Phillips)   £460

A needlework sampler, 'Anna
Fowler born March 2, 1739,
this sampler I did the year
1754', 13 x 19½in. £2,500

Needlework sampler, by
'Elizabeth Tonnecliff, her
work done in 1791', silk
yarns, 16 x 20¼in. £7,500

A needlework sampler
made by Sarah Johnson,
Newport, Rhode Island,
1769, 9 x 16in. £17,500

An early 18th century needle-work sampler, the linen ground embroidered in coloured silks, 46 x 21cm.   £1,000

A Boston School needlework sampler, made by Sarah Henderson in 1765, aged 12, 21 x 18½in.   £17,500

A fine and rare needlework sampler, by Sarah Doubt, Massachusetts, 1765, worked in red, green, blue, purple, yellow and white silk threads, 50.5 x 30cm. (Christie's New York)   £3,805

Needlework sampler, Boston area, second half 18th century, rows of alphabet and numbers over scenic panel with Adam and Eve, 11½in. high. (Skinner Inc.)   £5,215

A needlework sampler, Joanna Maxwell, Warren, Rhode Island, dated 1793, made by Joanna Maxwell, born May the 8 A D 1782 at Warren and further inscribed Wrought at Warren, September the 12 A D 1793 (Robt. W. Skinner Inc.)   £22,727

Needlework sampler, *Mary Leavitt her Sampler made (in the four)teenth year of her age A.D. 17(18)*, Salem, Massachusetts, 16½ x 7¾in. (Skinner Inc.)   £614

An early 18th century needle-work sampler by Suzannah Jeffery, the linen ground embroidered in mainly red, green, yellow and blue wools, 48 x 25cm. (Phillips)   £420

A late 18th century needle-work sampler by *Mary Brad-field, aged nine years, 1798,* the wool ground embroidered in coloured silks with carnations, morning glory and trailing summer flowers, 34 x 34cm. (Phillips West Two)   £700

An 18th century needlework sampler well decorated in coloured silks, 17 x 12½in.   £700

An early 19th century needlework sampler by Lehizo Maria
Dolores Gomez, the linen ground
embroidered in coloured silks
with a farmyard scene, 35x57cm.
(Phillips) £380

A framed pictorial needlework
sampler, inscribed 'Mary
Jagger 1807', England, 17¼ x
19½in. £300

A needlework sampler made
by 'Anna Braddock . . . A
work wrought in the 14th
year of her age, 1826', 22½
x 26in. £25,000

A sampler by Matilda Andrews,
1837, worked in coloured silks
with a verse *Lord search, oh
search,* 15 x 12in. (Christie's
S. Ken) £770

An early 19th century needlework sampler by Sarah
Mitton finish'd April 2nd in
the year of our Lord 1825,
31cm. x 33cm. (Phillips)
£320

A sampler by Ann Diggle,
Rochdale Free English School,
1820, worked in black silk
with a verse "the interest of
the poor", 18 x 17in.
(Christie's) £352

A needlework sampler, Elizabeth
Thurston A E 17 1802, Newburyport, Massachusetts, with rows of
alphabets, sentimental verse and
inscription, 24in. wide. (Robt. W.
Skinner Inc) £7,386

A sampler by Ann Watkins,
1811, worked in coloured
silks with a verse, and a scene
depicting Adam and Eve,
16 x 4in. (Christie's) £506

A needlework sampler, "Apphia
Amanda Young's sampler
wrought in the twelfth year of
her age July 22 A.D. 1833",
probably New Hampshire,
17in. wide. (Robt. W. Skinner
Inc.) £681

Early 19th century woolwork sampler, worked by Elizabeth Shufflebottoms 1841, 23½ x 23¾in. £400

A nicely worked needlework sampler, by Sarah Iesson, the linen ground embroidered in silks, 33 x 21cm. £700

Framed needlework pictorial verse sampler, by Eliza. A. Machett, New York, March 22, 1828, 16½ x 16in. £550

A needlework sampler by Mary Ann Cash, 1801, the linen ground worked in coloured silks, 37 x 30cm. £300

A George III linen sampler worked in polychrome threads with a verse and "Mary Hand finished this work in December '15, Piddletown 1801", 18 x 12in. (Hy. Duke & Son) £230

A mid 19th century needlework sampler by Sarah Redfern, 1.04 x 0.77m., framed and glazed. £700

A sampler by Charlott Webb, worked in brown silk with a verse "Happy the man", 16 x 12in., first half of 19th century. (Christie's) £242

Needlework memorial sampler, Sarah Jane Campbell, America, 19th century, the upper panel depicting a woman mourning beside a tomb, 21½ x 17¼in. (Skinner Inc.) £675

A needlework sampler worked in silk yarns on natural coloured linen, 'Susanah Cadmore, 1805', 12½ x 13¼in. £550

Early 19th century unfinished Shaker needlework sampler on natural linen, 8½ x 10¼in. £600

A mid 19th century Armenian needlework sampler by Souepile Kedeasian, the linen ground embroidered in red and pink threads, 45 x 58cm. £200

An American needlework sampler by Maria Alligood, 1802, 26¼ x 21¼in. £2,250

Needlework sampler, England, 'Margaret Smith, aged 12 AD 1848', worked in heavy wool yarns, 17 x 18in. £600

Needlework sampler, 'Rhoda Roger's Sampler wrought in the 11 years of her age 1804', Mass. £4,500

A William IV needlework sampler by Mary Belt, 1833, 1ft. 11½in. x 1ft. 9in. £1,500

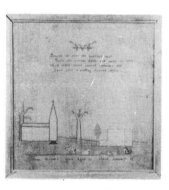

A fine sampler, by Martha Mabe, 1837, worked in coloured silks with a large house, caption and various spot motifs, 18 x 13in. (Christie's) £1,870

A needlework sampler worked in silk and wool threads on a linen ground, by Hannah S. Pidgeon, 1813, 17½ x 25¾in. £3,500

An early 19th century needlework sampler, 'Jane Slessors work aged 13 years January 16', New England, 17 x 17½in. £500

A sampler by Charlotte Way, Portland, 1841, worked in pale brown silk, 14 x 11½in. £300

Needlework sampler, *Eliza Emory*, Rindge, New Hampshire, dated *183-*, 16¾ x 17¼in. (Skinner Inc.) £1,006

Early 19th century Adam and Eve sampler by Eliz. Tredick, New Hampshire or Southern Maine, 11 x 16in. £1,750

A needlework sampler 'Susannah Styles finished this work in the 10 years of her age 1800', worked in silk yarns on wool ground, 13in. square. £750

Needlework sampler, 'Sally Butman her work in the 11th year of her age, 1801', Marblehead, Mass., 10.3/8 x 12½in. £12,500

Needlework sampler, marked 'Elizabeth C. Engle's work done in the 12th year of her age, August 23th, 1837', 17½ x 17½in. £600

An early 19th century needlework sampler, inscribed 'Rachel Fowler's work finished May 29, 1837', 40 x 32cm. £650

Needlework picture, entitled 'The Beggar's Petition', by Sarah Hadley, 1841, 24 x 24in. £2,000

Needlework sampler marked 'Wrought by Sally Alden June 14 1811', Mass., 16 x 21in. £3,500

An early 19th century needle-work sampler by S. Parker, aged 14 years 1817, 37 x 32cm. £800

A framed needlework verse sampler, 'Rebecca Miers', New England, circa 1830, 22 x 21in. £650

A needlework sampler, by 'Sarah Pell, Febrery 21, 1830', wool yarns on white wool fabric, 12½ x 16in. £700

Needlework sampler, England, dated 1826, silk yarns in a variety of stitches on natural linen ground, 13 x 15½in. £750

Early 19th century needle-work sampler, 'Phebe L. Slessor work aged 11 years', New England, 16 x 16in. £850

An early 19th century needle-work sampler by Elizabeth Bushby, March 6, aged 10 years, 1822, 45 x 42cm. £500

A sampler by Mary-Ann Hayter, aged 8 years, 1823, worked in coloured silks, 15 x 13in. £460

Framed needlework pictorial sampler, inscribed 'Harroit Hoyle, Aged 21, 1834', 24 x 24in. £2,250

A needlework sampler, 'Emily Furber her sampler aged 10, wrought March 16, 1827', 23 x 26in. £2,500

An early 19th century American needlework sampler, 19½ x 21in. £3,000

Sampler by Ann Foss of Houghton, Le Spring, 1813, 12½ x 17in. £650

A sampler by Emma Toogood finished June 28th, early 19th century. £425

A sampler by Peggy Veale, 1819, worked in coloured silks with a verse *God spake,* 18 x 13in., framed and glazed. (Christie's S. Ken) £605

An early 19th century needlework sampler by Sarah Mitton finish'd April 2nd in the year of our Lord 1825, 31cm. x 33cm. (Phillips) £320

A framed pictorial needlework sampler, inscribed 'Celia(?) Procter Montrose 1833', England, 16 x 20in. £425

'Life of a Man' needlework sampler, early 19th century, American. £6,000

A needlework family register worked by Lucia A. Daniels in 1832, 16 x 18in. £850

A George IV needlework sampler, by E.H., 1826, 17 x 12½in. £500

A sampler by Julia Matild Paisey, 1845, worked in dark silks, 16 x 12½in. £650

A needlework family register, 'Wrought by Hannah Winchell, 1822', 22½ x 23½in. £2,000

An early 19th century needlework sampler by Selina Doughty, 1835. £400

An early 19th century needlework sampler by Ann Essex aged 10, born Sept 18 1800, Surfleet Lincolnshire, 42.5cm. x 31cm. (Phillips) £420

An early 19th century needlework sampler, by Elizabeth Campling, aged 12 years, the linen ground embroidered in silks, 31.5 x 34.5cm. £350

A needlework sampler by Eliz. Matilda Whitcombe aged 11, 1846, embroidered in coloured silks on a wool ground, 43 x 32cm. £400

Sampler with alphabet verse and figures of plants and birds, dated 1824, 17 x 13in. £425

A needlework sampler by Susanna H. White, Marblehead, dated 1806, 14½ x 19in. £12,500

A needlework sampler by Mary Anne Hunter aged 14 years 1844, 26 x 16½in. £450

An early 19th century needle-work sampler by *C. May, aged 8 years, 1828,* the wool ground worked in mainly green, brown and ochre silk threads, 33 x 43cm. (Phillips) £400

Needlework sampler, worked by *"Ruthy Long Poor born Oct. 28 1801, Aged 13",* Newburyport, Massachusetts, 1814, 11¼ x 8¾in. (Skinner Inc.) £423

Needlework sampler, *Wrought by Mary Attwill Aged 10 Years, Lynn, September 3, 1812,* Massachusetts, worked with silk threads on a linen ground. (Skinner Inc.) £3,067

A sampler, by Elizabeth Rennie, 1811, worked in coloured silks with a verse *Stretched on the cross,* 17 x 13in., framed and glazed. (Christie's S. Ken) £495

Needlework sampler, *Wrought by Eunice Goodridge Aet 16 yrs. Fitchburg 1825,* Massachusetts (fading, staining), 20½ x 16½in. (Skinner Inc.) £387

An early 19th century needle-work sampler by Ann McGill, the canvas ground embroidered mainly in shades of green and brown coloured silks, 52x45cm. (Phillips) £350

Needlework sampler, *Orpha Starkwather 1804,* possibly Virginia or South Carolina, framed, 15½ x 18in. (sight), (minor discoloration). (Skinner Inc.) £1,032

Needlework sampler, *Chloe E. Trask's work wrought in the year 18...,* probably Massachusetts, worked in silk threads, 15¾ x 16½in. (Skinner Inc.) £352

A sampler by Emma Greaves, 1846, worked in coloured wools, with a verse *Jesus permit,* also with a large mansion flanked by formalised trees, 26 x 27in. (Christie's) £220

DOLLS & TOYS

Needlework sampler, *Betsy Patten born September 1802, aged 11 A.D. 1812 Mary Cummings instructress*, Westford, Massachusetts, 17 x 17in. (Skinner Inc.)   £244

Needlework family record, *Wrought by Sarah E. Foster Aged 11 years Roxbury, Dec. 24th 1830*, Massachusetts (good condition), 19½ x 16¼in. (Skinner Inc.)   £859

A needlework sampler, 'Sina Halls Sampler Wrought at Wallingford, August 10, 1811', worked in a variety of stitches on moss-green linsey-woolsey ground, 15¾ x 17½in.   £10,000

An early 19th century needlework sampler by *Louisa Gawby 1811,* in brightly coloured silks, designed with a verse titled *Advice,* 43 x 30cm. (Phillips West Two)   £320

An early Victorian child's needlework sampler, worked in full cross stitch in coloured wools, by Maria Rotherham aged 8 years, 1859, 61cm. square. (Henry Spencer) £140

An American needlework sampler, signed Jane Littlefield, circa 1810, worked in silk threads on a dark green canvas, 24in. high, 15½in. wide.   £4,000

Needlework sampler, *Sally Goss,* probably Pennsylvania, rows of alphabets above inscription and verse over a panel of flowering trees, 11¹/₂ x 15³/₄in. (Skinner Inc.)   £826

Needlework sampler, *Mary L. Montagu, A.D. 1828 AE 11 yrs.,* worked in silk threads in shades of black, green, blue and tan, 18³/₄ x 13³/₄in. (Skinner Inc.)   £81

A sampler by Sarah Thornback, 1826, embroidered in coloured silks with a verse *Jesus permit,* framed and glazed, 16 x 13in. (Christie's S. Ken)   £550

A sampler 'Wrought by Harriot Wethrell May Aged 10 years, Plymouth Massachusetts, June 10th 1830', 16¼ x 16½in. £1,750

An early 19th century needlework sampler by Elizabeth Eady aged 10 years 1834, 31.5cm. x 29.5cm., framed and glazed. (Phillips) £360

A sampler by Mary Swiney 1815, worked in coloured silks with a windmill flanked by weeping willows, 15 x 13in. (Christie's S. Ken) £242

An early 19th century sampler, *Mary Ann Healey's work July 28 1809*, the undyed tammy cloth ground designed with a central prayer worked in black cross-stitch, English, 41.5cm. x 30.5cm. (Phillips) £750

Needlework sampler, *"Wrought by Roxanne Lyard of Cabot, Vt. aged 20, born December the 23rd, 1801–21"*, rows of alphabets over inscription and panel, 12¾ x 14½in. (Skinner Inc.) £304

A mid 19th century needlework sampler, wool on canvas, depicting a colourful bead eyed bird in a stylised tree, by *'Emma Collinson Aged 9 years 1844'*, 47 x 43cm. (Phillips) £360

A Georgian needlework sampler by Maria Coster, in the tenth year of her age, 1819, 1ft.5in. x 1ft.1in. £800

A needlework sampler by Martha Evans, English or American, dated 1848, worked in polychrome wool yarns on an ivory silk ground, 23½ x 27½in. £500

A needlework sampler by Catherine Lewis, Wales, 1867, worked in polychrome wool yarns, 52 x 28in. £400

Needlework sampler, worked by *"Sarah Elizabeth Wright, Aged 18 Years"*, Massachusetts, dated *"1821"*, 15³/₄ x 17in. (Skinner Inc.) **£582**

A needlework picture, signed Anne Oram and dated 1824, worked in polychrome threads on natural ground, 10 x 12in. **£375**

A needlework family record, silk yarns in shades of blue, green, pale peach, ivory and black on natural linen ground fabric, 18¼ x 14½in. **£750**

An early 19th century sampler dated 1803, by *Ann Wilson Aged 11*, the tammy cloth ground worked in coloured silk threads with pious verse and family names, Scottish, 44.5cm. x 32cm. (Phillips) **£480**

An early Victorian needlework sampler by Martha Bitterson, signed and inscribed '*Martha Bitterson/ her work/Aged 9 years 1841*', 16½in. by 17½in. (Bearne's) **£430**

An early 19th century sampler of silk cross-stitch on tammy cloth, portraying a house with a green roof in a garden with a fence, worked by Jane Peskett aged 10 years, 1824, English, 40 x 32cm. (Phillips) **£440**

Needlework sampler, probably England, dated 1804, worked in shades of red, green, blue and cream silk threads, 12³/₄ in. wide. (Skinner Inc.) **£163**

Needlework sampler, *"Sally Harringtons Work 1808"*, New England, worked in silk threads, 25 x 19¹/₂in. (Skinner Inc.) **£1,084**

An early 19th century needlework sampler, 'Hannah L. Slessor aged 13 years', New England, 16½ x 15½in. **£750**

SCHUCO TOYS

The company making these toys was established in Germany in 1912 by H Mueller and H Schreyer. They traded as Schreyer & Co., but it is by their trademark Schuco that their products are best known. Schuco toys are very highly regarded, and some collectors consider them as being the most technically advanced of their type.

During the 20s and 30s they produced a range of novelty clockwork toys, which included animals that were wound up by an arm or leg rather than a key!

It was after the Second World War that Schuco started to produce an inexpensive range of clockwork tinplate cars. Some of these were amazingly complex, such as the Steerable Driving School car, which came complete with jack and tools to remove wheels.

Between the end of the war and 1951 Schuco toys were marked as having been made in the American Zone of Occupation, but thereafter were simply marked *Made in Germany*.

The company closed in 1977, but the brand name was bought by Gama.

Charlie Chaplin, with clockwork mechanism, in original clothing, walking stick and bowler hat, by Schuco, circa 1933, 6¾in. high. (Christie's S. Ken) £330

Schuco, felt and velvet rabbit, the orange creature with large ears, green trousers, dancing with its pink infant, 15.5cm. (Phillips) £130

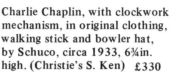

Schuco tinplate Donald Duck, right foot fatigued, boxed, with label. (Phillips West Two) £460

Schuco clockwork felt covered fox dressed in red jacket, blue trousers and yellow tie, carrying a lithographed tinplate clockwork suitcase, 13cm. (Phillips) £115

Donald Duck, a felt covered and painted tinplate toy, with clockwork mechanism, by Schuco, circa 1936, 6in. high. (Christie's S. Ken) £242

A Schuco 6080 Elektro-Construction tinplate fire engine, in original box, circa 1955. £325

Schuco, felt and velvet mouse drinking from a flagon, 11cm. (Phillips) £110

SCRAPS

In the 18th century it was ladies who most commonly enjoyed collecting scraps of paper and pasting them into albums. By the mid 19th century there was a growing market for specially produced printed scraps and these were printed in sheet form but could be cut and arranged as desired.

Early scraps were coloured by hand, but by the mid 19th century fine colour work could be done quickly and cheaply on printing presses. Sheets were often embossed and glazed and up to 14 plates could be used to give a huge range of shapes and colours.

By the end of the century scrap collecting had become a mainly childish pursuit, and subject matter changed accordingly. Also in the 20th century styles changed, becoming less sentimental and such objects as cars and aeroplanes began to feature as these became commonplace. Quality declined after the first World War. British manufacturers produced a multitude of designs, but many scraps continued to be imported from Germany, and these were especially prized by youthful collectors as late as the 1950s. Alternatively, scrap books could be filled with Christmas or birthday cards, picture postcards or even advertising material – just about anything that could be cut out in fact.

Early albums were often finely bound with coloured pages. Many were imported from Germany, but such British companies as George Chapman (estab. 1883) also produced fine examples.

As the quality of scraps declined, so too did that of the albums, which came to be made of cheap paper, and aimed mainly at the juvenile market.

Girl In Yellow With Songbird, 4in. high. £3

Black and White Retriever, 2in. high. £2

Children With Flower Baskets, 4in. high. £8

Eggs In A Basket. £1

Child With Hat, 5in. high. £3

Victoria Cross by Harry Payne, 6in. wide. £5

Floral Bells, 4½in. across. £2

Love Birds, 3in. high. £1

'O' was an Organman, 'P' was
a Parson, 6in. high.   £8

Forget-me-nots. 3½in.
high.   £3

The King and The Lady.
                    £8

'S' was a Sailor, 'T' was a
Tinker.   £8

Red Roses, 3½in. high.
                    £5

Tom Pinch and his sister
Ruth.   £8

'M' was a Miser, 'N' was a
Nobleman.   £8

Love Birds, 3in. high.
                    £3

'U' was an Usher, 'V' was a
Veteran, 'W' was a Watch-
man, 'X' was Expensive.   £8

Peasant Girl with Dove,
4½ in. high.   £5

'Y' was a Youth, 'Z' was
a Zany.   £8

'G' was a Gamester, 'H' was
a Hunter.   £8

'C' was a Captain, 'D' was a
Drummer.   £8

Rose in Hand, 7 in. high.
                               £5

Mr Serjeant Buzfuz, Mrs
Bardell and Master Tommy
Bardell.   £8

'I' was an Italian, 'J' was a
Joiner.   £8

Love Birds on the Bough,
3 in. high.   £2

'E' was an Earl, 'F' was a
Farmer.   £8

Cupid with Arrow, 3½in.
high.   £2

Newman Noggs and Nicholas
Nickleby's Children.   £8

Gabriel Varden and Sim
Tappertit.   £8

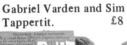

Victoria Cross Gallery, Serg't.
Joseph Malone.   £8

Father Christmas with
Presents.   £5

Mr Tupman, Miss Wardle and
the Fat Boy.   £8

Old Mr Turveydrop and
Peepy and Guppy.   £8

Girl in Red Dress, 5in.
high.   £4

Joe Gargery and Pip.   £8

Girl with Plum Pudding,
2½in. high.   £3

Miss Jenny Wren and Mr Riah.
                              £8

Little Dorrit and her Lover,
John Chivery.   £8

Mr Dick and Betsy Trotwood.
                              £8

Victoria Cross Gallery, Sergeant
H. Ramage.   £8

The Lucky Clown, 12in.
high.   £15

Agnes Wickfield and Uriah
Heep.   £8

Girl in Blue Gown, 5in.
high.   £4

Dick Swiveller and The Mar-
chioness.   £8

Girl in a Feathered Hat,
4in. high.   £3

Winged Cherub, 4in. wide. £6

Girl in a Green
Dress, 4in. high.
             £3

Girl with a Songbird,
3½in. high.   £3

Kitten in a Floral Basket, 9in.
high.   £10

1st Bengal Cavalry,
4in. high.   £2

The 17th Lancers,
4in. high.   £2

Romeo and Juliet,
2½in. high.   £3

H.R.H. The Duchess
of York.   £5

H.M.G.M. The Queen in 1837
10in. high.   £12

Girl in a Bonnet,
4in. high.   £3

Eggs in the Nest,
1in. high.   £1

Rabbit in the Grass, 2in. wide.
£2

Pansies, 2in. high.
£1

Schoolgirl Feeding
Birds, 2in. high. £1

1930's Boy with
Flowers, 3in. high.
£1

An Oak Tree, 9in. high.   £5

Cherub on a Cloud.
£3

Girl with Clown Doll,
3in. high.   £5

H.R.H. The Princess
of Wales.   £5

H.M.G.M. The Queen in 1897,
10in. high.   £10

Girl in Pink, 5in. high.
£5

German toy chain-stitch machine of pressed metal with elaborate floral decoration, pre-1914. £50

'Little Wanzer' lock-stitch machine by the Wanzer Sewing Machine Company, on white marble base, circa 1875. £120

Small chain-stitch machine sold by James Weir, Soho Square, post 1872. £120

A rare Nuremburg Clown sewing machine, No. 4024, the seated cast iron figure with nodding head and working arms operated by a porcelain handled crank, on iron base with lions paw feet, 8¾ in. high. (repainted) (Christie's S. Ken) £2,860

German Casige child's sewing machine, 1918. (Auction Team Köln) £224

German Casige child's sewing machine made in 'British Zone', circa 1950. (Auction Team Köln) £65

'The Handy', small lock-stitch machine by Harpur & Mason with patent number for 1886, in tin carrying case. £200

A cast iron Mueller No. 12 child's sewing machine with chain stitch gripper, Berlin, post-1901. (Auction Team Koeln) £92

Small lock-stitch machine by the Dorman Sewing Machine & Engineering Co. of North-ampton. Design registered in 1889. £200

The ABC nine-pin and spelling blocks by McLoughlin Bros., New York, 1870-80. £125

A 17th century wooden skittle doll carved as a Puritan woman, 6in. high. £250

A Harlequin set of nine Steiff skittles, circa 1908, on circular wooden bases. £5,000

Six turned polychrome Ring Toss Game figures, New England, late 19th century, 14½in. high. £2,000

A group of felt-covered animal skittles, complete with two balls, the largest 11in. high, circa 1910. £400

SPACE TOYS

Space, the last great frontier, started to capture the public imagination in the 1950s, and it was then that space toys began to be made. Examples dating from that pre-space-race period have a particular charm in that they are based on the designer's ideas of what astronauts and space vehicles might look like, or from impressions they had gleaned from science fiction films. Battery operated, these toys are now quite rare.

Easier to come by are a range of diecast, space related toys issued by Dinky in the 1960s and 70s. These are based on such popular series as Star Trek and Thunderbirds.

Space related toy watches are also worth looking out for, especially if they feature the 1950s hero of the Eagle comic, Dan Dare.

The popularity of space toys is often related to the popularity of the series or film on which they are based. Apart from that, it is important that the toy should be complete, and an accompanying original box also adds to the value.

SH-Japanese battery oper-ated Space Station, boxed.
£300

ALPS, TPS, battery operated Mercury Explorer spaceship with magic colour dome finished in very bright primary colours, 20cm., boxed.
(Phillips) £60

'Sparkling Rocket Fighter Ship', a printed and painted tinplate rocket fighter, by Marx, American, 1950's, 12in. long. (Christie's) £209

A Nomura two stage rocket launching pad toy, Japanese, 1960's, tin base lithographed with scene of control room operation, operative seated at TV screen, 7½in. high.
£150

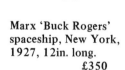

Marx 'Buck Rogers' spaceship, New York, 1927, 12in. long.
£350

TM, battery operated Super-sonic Moon Ship, boxed.
£150

A Marx Buck Rogers space-ship, Pat. 1927, lithograph-ed tin, 12in. long. £300

Karl Bub, clockwork Atom Rocket Ship, boxed. £150

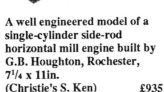

A well engineered and presented model stationary steam set built by D.J. Moir, 1976, overall, 24 x 30¼in.
(Christie's S. Ken) £990

A well engineered model of a single-cylinder side-rod horizontal mill engine built by G.B. Houghton, Rochester, 7¼ x 11in.
(Christie's S. Ken) £935

A finely engineered model of an early 19th century four column single cylinder beam pumping engine originally designed by D. E. Alban, 9½ x 9in. (Christie's S. Ken) £605

A well engineered Marklin horizontal steam plant having twin spirit-fired boilers served by single stack chimney, 46cm. x 38cm.
(Phillips) £2,185

Ducrette and Roger of Paris, a well detailed brass, vertical hot-air engine with glass enclosed piston driving flywheel, 39cm. high.
(Phillips) £380

A Marklin for Gamages live steam spirit fired horizontal stationary steam engine, with brass boiler, chimney, original fittings, German, circa 1920, 12½in. wide. (Christie's S. Ken) £385

Doll et Cie spirit fired vertical steam engine, with lubricators, pressure gauge, whistle and taps, overall 41cm. high.
(Phillips) £345

A Märklin spirit-fired 'Three in One' convertible steam engine, single-cylinder over-type, in original box without lid, 1920's, 8in. long.
(Christie's S. Ken) £396

A finely engraved model Stuart No. 1 single-cylinder vertical reversing stationary engine built by A.L. Holloway, Sidcup, 14½ x 8¾in.
(Christie's S. Ken) £440

411

An ingenious and well presented model steam driven Stone Sawing Plant, built by R. J. Sare, Northleach, 13½ x 24½in. £400

A finely engineered model twin cylinder compound undertype stationary steam engine built to the designs of A. H. Greenly, by P. C. Kidner, London, 14½ x 24½in. £1,750

A 1:12 scale model of a six horse-power pyramidical columned condensing rotative beam engine built by Messrs Fenton Murray & Co., circa 1810, 12 x 15in. £500

An exhibition standard model of the three cylinder compound surface condensing vertical reversing marine engine, fitted to S.S. 'Servia', and modelled by T. Lowe, 1907, 14½ x 12½in. £4,500

A live steam, spirit fired tinplate vertical steam engine, by Bing, circa 1928, 12½in. high, in original box. £125

A well presented model single cylinder vertical reversing stationary engine, built from Clarkson castings, 17½ x 9¾in. £800

An Exhibition Standard model of a single cylinder overcrank stationary engine, by A. Mount, London. £400

A late 19th century full size four-pillar twin-cylinder compound vertical reversing launch engine, 31½ x 24in. £2,000

An unusual model of a steam driven 19th century twin bore Deep Well Engine House and Pump, built by R. J. Sare, Northleach, 16½ x 18½in. £275

Engineering model of an inclined compound surface paddle engine, 16½in. wide.   £1,500

An early single vertical cylinder open crank gas engine, probably American, 24 x 9in.   £225

A model Stuart triple expansion vertical reversing marine engine built by G. B. Houghton, Rochester, 7 x 8¾in.   £750

A well presented approx. 1:20 scale model of the Weatherhill Pit Winding Engine of 1833, built by W. K. Walsam, Hayes, 19 x 14½in.   £700

Late 19th century model of the three cylinder compound vertical surface condensing mill engine 'Asia', 16¼ x 13¼in. £2,000

An early 19th century small full size single cylinder six pillar beam engine, 31 x 34in.   £1,000

A 1:20 scale brass model of the Fenton, Murray & Wood 6 N.H.P. underlever beam engine of 1806 built by G. L. Dimelow, Ashton-under-Lyne, 9¾ x 9¼in   £700

An horizontal cylinder stationary steam engine, built by Negelin & Hubner, 28 x 64in.   £600

A contemporary early 19th century brass and wrought iron single cylinder six pillar beam engine, built by Chadburn Bros., Sheffield, 19 x 19¼in.   £2,250

An exhibition standard 3in. scale model of
the Savage horse-drawn Electric Light Engine
No. 357, built by C. J. Goulding, Newport,
27 x 47in.　　　　　　　　　　£3,000

An engineered model enclosed compound generating set, 13½ x 22in.
　　　　　　　　　　　　　£400

An early 20th century model single cylinder
surface condensing 'A' frame beam engine,
19½ x 24in.　　　　　　　　　£2,000

A Stuart Major Beam engine, cylinder, 2¼ x
4in., on wood stand in glazed case.　£700

A detailed steam driven model of a Bengali
Dye Mixing plant, built by A. Sare, Northleach,
measurements overall 18½ x 24in.　　£900

A finely engineered and well presented model
'M E', centre pillar beam engine, built by
K. R. F. Kenworthy, measurements overall
13 x 17½in.　　　　　　　　£1,000

An early 20th century single cylinder horizontal mill engine, complete with mahogany
lagged brass bound cylinder, 2½ x 3in. £300

An early 18th century tinplate and cast-
iron model single horizontal cylinder gas
engine by Bing, 10 x 16in.   £700

An exhibition standard model of the three
cylinder compound surface condensing
vertical reversing marine engine fitted to
the Cunard Liner S.S. 'Servia' and modelled
by Thos. Lowe, 1907, 14½ x 12½in. £4,000

A fine contemporary late 19th century small,
full size, single cylinder horizontal mill engine,
measurements overall 18 x 25in.   £750

A model of an early 20th century twin
cylinder horizontal mill engine, complete
with mahogany lagged copper bound
cylinders, 2½ x 5in.   £700

A model of a three cylinder horizontal
reversing stationary engine, built by W.
G. Duggan, Benton and D. Ash. £700

A large well engineered
horizontal twin cylinder steam
plant driven by a separate boiler,
the twin cylinders mounted in
tandem, lacks boiler, overall
64cm. long.
(Phillips)   **£500**

A well engineered display
model of a twin overhead cam-
shaft, fuel injected V-8 car
engine, finished in red, black
and polished brightwork,
4¼ x 5½in. (Christie's)   £330

A Marklin live steam spirit
fired horizontal stationary
steam engine, in original paintwork, circa 1921, 52in. high.
(Christie's S. Ken)   £770

A German spirit fired model
of a horizontal steam engine,
bearing the trademark M.G. &
Cie, Wurtemberg, size of base
18½in x 20½in. (Lawrence Fine
Arts)   £1,100

A rare late nineteenth live
steam, spirit fired, stationary
steam set, with brass pot
boiler and fretwork firebox,
8½in. high, possibly American.
(Christie's)   £165

A Schoenner live steam spirit
fired tinplate overtype engine,
with brass boiler and original
fittings, 17½ x 15¾in., circa
1910. (Christie's)   £990

A Marklin live steam, spirit
fired horizontal stationary
steam engine, with brass
boiler and chimney,
13¼ x 11 x 16½in., German,
circa 1920. (Christie's)
                         £1,320

**An extremely fine, mid-19th
century brass, wrought and cast
iron model of a four-pillar
stationary steam engine and
boiler, overall measurements:
boiler, 22 x 30in., engine 23 x
12½in.**
(Christie's S. Ken)   **£6,600**

An early 19th century wrought
iron and brass, single cylinder,
four pillar overcrank model
engine with cylinder approx.
2in. bore x 2in. stroke,
19 x 11¼in. (Christie's S. Ken)
                         £242

German plush pull toy of a baby elephant by Steiff, 14in. overall. £300

A Steiff golden velvet bulldog, with black stitched muzzle, orange felt tongue and glass eyes, 9.5cm. high. (Henry Spencer) £210

A plush covered lion cub, 9in. long, circa 1925 with Steiff button. £150

A Roly Poly blue and white rabbit with glass eyes and Steiff button in ear, 10$^{1}/_{2}$in. high with ears extended. (Christie's S. Ken) £880

A golden short plush covered lion on wheels, with curly plush blonde mane, by Steiff, circa 1913 (missing ears, growl inoperative). (Christie's S. Ken) £330

Mid 20th century life-size young donkey, probably Steiff, 39in. high, 39in. long. £200

A felt rooster with wire framed feet, yellow, red and green feathers with Steiff button and original white tag, 1117, circa 1905–26. (Christie's S. Ken) £550

A large Steiff rocking elephant, 45in. long, German, circa 1925. £650

A Steiff Mickey Mouse, the velvet covered head with felt ears and wide smiling mouth, 7in. (Phillips) £299

TEDDY BEARS

Most people are now familiar with the account of how the Teddy bear got its name. This tells how, while on a hunting trip in 1902, President Theodore Roosevelt could not bring himself to shoot a bear cub which had been conveniently tethered to a post by some well-meaning aide (the President having just shot its mother). Such fore'bear'ance on the part of the noted hunter appealed to the popular press, and the incident was captured in a cartoon of the day. Seeing this, one Morris Michtom, of the Ideal Toy Corp. who had created some toy bears, asked permission to call them after Theodore, so the Teddy bear came into being.

Roosevelt obviously felt the connection did no harm to the Presidential image, and when his daughter married in 1906, the wedding breakfast tables were decorated with tiny bears made by the Steiff toy company.

Margrete Steiff had been making felt animals at Geingen in Germany for some time and was joined in 1897 by her ambitious nephew Richard. They exhibited at the Leipzig Fair in 1903 and the popularity of their toys was so great that the factory simply could not keep up with demand.

Pre-1910 Steiff bears tend to be rather elongated for modern taste, with pointed snouts and humps. The Steiffs had the good marketing sense to put a characteristic button in each of their product's ears, thus making them instantly recognisable. They are now the most valuable bears for collectors.

Many firms in Britain too produced Teddy bears. Few, however are marked, and attribution is often impossible. Those by Merrythought now have quite a following among collectors.

A plush covered polar bear with button eyes, felt pads and joints at hips, 16in. long, with Steiff button, circa 1913. (Christie's) £385

Early white mohair teddy bear, Germany, circa 1906, 13½in. high. £750

A honey plush covered teddy bear with boot button eyes, wide apart ears, 13½in. high, with Steiff button in ear (one pad moth eaten). (Christie's) £440

A silver plush covered teddy bear with button eyes and felt pads, 14in. high, with Steiff button. (Christie's) £550

A plush covered bear on wheels with swivel head, boot button eyes, stitched nose and slight hump, with Steiff button in ear, 8½in. long. (Christie's S. Ken) £385

A long cinnamon plush cover, teddy bear with large button eyes, central face seam, wide set ears, 21in. high, circa 1905, probably Steiff. (Christie's) £1,540

A dark plush teddy bear with straw stuffed body and elongated arms, back hump and felt pads, probably by Steiff, 40cm. high. £700

A dark golden plush covered Roly Poly bear with boot button eyes, pronounced snout and wide apart ears by Steiff, circa 1909, 5¹/₂in. high.
(Christie's S. Ken) £418

A Steiff Centennial teddy bear, for the German market, golden mohair, black button eyes and ear button, 17in. high, 1980. £350

A straw gold plush covered teddy bear with elongated limbs, pronounced snout, glass eyes, and Steiff button in ear, probably circa 1909, 24in. high.
(Christie's S. Ken) £1,980

A plush covered pull-along bear mounted on a wheeled frame, 23in. long, with raised letters, Steiff button, circa 1920. (Christie's) £418

An early 20th century golden plush Steiff teddy bear, with Steiff metal button in the ear, swivel joints with felt pads, 51cm. high.
(Henry Spencer) £1200

A light brown plush covered teddy bear with boot button eyes, 21in. high, by Steiff, circa 1905. (Christie's) £300

A cinammon plush covered bear with large black boot button eyes, 29in. long, Steiff button in ear, circa 1904.
(Christie's) £1,870

A plush-covered teddy bear with round ears, button eyes, pronounced hump and long paws, probably by Steiff, 21in. high. £500

DOLLS & TOYS

A cinnamon plush covered teddy bear, with boot button eyes, 24in. high, probably Steiff, circa 1908. (Christie's) £1,540

A Steiff gold mohair plush teddy bear with wide apart rounded ears, black boot button eyes, 16in., 1911. (Phillips) £800

An early 20th century Steiff blond plush teddy bear. (Spencer's) £2,800

A white plush covered teddy bear with elongated limbs, pronounced snout, glass eyes, hump and Steiff button in ear, circa 1930's, 18in. high. (Christie's S. Ken) £990

A pale golden plush covered teddy bear with boot button eyes, wide apart ears, elongated limbs, hump, cut muzzle, stitched nose with four claws, felt pads and growler, with Steiff button in ear, circa 1911, 28in. high.(Christie's S. Ken.) £2,090

A beige plush covered teddy bear with felt pads, hump and squeeze growler, small blank Steiff button in ear, circa 1903-4, 10in. high. (Christie's S. Ken.) £605

A dark gold plush covered teddy bear with brown glass eyes, 19½in. high with Steiff button, circa 1920. (Christie's) £300

A long plush-covered teddy bear with black button eyes, with Steiff button in the ear, 25in. high. £2,000

A blonde plush covered teddy bear with boot button eyes, wide apart ears, 13in. high, Steiff button in ear. (Christie's) £660

German teddy bear by Steiff of pale plush colour, renewed pads, snout and nose, circa 1909.   £1,500

A blonde plush covered teddy bear with boot button eyes, dressed as a sailor in blue trousers, white jersey and blue beret, by Steiff, 8½ in. high. (Christie's S. Ken)   £286

A blonde plush covered teddy bear with boot button eyes, 17 in. high with Steiff button in ear. (Christie's)   £440

A Steiff gold plush teddy bear, circa 1912, with black boot button eyes, rounded pricked ears, hump back, swivel joints, and growl box, 68cm. long. (Henry Spencer)   £380

A strawberry blonde plush covered teddy bear with boot button eyes, 12 in. high, with plain Steiff button in ear, circa 1903/1904. (Christie's)   £528

'Edward Bear', a blonde plush covered teddy bear with boot button eyes, cut muzzle, elongated limbs, with Steiff button in ear, circa 1905, 10 in. high. (Christie's S. Ken)   £825

A Steiff blonde plush teddy bear, with metal disc in left ear, 17 in. high.   £1,500

A golden plush covered centre seam teddy bear with boot button eyes, by Steiff, circa 1905, 20 in. high (lacks stuffing in arms from loss of front paw pads). (Christie's S. Ken)   £715

A golden plush covered teddy bear with boot button eyes, wide apart ears, and Steiff button in ear, 16 in. high. (Christie's)   £1,210

A Steiff pale plush teddy bear with black thread stitched nose and straw stuffed body, with button in left ear, 33cm. high. £750

A golden plush covered teddy bear, the front unhooking to reveal a metal hot water bottle, by Steiff, 17in. high. £1,500

A dark plush teddy bear with wide apart rounded ears, black button eyes and pointed snout, probably by Steiff, 34cm. high. £600

A good early golden plush Steiff teddy bear, with black boot button eyes, pointed brown stitched snout, rounded pricked ears, back hump, swivel joints, felt pads and a growl box, 38.5cm. long. (Henry Spencer) £2,600

An early golden plush covered teddy bear, with boot button eyes, hump, excelsior stuffing and elongated limbs, wearing tortoiseshell rimmed spectacles, with small blank Steiff button in ear, circa 1903/4, 20in. high. (Christie's S. Ken) £385

Noel, a rare black plush covered teddy bear, with boot button eyes mounted on red felt, elongated limbs and wide apart ears, by Steiff, circa 1910, 20½in. high. (Christie's S. Ken) £2,860

A golden plush covered teddy bear with pronounced hump, pointed snout and with Steiff button in ear, 29in. high. £4,000

A Steiff pale plush teddy bear with rounded wide-apart ears, black button eyes and large felt pads. (Phillips) £320

A gold plush teddy bear, with metal Steiff disc in left ear, German, circa 1907, 25in. high. £3,000

TEDDY BEARS
STEIFF

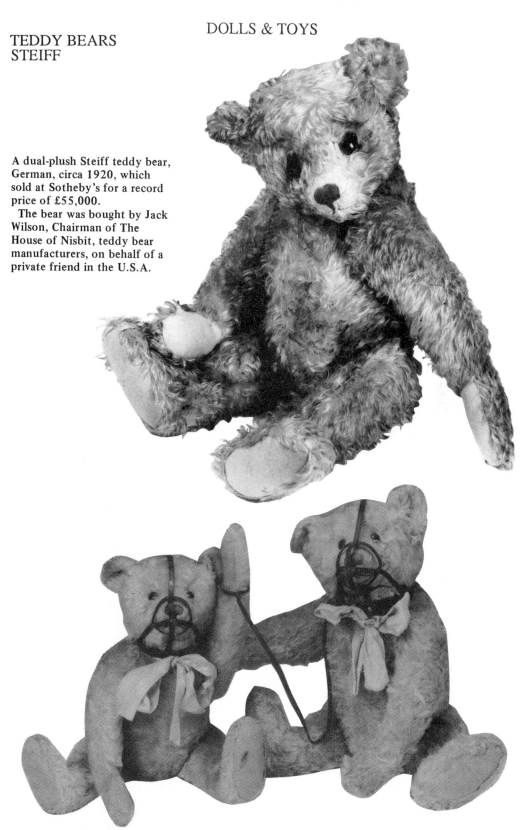

A dual-plush Steiff teddy bear, German, circa 1920, which sold at Sotheby's for a record price of £55,000.

The bear was bought by Jack Wilson, Chairman of The House of Nisbit, teddy bear manufacturers, on behalf of a private friend in the U.S.A.

Steiff muzzled teddy bears, circa 1913, 'Archibald' on the left is worth about £6,500 while the 20in. example on the right is worth about £10,000.

TEDDY BEARS
STEIFF

A very rare short red plush teddy bear, called Alfonzo, with button eyes, excelsior stuffing and felt pads dressed as a Russian, having belonged to Xenia Georgievna, Princess of Russia and second cousin to Tsar Nicholas II. Xenia was stranded in England following a summer holiday at Buckingham Palace when war broke out in 1914, 13in. high with Steiff button (voice box inoperative, front paws recovered in chamois leather), 1906-1909.
(Christie's)   £12,100

A fine Steiff black mohair plush teddy bear with wide apart rounded ears, black boot button eyes mounted on red felt discs, cut stitched snout, on an excelsior filled body with swivel joints, hump back and elongated felt pads, 19in., button in ear marked Steiff, circa 1912.

A similar example may be referred to in the 'History of the Teddy Bear and his Friends, Button in Ear' by Jurgen and Marianne Cieslik, where it is stated that 494 of this type, serial no. 5335 were produced, for the English market and available in five sizes ranging from 14in. to 19in.
(Phillips)   £8,000

TEDDY BEARS
STEIFF

A cinnamon plush covered teddy bear, with boot button eyes, wide apart ears, elongated limbs, hump and cut muzzle, with Steiff button in ear, 13in. high. (Christie's S. Ken) £2,200

A golden plush covered teddy bear with hump and Steiff button in ear, 14in. high. (Christie's) £352

A pale golden plush covered teddy bear with embroidered snout and slight hump, 15½in. high, with Steiff button. £1,500

A golden plush covered teddy bear with boot button eyes, cut muzzle, hump and elongated limbs, with Steiff button in left ear, 19in. high. £850

An early 20th century German blond plush large teddy bear, with black wooden eyes, stitched pointed snout, hump back and moving arms, 52cm. high, probably Steiff. (Spencer's) £1,200

A rare central seam golden plush covered teddy bear, with boot button eyes, wide apart ears, elongated limbs, hump and pronounced snout, by Steiff, circa 1905, 20in. high. (Christie's S. Ken) £990

An early golden plush covered teddy bear with boot button eyes, Steiff button in ear, 8½in. high. (Christie's) £605

A dark golden plush covered teddy bear wearing a leather muzzle with lead, with Steiff button and white tag in ear, circa 1910, 12½in. high. (Christie's S. Ken) £550

A honey plush covered teddy bear with boot button eyes, 14in. high, Steiff button in ear, circa 1903. (Christie's) £820

An early 20th century jointed teddy bear of blonde mohair, 19in. high. £250

A golden plush covered teddy bear in the form of a child's muff, 15in. high. £250

1930's German teddy bear with jointed limbs, 14in. high. £250

Page Hop: with short plush head and paws, dressed in red felt uniform jacket and cap, black trousers, with boot button eyes, by Schuco, circa 1923, 11in. high.
(Christie's S. Ken) £770

A teddy bear of grey plush with brown button eyes, embroidered nose, hump back and long paws, 13in. high. £500

A golden curly plushed covered teddy bear with cut muzzle snout, glass eyes, rexine type pads, with original Chad Valley swing ticket and label on foot pad, 21in. high.
(Christie's S. Ken) £275

An early 20th century German gold plush teddy bear with black boot button eyes, stitched muzzle, felt paws, hump and growl box, 38cm. high. £100

An Edwardian plush model bear on wheels, 1ft.4in. high, one ear and one eye missing. (Hobbs & Chambers) £100

A pale plush covered teddy bear with brown glass eyes, cut muzzle and reinforced felt feet, 22in. high. (Christie's) $374 £198

A musical teddy bear with swivelling head operated via his tail, 43cm. high. £350

A honey plush covered pull-along bear on metal wheels, 6in. high, circa 1908. £350

A dual-coloured teddy bear, with black and beige tufted mohair plush, circa 1950, 25in. high. £45

An early 20th century blonde plush, straw filled teddy bear with black and orange glass eyes, 50cm. high. (Henry Spencer) £220

A golden plush covered teddy bear with cut muzzle, dark orange glass eyes, English, circa 1930's, 9½in. high (squeaker inoperative). (Christie's S. Ken) £176

German straw-filled teddy bear with hump back, pad feet, long nose and button eyes, 11in. high. £300

A cotton plush covered teddy bear, with clear glass eyes, felt pads and embroidered claws, 13½in. high, circa 1917. (Christie's S. Ken) £330

A brown plush covered bear on all fours, with swivel head, cut muzzle, glass eyes, stitched nose and pronounced hump, 9in. long. (Christie's S. Ken) £121

'Page Hop': a golden plush Yes/No bear dressed in red jacket, black felt trousers with bellboy cap, original Schuco swing ticket and price tag, circa 1928, 14½in. high. (Christie's S. Ken) £2,530

Late 19th century clock-work brown bear, real fur pelt, possibly France, 7in. high. £200

German gold plush teddy bear with stitched pointed snout, hump, black shoe button eyes, circa 1910, 21in. high. (Hobbs & Chambers) £200

A straw filled ginger teddy-bear, with ball and socket joints, 74cm. high. £75

A dark golden plush covered teddy handbag, with black button eyes, pronounced snout, and moveable joints, 8in. long, pads replaced, possibly by Schuco.
(Christie's S. Ken.) £770

An early 20th century German cinnamon plush teddy bear, with long arms and black leather paws, 66cm. tall.
(Spencer's) £700

A dark golden plush covered teddy bear with elongated limbs, low set wide apart ears, and red, white and blue ribbon rosette on chest, 12in. high.
(Christie's S. Ken) £385

An orange plush teddy bear with smiling mouth, small hump back and swivel joints, 16in. high, circa 1930. £150

A short golden plush covered standing clockwork bear, with broom handle attached to his right paw, 8in. high, circa 1933. (Christie's) £418

A gold short plush covered teddy bear, slight hump, 15½in. high, circa 1926. £250

A teddy bear covered in beige coloured mohair, with glass eyes, rounded ears and shorn muzzle with stitched snout, circa 1920, 15½in. high.
(Christie's)   £77

Blonde mohair jointed teddy bear, 1910, 17in. high. £300

A golden plush-covered musical teddy bear, playing Sonny Boy by Al Jolson, 20in. high, circa 1930. £750

A golden plush covered teddy bear with felt pads, stitched nose, enlarged torso and forward placed ears, 15in. high.
(Christie's S. Ken)   £154

An early gold plush tumbling teddy bear, the body of wood and cardboard, containing a key-wind mechanism, 9in. high.   £100

A deep golden plush covered teddy bear with boot button eyes, elongated limbs, wide apart ears, felt pads and hump, 22in. high.
(Christie's S. Ken)   £462

A clockwork somersaulting teddy bear dressing in gold felt jacket, blue trousers and white vest, by Bing of Nuremberg, 9in. high. £850

A blonde plush covered teddy bear, with Gebruder Bing button on side, Nuremberg, circa 1910, 11½in. high.
(Christie's)   £495

A chubby long blonde mohair teddy bear, fully jointed with glass eyes, 20in. high.   £200

TEDDY BEARS

Pre-war fur fabric teddy bear, 15in. high. £50

A long blonde plush covered teddy bear, with small hump, large feet and growler, 20in. high. (Christie's S. Ken) £385

Tan mohair teddy bear with shoe button eyes, circa 1910, 12¾in. high. £200

An unusual red plush covered teddy bear with pronounced snout, 16½in. high (eyes missing, plush worn, pads replaced) with an illustrated manuscripted story book of the bear's adventures written by the family's French governess in 1938. (Christie's S. Ken) £1,100

Edwardian gold plush teddy bear with black stitched snout, black and brown glass eyes, partly straw filled with squeaker, 19in. high (Hobbs & Chambers) £290

A rare 'laughing Roosevelt teddy bear', with dark golden mohair plush, glass eyes, jointed arms and legs, by Columbia Teddy Bears Manufacturers, circa 1907, 23in. high. (Christie's S. Ken.) £495

An early gold plush teddy bear, with protruding black stitched snout, glass eyes, rounded ears and back hump, 15in. high. (Lawrence Fine Arts) £396

Early amber plush teddy bear and accessories, circa 1910, 15in. tall. £200

A golden plush covered teddy bear with elongated limbs, cut muzzle, glass eyes, wide apart ears, hump and growler, 21in. high. (Christie's S. Ken) £715

TEDDY BEARS

A blonde mohair plush
teddy bear with voice box,
circa 1910, 18½in. high.
£350

An English gold mohair plush
teddy bear, with small rounded
ears, stitched snout on an
excelsior filled body with swivel
joints, 18in.
(Phillips)   £80

A fawn plush covered Yes/No
teddy bear with cut muzzle, glass
eyes, down-turned paws and felt
pads, sits 11in. high.
(Christie's S. Ken)   £528

A blonde plush covered teddy
bear, with boot button eyes,
long arms and felt pads, 10½in.
high, circa 1910. (Christie's)
£308

A golden short plush covered
teddy bear with boot button
eyes, hump, low set ears,
horizontally stitched nose, felt
pads, firm stuffing and long
straight legs, probably early
American, 29in. high.
(Christie's S. Ken.)   £880

A blonde plush covered teddy
bear with cut muzzle, felt pads,
squeaker and slight hump,
probably by Merrythought, 16in.
high.
(Christie's S. Ken)   £220

'Winnie the Pooh', a honey plush
teddy bear with small wide apart
rounded ears, on an excelsior
filled body with short limbs,
16½in.
(Phillips)   £40

A long plush mohair covered
teddy bear, with boot button
eyes, wide apart ears, hump
and elongated limbs, 22in. high.
(pads replaced) (Christie's S.
Ken)   £2,640

A tan mohair bear with wired
limbs, blonde plush ears,
snout and feet and glass eyes,
Germany, circa 1930, 11in.
high.   £100

An exhibition standard 2in. scale model of a Burrell 5 N.H.P. double crank compound three shaft, two speed Showman's Road Locomotive, 20 x 30½in.   £6,500

A 3in. scale model of a single cylinder two speed, four shaft Clayton & Shuttleworth traction engine, built by K. Prout, 31 x 56in.   £4,000

A 2in. scale model of a single cylinder single speed three shaft general purpose traction engine, cylinder approx. 1¼in. bore x 2in. stroke, 19½ x 28in.
(Christie's S. Ken)   £1,210

A 3in. scale live steam coal-fired Burrell single-cylinder agricultural traction engine 'Myrtle', by Dennis Hurn, 45in. long overall.   £3,000

An exhibition standard 1½in. scale model of the Allchin single cylinder two-speed four-shaft General Purpose Traction Engine (Royal Chester).   £2,000

A 2in. scale model of a single cylinder three shaft two speed Davey-Paxman general purpose agricultural traction engine built by A. R. Dyer & Sons, Wantage, 23½ x 38in. £2,500

A 4½in. scale model of a Burrell single cylinder, two-speed, three-shaft general purpose traction engine, built by Lion Engineering Co., 1971, length of engine 68in. £5,000

A sturdily constructed 2in. scale model of a Fowler twin crank compound three speed, four shaft road locomotive built by S. W. Brown, Newbury, 23 x 37in.   £3,000

A finely engineered, exhibition standard 1in. scale model of the single cylinder two speed four shaft general purpose agricultural traction engine 'Doreen', built to the designs of 'Minnie', by H. A. Taylor, 1980, 11½ x 18in.   £1,750

An exhibition standard 2in. scale model of the Burrell 5 n.h.p. double crank compound two speed three shaft 'Gold Medal' tractor, engine No. 3846, Registration No. AD7782 'Pouss-nouk-nouk', built from works drawings by P. Penn-Sayers, Laughton, 19¾ x 27¼in. £8,000

A 1½in. scale model of a Burrell single crank compound two speed three shaft general purpose agricultural traction engine, built by J. B. Harris, Solihull, 15½ x 25in.   £2,500

A finely engineered and well presented 3in. scale model of a Burrell single-cylinder, traction engine built by R. Simmons, Stowmarket, 29 x 44in. (Christie's S. Ken)   £8,250

A scale model of a Ferguson TE20 tractor and plough, 15¾in. long overall.   £400

3in. scale model of a single cylinder Burrell agricultural traction engine, by K. B. Thirsk, Driffield, 1973, 45in. long.   £5,000

A finely engineered unique steam-powered Crawler Tractor built on a Ransome's MG 6 chassis by A. Pickering, 1985. Overall length 90 x 43in.
(Christie's S. Ken)   £9,900

A fine exhibition standard 2in. scale model of the Burrell 5 m.p.h. double crank compound three shaft, two speed, agricultural tractor, built by D. Burns, Pennington, Australia, 19¾ x 29in.
(Christie's S. Ken)   £6,050

A well engineered 3in. scale model of a Suffolk Dredging tractor, built by C. E. Thorn, 27 x 30in.   £600

Lesney Massey Harris 745D tractor.   £150

VANS & TRUCKS

A Shackleton clockwork blue and red painted Foden flat truck with rubber tyres, 31cm. long. (Henry Spencer)
£160

A rare Dinky pre-war 2nd Series 28m Wakefield's Castrol Oil Van, with metal wheels, tinplate radiator, finished in green and inscribed in red. (Christie's)
£660

Dinky Supertoys 514 Guy Van, advertising 'Slumberland', in original paintwork, with box. (Christie's)
£165

Hornby 'O' gauge No 2 breakdown crane, boxed. (James of Norwich)
£40

Dinky Supertoys 923 Big Bedford Van, advertising 'Heinz 57 Varieties', with Baked Beans tins on sides, in original box. (Christie's)
£165

Dinky Supertoys 918 Guy Van, advertising 'Ever Ready', in original paintwork, with box. (Christie's)
£154

Dinky Supertoys, No. 957 Ruston Bucyrus Excavator, in original box. (Christie's S. Ken)
£154

A Dinky 920 Guy Warrior Van 'Heinz' Tomato Ketchup, boxed.(Phillips)
£800

Spot-On, 265 Tonibell Ice Cream van, with server, in original box.   £75

A tinplate Lineol ambulance, No. WH 2517, German, circa 1938, 12in. long.   £500

Dinky 28M green delivery van advertising 'Atco Motor Mowers'.   £300

Dinky Supertoys, 919 Guy van, advertising 'Golden Shred', in original paintwork, with golly, in original box.   £525

A Wells tinplate ambulance, clockwork mechanism driving rear axle, 6½in. long, English, circa 1935.   £200

Spot-On – 110 2B A.E.C. Major Brick Lorry (E to M), boxed.   £250

Tekno, Mercedes Tuborg Pilsner Delivery lorry, boxed.   £85

Buddy L sheet metal railway express truck, green cab and open hauler, circa 1950, 21in. long.   £150

Dinky Supertoys, 514B Guy Van, advertising 'Lyons Swiss Rolls', in original paintwork and box. £400

Pre-war yellow-bodied Dinky delivery van, advertising Kodak film. £500

Dinky 28/3a Hornby Trains Delivery Van, finished in red, advertising 'Hornby Trains British and Guaranteed', in gold decals. £300

Dinky model Guy van, 'Weetabix', No. 514, boxed. £550

A Mettoy 'OK Biscuits' spring drive tin delivery van, brightly coloured in yellow and red, 10cm. x 24cm. (Phillips) £70

A Dinky Series 28 first pattern delivery van, painted in black and red with gilt decals, 'The Manchester Guardian', circa 1935. £350

A Dinky series 25D petrol tanker, 4½in. long, English, circa 1939. £200

Dinky van advertising Pickfords. £425

A printed and painted tinplate "Carter Paterson" delivery van, with clockwork mechanism, 9¾in. long, by Tipp, circa 1930. (Christie's) £880

Dinky Supertoys Foden 'Mobilgas' tanker, fair condition. (Lawrence Fine Arts) £55

Dinky Supertoys, 923 Big Bedford Van, advertising 'Heinz 57 Varieties', with Baked Bean tin on sides, in original paintwork. (Christie's)

£154

Dinky Supertoys No. 930 Bedford Pallet Jekta van, in original box. (Christie's S. Ken) £176

A Dinky 918 Guy van, advertising 'Ever Ready', in original paintwork. (Lawrence Fine Arts) £110

Citroen, painted tinplate clockwork petrol tanker finished in red and silver, 44cm., with electric lighting. (Phillips) £800

A wooden toy military ambulance, with opening rear doors and stretchers, 19in. long, marked *The Priory Toys*. (Christie's S. Ken) £110

A Dinky 917 Guy van, advertising 'Spratt's', in original paintwork, fair condition, unboxed. (Lawrence Fine Arts) £132

Citroen, clockwork painted tinplate delivery lorry finished in red with black lining with electric lighting, boxed with key, 43cm. (Phillips) £480

Pre-war 33R, railway
mechanical horse and trailer
van, 'LNER' (chipped).
(Christie's S. Ken)   £187

Dinky Supertoys, No. 948
Foden 14-ton tanker Regent,
in original box. (Christie's
S. Ken)   £286

Greppert and Kelch, spring
action lithographed tipper
lorry finished in orange and
black, 21cm. long. (Phillips)
£240

A Chad Valley lithographed
tinplate clockwork Delivery Van,
in original box, 1940's, 10in.
long.
(Christie's S. Ken.)   £715

A well engineered approx. 3in.
scale model of a six-wheeled
undertype steam engine wagon
'Lensford Dragon' built by
A. Pickering, 30 x 69in.
(Christie's S. Ken)   £5,500

Dinky rare 923 Heinz big
Bedford van, tomato ketchup
bottle variant, in original box.
(Christie's S. Ken)
£1,045

Dinky 943 Esso Leyland Octopus
tanker, in original box.
(Christie's S. Ken)   £220

Dinky Lyons 'Swiss Rolls'
Guy van No.514, boxed.
(Hobbs & Chambers)   £320

A well built approx. ¼ scale
model of the Scammell timber
tractor, Reg. No. HDW471,
built by K. Bryan, Nottingham,
42 x 77in. (Christie's S. Ken)
£6,050

Early 20th century child's toy pick-up truck painted black. £85

A Britains Army Ambulance, with driver, in original box. £125

A Dinky model Guy van with upright radiator grill, unboxed. £75

A searchlight lorry with adjustable electric searchlight, in the original box. £250

Dinky van advertising Oxo. £300

Dinky Supertoy, No. 514C Guy van, advertising 'Weetabix', in original paintwork and box. £400

Dinky Guy 'Spratts' van, no. 514, boxed. £300

Spot-On, 271 Express Dairy van, with driver and milk crates, in original box. £40

Dinky Supertoys, 919 Guy van, advertising 'Golden Shred', in original paintwork, un-boxed, slightly chipped.   **£125**

A Distler lorry and trailer with clock-work mechanism driving the rear axle, German, circa 1935, 19¾in. long.   **£500**

Minic pre-war No. 30M 'Minic Transport' Artic, in original paintwork, with transfers, petrol can and white rubber tyres.   **£85**

A Chad Valley games van with clockwork mechanism, English, circa 1930.   **£175**

A 2in. scale model of a Garrett 'undertype three-way tipper, live-steam wagon, 30in. long.   **£1,200**

Spot-On — 110/4 4000 gallon Auto Petrol Tanker (M), boxed.   **£450**

Lehmann tinplate postal delivery van, No. 786, German, circa 1927, 7¼in. long.   **£700**

Dinky van advertising Hornby trains.   **£425**

Late 19th century Folk Art painted and carved mechanised wooden model of five bearded men at work, America, base 18½in. long. £714

Miniature carved and painted squirrel, America, early 20th century, 3½in. high. (Skinner Inc.) £110

Carved and painted horse and sulky with driver, early 20th century, mounted above a shaped wooden stand (imperfections), 11¾in. long. (Skinner Inc.) £982

Mid 19th century child's wooden velocipede, probably New York State, 31in. long. £220

Carved and painted parrot with metal hoop, possibly Canada, late 19th century (paint wear), 18½in. high. (Skinner Inc.) £1,718

Automated wood and brass horse and sulky with driver, America, first half 20th century, the carved and painted driver, articulated horse with leather tack, 24in. long. (Skinner Inc.) £2,135

A 19th century beechwood rattle, 10½in. long. £125

A wooden group of miniature human and animal figures, platform 5 x 9in. (Robt. W. Skinner Inc.) £225

A 19th century sycamore bilboquet, 11¼in. high. £125

INDEX